TRANSNATIONAL SOCIAL WORK

Opportunities and challenges of a global profession

Edited by Allen Bartley and Liz Beddoe

First published in Great Britain in 2018 by

Policy Press
University of Bristol
1-9 Old Park Hill
Bristol
BS2 8BB
UK
t: +44 (0)117 954 5940
pp-info@bristol.ac.uk
www.policypress.co.uk

North America office:
Policy Press
c/o The University of Chicago Press
1427 East 60th Street
Chicago, IL 60637, USA
t: +1 773 702 7700
f: +1 773-702-9756
sales@press.uchicago.edu
www.press.uchicago.edu

British Library Cataloguing in Publication Data
A catalogue record for this book is available from the British Library

Library of Congress Cataloging-in-Publication Data
A catalog record for this book has been requested

ISBN 978-1-4473-3336-4 hardcover
ISBN 978-1-4473-3338-8 ePub
ISBN 978-1-4473-3339-5 Mobi
ISBN 978-1-4473-3337-1 epdf

Cover design by Hayes Design
Front cover image: www.alamy.com
Printed and bound in Great Britain by CPI Group (UK) Ltd, Croydon, CR0 4YY
Policy Press uses environmentally responsible print partners

Contents

Acknowledgements

Projects of this sort inevitably require investments of time that extend beyond what can fit into a 'normal' workday or week. In that respect, our families have made a contribution to this book in the sacrifice of our time and presence of mind that they might otherwise have enjoyed.

Our thanks to Dr Shajimon Peter for maintaining momentum on our shared project to engage the whole of the social work profession in Aotearoa New Zealand in the issues to deal with transnational social workers while we completed this book. We also acknowledge the work of Sue Osborne who has provided editorial support for referencing and style.

Our journey into research with and about transnational social workers began in 2009 with a Faculty Research Development Fund (FRDF) grant, from the Faculty of Education and Social Work at the University of Auckland. Professor Christa Fouché was the principal investigator on that project. We are grateful to Christa for her leadership and to the FRDF for providing the impetus to launch us into this work. Our thanks, too, to the research participants who gave so generously of their time and their insights.

Finally, this collection could not have been produced without our contributors. We were delighted that all we approached accepted our invitation to contribute and they represent the leading scholars in this important area of research. This book thus represents a collaborative effort to share and advance international understanding of the transnational social work space.

List of tables and figures

List of abbreviations

AASW	Australian Association of Social Workers
AHMAC	Australian Health Ministers' Advisory Council
AHPA	Allied Health Professions Australia
AHPRA	Australian Health Practitioners Regulation Agency
ANZASW	Aotearoa New Zealand Association of Social Workers
ASWEAS	Australian Social Work Education and Accreditation Standards
CASW	Canadian Association of Social Workers
COAG	Council of Australian Governments
EASSW	European Association of Schools of Social Work
GSCC	General Social Care Council
HCPC	Health and Care Professions Council
IASSW	International Association of Schools of Social Work
IFSW	International Federation of Social Workers
JUC SWEC	Joint University Council Social Work Education Committee
NASRHP	National Alliance of Self-Regulating Health Professions
NISCC	Northern Ireland Social Care Council
NRAS	National Registration and Accreditation Scheme
NSPCC	National Society for the Prevention of Cruelty to Children
NSWQB	National Social Work Qualifications Board
SCWRU	Social Care Workforce Research Unit
SWRB	Social Workers Registration Board
TSW	transnational social worker

Notes on contributors

Donna Baines is Professor and Chair of Social Work and Policy Studies, University of Sydney, Australia. Her research is on paid and unpaid care work in the context of changing social policy and anti-oppressive theory and practice. She recently published the third edition of *Doing anti-oppressive practice. Social justice social work* (2017, Fernwood) and has had articles appear recently in *British Journal of Social Work*, *Critical Social Policy* and the *Journal of Industrial Relations*.

Allen Bartley is Head of the School of Counselling, Human Services and Social Work in the Faculty of Education and Social Work, University of Auckland, New Zealand. As an 'embedded sociologist' in the social work programme, Allen's teaching has addressed sociology and social theory, social welfare law, and research methodologies and methods. Born and raised in the US, Allen migrated to Aotearoa New Zealand in 1992 – an experience that has motivated his research interest in migration, transnationalism and the adjustment experiences of transnational families.

Liz Beddoe is Associate Professor in the Faculty of Education and Social Work, University of Auckland, New Zealand. Liz's teaching and research interests include critical perspectives on social work education and professional supervision. Liz has published articles on supervision and professional issues in New Zealand and international journals. Recent books include the co-authored (with Allyson Davys) *Challenges in professional supervision* (2016, Jessica Kingsley Publishers) and *Social work practice for promoting health and wellbeing: Critical issues* (2014, Routledge), and (with Jane Maidment) *Social policy for social work and human services in Aotearoa New Zealand: Diverse perspectives* (2016, Canterbury University Press).

Marion Brown is Associate Professor at the Dalhousie University School of Social Work, Canada, and registered social worker. Her research focuses on the experiences of internationally educated social workers, professional identity development in interprofessional teams and critical pedagogies in social work education. Marion has worked in a variety of settings, including community-based non-profit programmes, clinical counselling practice and assessment services, in roles from front-line to supervisory.

Stephanie Éthier is a PhD student at the University of Montreal's School of Social Work, Canada. Under the supervision of Dr Annie Pullen Sansfaçon, she has completed a master's degree investigating how social workers transfer their knowledge across national borders, particularly to the Montreal context of practice. Before turning to research, Stephanie practised social work for nearly 15 years in several different areas.

Amy Fulton is a postdoctoral scholar with the Alberta Resilient Communities (ARC) project at the Faculty of Social Work, University of Calgary, Canada. As a social worker and researcher in Alberta, her research focus is on community-based inquiry related to the contextualised social work and human services professional practice realities and educational landscape in Alberta. Her dissertation presented a comparative gender analysis of the professional adaptation experiences of migrant social workers in Alberta. Dr Fulton's areas of research interest include social worker migration and adaptation, disaster social work, and social work education.

Sue Hanna is the Workforce Development Team Leader for Social Care at the London Borough of Tower Hamlets, UK. She was a social work educator in New Zealand and England for many years and her interest in transnational social work developed after she immigrated to the UK in 2010. In 2011, she was awarded a research grant by the Nuffield Foundation to investigate the experiences and perspectives on practice of London-based transnational social workers and their managers. The results of this study provide the basis for this current book chapter.

Gai Harrison works as a social work clinical educator for Metro North Hospital and Health Service, Brisbane, and is an honorary senior lecturer in social work at the University of Queensland, Australia. Prior to taking up her position as clinical educator, she worked in higher education in both Australia and England for 12 years. Her current role involves coordinating staff training and professional learning placements for social work students. Her research and teaching interests span social work education, field education, human services workforce issues, migration and working with difference.

Karen Healy is a Professor in the School of Nursing, Midwifery and Social Work, in the Faculty of Health and Behavioural Sciences at the University of Queensland, Australia. From 2011 to 2017, Karen was the National President of the Australian Association of Social Workers (the national accrediting body for professional social work in Australia). Karen is also National Director for The Benevolent Society, Australia's oldest not-for-profit community service organisation. Karen's research focuses on promoting a healthy start to life for vulnerable children, young people and families. In 2016, she was appointed a member of the Order of Australia (AM) for her contribution to social work particularly in child protection, higher education and research.

Shereen Hussein is a Research Professor at King's College London, UK. She is a demographer with a sound statistical and economic background. Her current research focuses on ageing demographics and long-term care (LTC) demand and migration within the UK and Europe. She has led research streams on: migrant workers and global care; transnational health and care professional workers; diversity, structure and wage differentials in the LTC sector; and several national evaluations of new models of working. Shereen has an international research presence in Europe and Scandinavia, the Middle East, the Russian Federation, and Australasia, collaborating with organisations such as the World Health Organization, United Nations Children's Fund (UNICEF) and the World Bank.

Karen Lyons is an Emeritus Professor at London Metropolitan University, UK. For 26 years, she was a social work educator at the University of East London, where she developed award-bearing courses in international social work. Her doctoral research (into British social work education), together with experience in the International Association of Schools of Social Work (IASSW) and as the Editor of *International Social Work*, resulted in contributions to the development of social work education, for example, in Lithuania and (currently) Malawi. Her most recent writing, on international labour mobility and transnational social work, echoes and extends earlier research activity in relation to the national professional workforce.

Kate Matheson is a registered social worker currently working in health-care policy, living on Nova Scotia's South Shore, Canada. Kate's experience varies from non-profit, community work to clinical mental health. Kate has recently joined the Nova Scotia College of Social Workers Council and sits on the College Candidacy Committee, which is exploring registration and licensing in Nova Scotia.

Litea Meo-Sewabu is from Fiji and has lived in New Zealand for the past 11 years. She is currently the coordinator for the Pacific Research and Policy Centre at Massey University. Prior to her current role, she taught at the School of Social Work on Pacific well-being, community development and indigenous research. Her current research explores Pacific customary land with a team of researchers at Massey University as part of a Marsden-funded project. Her doctorate explored the understanding of health and well-being among indigenous Fijian women in a village in Lau and in a transnational community in Aotearoa New Zealand.

Erna O'Connor is assistant professor of social work, director of the Master in Social Work programme and fieldwork coordinator at the School of Social Work and Social Policy, Trinity College, Dublin, Republic of Ireland. Prior to joining the university, she worked as a social worker in drug treatment services and a social worker and social work team leader in hospital-based social work. Her teaching and research interests include health-related social work, reflective and relationship-based practice, practice learning, and transnational social work.

Angelika Papadopoulos is a lecturer in the School of Global Urban and Social Studies at RMIT University, Australia, and teaches theory, practice and research in the social work programmes. Prior to becoming an academic, she was a philosopher, musician and worked in dispute resolution. Her research interests focus on understanding social policy shifts in the 21st century and their impact on human existence and possibilities.

Annie Pullen Sansfaçon is Associate Professor at the University of Montreal's School of Social Work, Canada. Her work focuses on the development of anti-oppressive theories, approaches and methodologies to promote ethical and emancipatory practice in social work. Her most recent projects include research that aims at understanding the experiences of the adaptation of internationally educated social workers, as well as research on the experiences of oppression of trans children and their families.

Helen Simmons is a Pākehā New Zealander and is employed at Massey University as a Senior Professional Clinician in the School of Social Work. She has worked alongside her co-authors and other colleagues over a number of years developing and delivering programmes to enhance cultural competence.

Antoinette Umugwaneza is from Rwanda. She came to New Zealand in 1996 as a refugee. She has a Bachelor in Economics and Social Sciences from the National University of Rwanda and a Diploma in Counselling from UCOL, New Zealand. She currently works as a resettlement case worker and cultural advisor for New Zealand Red Cross in Palmerston North.

Trish Walsh is assistant professor of social work in Trinity College, Dublin, Republic of Ireland. Prior to joining the School of Social Work in Trinity College, Dublin, she worked in practice in the UK and Ireland in child welfare, mental health and family therapy. Her interest in patterns of social work transnational mobility stems from her time as a member of the board of the Irish National Social Work Qualifications Board from 2006 to 2011.

Wheturangi Walsh-Tapiata is an indigenous woman from Aotearoa New Zealand. She has taught in social work education for many years and is currently the Pouārahi (national programme lead) for the health and social work programmes based at Te Wānanga o Aotearoa, one of the three indigenous universities in Aotearoa New Zealand.

George Wilson's main research interests are in social work education and mental health, and he has published extensively in both these fields. Dr Wilson has a special interest in comparative social work research and has been involved in a number of studies that have focused on educational policy and practice in Northern Ireland and the Republic of Ireland. Dr Wilson was formerly programme director of the MSc in Strategy and Leadership (Social Work) in Queen's University, Belfast, and currently works as an independent researcher and part-time lecturer at Queens

ONE

Transnational social work: opportunities and challenges of a global profession

Allen Bartley and Liz Beddoe

Introduction

The professional experiences of transnational social workers (TSWs) form the central focus of this book. The Oxford online dictionary defines 'transnational' as 'extending or operating across national boundaries' and our usage of the term delineates social workers who have gained their professional education in one nation and who relocate to practise (or aspire to practise) in another. Since the turn of the millennium, there has been a growing recognition that 'transnationalism' is an increasingly appropriate concept to describe the activities of some migrants and migrant communities, expanding the term's application beyond merely describing the activities of corporations and flows of capital (Faist, 2004; Levitt and Jaworsky, 2007; Portes et al, 2007; Patterson, 2009). The two are not unrelated, of course: in 'freeing' capital to move easily across the world economy, nation-states have also increasingly facilitated the movement of labour – across all strata of the economy, from agricultural labourers to chief executives (Portes, 2003; Nora Chiang, 2008; Faulconbridge and Muzio, 2011; Seabrooke, 2014). That technological advances have made international travel and communication far simpler and cheaper than for previous generations – combined with the relative ease of shifting capital across international borders – has meant that migrant individuals, families and communities are able to sustain intense contact and exchange between both sending and receiving societies, maintaining degrees of simultaneous embeddedness in both (Glick Schiller et al, 1992; Portes et al, 1999). Their 'shift' across international borders may be temporary or long-term. Their decision to cross borders may be informed by push and/or pull factors: political or religious conflict; violence; economic need; employment opportunities; new or existing family relationships with transnationals; career advancement; adventure; and discovery of heritage and ancestry (Beddoe and Fouché, 2014).

An increasingly pressing demand in the study of globalisation and transnational migration is the need for particular professions to address the complex dynamics within each profession that are brought about by transnational labour market mobility (Verwiebe and Eder, 2006). Prior examinations of transnational labour flows have tended towards a bifurcated focus of either low-waged, unskilled or semi-skilled labour migrants on the one hand, or members of the transnational capitalist class on the other: professional, managerial or entrepreneurial elites. However, less attention has been paid to the skilled transnational migrants who fall into other categories between these extremes (such as teachers, health and allied health professionals), or to the institutional spaces that they occupy.

Social work is a particular example of an increasingly transnationally mobile profession, and one that highlights unique challenges to the globalisation discourse. There is an assumption that the principles, values and theoretical approaches that underpin social work are sufficiently common in many countries as to enable the growing mobility of social work professionals across international borders, although this idea of a universal social work is contested, as will be explored throughout this book. Social work is an occupation that frequently appears on national skills shortage lists in the UK, Australia, Canada and Aotearoa New Zealand; this makes it easier for employers to recruit social workers from other countries, and for TSWs to obtain work permits and permanent residency status in foreign jurisdictions. Such ease of labour market mobility has the potential to create transnational professional spaces (Bartley et al, 2012) in which multiple fields of practice are connected by sustained networks of ties across national borders. However, transnational professional spaces also create challenges involved in transplanting models of practice, professional dispositions and knowledge of law and policy from familiar fields to foreign jurisdictions. These challenges confront government policymakers, social service employers, service users and user communities, and the whole of the social work profession, as well as the growing number of transnational professionals themselves.

The opportunities and challenges presented by the steady growth of transnational social work labour market mobility have only recently begun to be explored systematically in the key social work labour markets of the UK (White, 2006; Welbourne et al, 2007; Hussein et al, 2011; Lyons and Hanna, 2011; Moriarty et al, 2012; Hanna and Lyons, 2014; Hussein, 2014); Ireland (Walsh et al, 2010); Canada

(Pullen Sansfaçon et al, 2014; Brown et al, 2014; Fulton et al, 2016); Switzerland (Bolzman, 2015); Australia (Zubrzycki et al, 2008; Harrison, 2013; Papadopoulos, 2017); and Aotearoa New Zealand (Bartley et al, 2011, 2012; Fouché et al, 2013, 2014, 2015; Simmons et al, 2014). All of these authors reinforce the point that social work is a unique profession in which to explore transnational dynamics. Unlike many other global labour markets, social work involves the movement of professionals in every direction – south to north, north to south, east to west and west to east – and 'churn' within and across jurisdictions. Other elements also distinguish social work from other transnational labour markets: as argued by many in this book, the unique nature of social work practice – including the intensely interpersonal nature of the work and the central role played by culture and other forms of social identity in the everyday context of professional interactions – makes social work different from most other professions, and creates some unique contours for this particular transnational professional space.

There are many common themes that emerge from this international body of literature. First, many TSWs experience a degree of professional dislocation. They may face challenges in finding meaningful employment where their skills can be fully utilised. Second, they frequently experience complex and protracted communication with professional bodies over the appropriate recognition of their professional qualifications and experience. Third, they too often experience very limited professional induction and professional development in their new professional contexts. Lastly, they must negotiate – in both their private and professional lives – the complexity of the new socio-political and cultural environment. In social work, this cannot be relegated to weekends and holidays: immersion in the culture and politics of social services, justice, health and education is central to practice. All of these aspects pose challenges to the professional identity of TSWs.

Nuttman-Shwartz (2017, p 1) observes that 'professional identity combines the definition of a profession and the nature of identity with the processes involved in acquiring the identity, both by the individual and by members of a professional group'. At the heart of these 'processes' is the convoluted nature of social work's relations and status within its many contexts. In the early 2000s, there was much written about social work becoming an international or global profession, linked inextricably to globalisation as an economic phenomenon (see, eg, Khan and Dominelli, 2000). This perspective was confronted by others: a challenge mounted by Pugh and Gould (2000), for example, argued that the globalisation approach was overly reliant on economic determinism; additionally, Webb (2003, p 202) asserts:

Appeals for global social work seem to be little more than a vanity. Local cultural orders of reflexivity – concentrating as they do on the raw stuff of interactions, plans and morality – recognize the need for a shared culture of depth understanding that comes with being native to that culture as a language user and agent of the kinesics and proxemics of 'being-here'.

In the decade since early discussions of social worker mobility were published (Lyons and Littlechild, 2006; White, 2006; Welbourne et al, 2007), the concerns noted within the professional literature have crystallised around two significant sets of factors, bringing together the four themes described earlier. These can be roughly categorised as the profession/employer perspective and the migrant professional experience. In spite of increasing international mobility, Bolzman (2015, p 5) argues that 'new transnational social realities do not necessarily match with these laws and policies' as social work continues to be influenced mainly by a strong national dimension and, furthermore, 'is not very sensitive to the transnational dimension'. Thus, the tensions and challenges remain largely unresolved.

Our aim in editing this collection is to bring together the leading researchers in this field to explore the current state of play from five jurisdictions; all these countries share English as a common language. It happens that these anglophone countries provide the context in which current research on TSWs is actively being undertaken. This is not to say that social workers do not migrate to, and seek to practice in, other countries; however, research in other jurisdictions has not yet emerged. This helps to explain what appears at first to be the surprising absence of the US in this book. Each US state maintains its own licensing regimes that make inter-state mobility difficult for US social workers, and perhaps suppresses the demand for overseas-qualified social workers. This dynamic makes the US a unique case among anglophone jurisdictions, and perhaps explains the lack of research on transnational socials workers practising there. By introducing and comparing the social work labour market contexts in the five jurisdictions (UK, Ireland, Canada, Australia and Aotearoa New Zealand), the book aims to:

• provide detailed descriptions and analysis of the opportunities and challenges presented by transnational social work labour market mobility in each jurisdiction;

- present and discuss the findings of research into the experiences and perceptions of TSWs, in dialogue with the related professional and policy contexts; and
- inform the development of relevant policy and educational responses to the phenomenon of transnational social work mobility.

Our contributors draw on the latest research into the experiences of TSWs, social work employers and the policy contexts that impact on transnational labour market mobility. As such, we hope that this collection will be of interest to the following groups:

- *students*, many of whom will have the opportunity to consider transnational mobility at various points in their social work careers;
- *social service employers and managers*, who will work with practitioners with foreign qualifications and experience, and whose agencies may actively recruit from foreign jurisdictions;
- *social work educators* involved in training students for both local and international fields of practice;
- *professional bodies and registration authorities*, who must be better equipped to engage with transnationally mobile professionals, to assess foreign qualifications and experience, and to articulate essential points of commonality and difference across international fields of practice;
- *economists* and others who study international labour market dynamics; and
- *policymakers*, who must understand and anticipate the interrelated consequences of immigration policies, labour market dynamics, the politics of professionalisation and professional recognition, and the intensely local nature of the social work practice context.

The structure and content of the book

As identified earlier, any discussion of the opportunities and challenges of transnational social work tends to highlight four main elements. The first two of these are obvious: there are the perspectives and imperatives of the service agencies that employ social workers; and then – often presented as being at odds with these – there are the experiences of the transnational professionals themselves. A third perspective is offered by the professional bodies: whether they are statutory and regulatory, or voluntary associations, their role is framed as either facilitating and obstructionist, accommodating or penalising national differences, or variously expansionist or protectionist in outlook. The final element is, inevitably, a suggestion of the responses required. However, finding workable responses is itself a challenge given the range of stakeholders involved. It is difficult to imagine a single strategy or set of initiatives that would satisfy the imperatives of employers to fill skills shortages while simultaneously upholding the accreditation standards of the profession and providing reasonable opportunities for transnational migrants who have chosen to uproot from one nation to contribute to another, all the while providing meaningful, appropriate and competent services to the individuals, families and communities who need them. Readers might be surprised to find almost no discussion of the experiences of service users with regard to transnational social work practitioners. The reason for this is that research simply has not yet been conducted that captures service users' voices in this area. However, as a number of chapters in this book argue, there is growing evidence that service users are not well served when transnational practitioners – however well-qualified and experienced they may be – are ill-prepared for the specific social and cultural nuances that they encounter in new practice contexts. It must also be noted that in each of the five jurisdictions under discussion in this volume, questions about the incorporation of TSWs take place in a context in which the profession is already grappling with other significant questions. One of the most pressing of these questions concerns the nature of the social work profession itself, and whether (or to what extent) it can or should regulate itself (in terms of defining what social work is, what social workers do and the values/ethics frameworks that inform their practice) in the face of what we identify in this volume as the increased intrusion into the profession by neoliberal state regimes. Donna Baines foregrounds these issues in Chapter Three, and Hanna and Lyons highlight in Chapter Five that TSWs in England observed the de-professionalising impact of such state intrusion; however, this tension is at play in each jurisdiction under study. It is perhaps not a coincidence that statutory social work in each of these jurisdictions experiences such labour force churn as to motivate the apparent demand for overseas-qualified practitioners in the first instance. In this context, we aim to both explore the challenges faced by the stakeholders in social worker mobility and to consider some of the potential to mitigate these challenges.

Part One: Setting the transnational context

The book has been organised into four parts. The first part provides an overview of the context and introduces the wider context within which transnational labour mobility in social work takes place. In

Chapter Two, Karen Lyons explores the opportunities and challenges of a global profession from an international perspective. Beginning with a theme addressed in numerous places in this book, Lyons questions the extent to which global definitions, codes and standards are widely understood or applied, weakening their possible utility for TSWs. Lyons notes that many social problems are international, often with common issues and client populations; however, on the local level, the way in which services are funded and organised, and the configuration of social work roles within such services, is where wide variation occurs, with implications for education and local practices. Finally, Lyons discusses the strengths of TSWs but notes that these practitioners are often undervalued due to their positioning as lacking local knowledge and the related skill sets.

Donna Baines, in Chapter Three, sets out the increasingly mobile nature of the social work workforce against a backdrop of widespread neoliberal social policy and the presence of management models such as New Public Management. Baines argues that these global processes overlap with local contexts to both create and limit possibilities for social work practice that is led by social justice principles and a human rights orientation. Drawing on qualitative case-study data collected in Canada, Australia, the UK and New Zealand, this chapter encompasses three themes. First, Baines briefly sketches the history of colonialism and immigration that shaped, and shapes, these four countries. Second, she discusses the standardising influence of managerialism on social work practice possibilities in the four countries, in particular, exploring the increasing use of immigrant 'volunteer' labour and other forms of unpaid labour, including student placements and internships, as a response to the ongoing underfunding of social services and policies of 'permanent' austerity. The chapter finally addresses the implications for social work practice and possibilities for social-justice-based social work.

Part Two: Practitioner perspectives

The four chapters in this section of the book each focus on the experiences of TSWs in a single jurisdiction. In doing so, the authors demonstrate both the uniformity of the sorts of opportunities and challenges faced by TSWs (including the confrontation with 'race', class and the ongoing impact of colonialism), and the particular ways in which these are manifested in local contexts. Addressing the Canadian experience in Chapter Four, Marion Brown, Annie Pullen Sansfaçon, Stephanie Éthier and Amy Fulton apply Bourdieu's concept of forms of capital (particularly cultural capital) to assess the complicated ways in which the various forms of cultural capital accrued by individual transnational professionals are subject to a kind of 'variable exchange rate' in Canada. In doing so, they provide insights into the tensions between the neoliberal framing of what makes for 'successful' migrant adaptation and the recognition of the social and institutional forces at play in those processes.

The social and institutional impact on the experiences of individual TSWs is also examined in the English context by Sue Hanna and Karen Lyons in Chapter Five. Here, we see TSWs working to adjust to a practice context that is, in itself, experiencing significant upheaval as managerialist and technocratic imperatives have transformed statutory child protection social work and threaten to undermine the professional status of social work. While many of the insights and concerns of the transnational participants in the authors' study may actually be shared with their UK-trained social work colleagues, such as the stifling bureaucracy and the lack of adequate professional supervision, TSWs demonstrate their resilience in adapting to these conditions while also adjusting to an unfamiliar cultural context and a professional milieu in which their expertise and skills may be underutilised or altogether unrecognised.

In Chapter Six, Allen Bartley reports on the experiences of TSWs in Australia. The focus in this discussion is on the relationship between the transnational professionals and their first Australian social work employer. Specifically, Bartley suggests that both professionals and employers demonstrate a surprising naivety when considering (or, more appropriately, *not* considering) the manifold differences between Australian practice contexts and those of the many countries from which TSWs have come, as well as preparing and providing (or not) induction and ongoing professional development activities to bridge foreign-qualified and experienced professionals into the local context.

Beddoe, in Chapter Seven, reports on research on TSWs undertaken in Aotearoa New Zealand. While much has been written about social worker migration to the northern hemisphere, prior to the current decade, little was known about the experiences of social workers, with professional qualifications gained elsewhere, who were practising in Aotearoa New Zealand. Aotearoa New Zealand is a unique cultural context, bringing particular challenges to TSWs, who may arrive knowing little about the country's history of colonisation and the ongoing struggles of the indigenous Māori population. A programme of research used both qualitative and quantitative strategies in a three-phase project to gain greater insight into transnationals' experiences. An overview of findings in this chapter contributes greater understanding of the transitional experience for migrant professionals. Beddoe identifies themes of 'enduring professional dislocation', arising from limits to the portability of any 'universal' constructs of social work and demonstrating the need for structured support and education for TSWs.

Part Three: Employer/stakeholder views

The subsequent three chapters shift the focus from the experiences of the transnational professionals themselves to a range of institutional and regulatory factors that shape (or, in the case of Chapter Ten, that *could* shape) the experiences of TSWs and their integration into unfamiliar national contexts. In Chapter Eight, Shereen Hussein presents a picture of the changing nature of British social work (especially statutory child protection work) amid wider changes in Britain's immigration and labour market policies. As Hussein discusses, many of these policies have now been thrown into uncertainty in the wake of the 'Brexit' referendum. While the regulatory and accreditation processes may be subject to change, demand in the UK for skilled and experienced foreign social workers continues, and Hussein's work highlights the continuing centrality of British social work employers in facilitating the successful adaptation of transnational professionals.

Gai Harrison, in Chapter Nine, continues the theme of the importance of employers' deliberations and decision-making in shaping labour market outcomes for TSWs in Australia. Harrison refers to the 'informal recognition' of foreign qualifications and experiences as holding greater weight in the labour market than any formal assessment undertaken by the professional authority – in this case, the Australian Association of Social Workers (AASW). Harrison's analysis suggests that in a policy environment that favours the immigration of skilled workers and international students, the uncertainty of the labour market demand for social workers and local reticence to recognise non-Australian qualifications and professional experience create risks for transnational professionals that have yet to be explored in detail.

Chapter Ten provides a welcome contribution to the discussion about TSWs: that of indigenous voices. Writing from the context of Aotearoa New Zealand, Wheturangi Walsh-Tapiata, Helen Simmons, Litea Meo-Sewabu and Antoinette Umugwaneza present the various elements of the traditional Māori ritual of welcome, called pōwhiri. In extending their own generous welcome, the authors describe the cultural significance of each step of the ceremony, familiar to many Aotearoa New Zealand social workers and social work students, and explain why TSWs should always experience such a welcome on their arrival in a new employment setting. Walsh-Tapiata and her collaborators then shift to view the pōwhiri as a metaphor, and explain how each element of the welcome might be internalised by transnational professionals to strengthen their cultural competence to work with Māori people.

In Chapter Eleven, the focus moves again to Canada, where Annie Pullen Sansfaçon, Marion Brown and Stephanie Éthier provide a novel insight into the ways in which the TSWs in their study maintained their fundamental social work values (established in their origin countries) while adjusting to the new practice contexts in Canada. Their study found remarkable consistency in professionals' assessment of a series of case-study vignettes, while revealing considerable variety in participants' preferred intervention goals and strategies. The authors suggest that a focus on shared professional values may help to facilitate the professional adaptation of transnational professionals.

Part Four: Policy challenges, professional responses

The final section in the book begins to move us in the direction of dialogue across the profession. Marion Brown, Annie Pullen Sansfaçon and Kate Matheson demonstrate the impact of such a dialogue in the Canadian context in Chapter Twelve. There, they report on a pair of 'knowledge exchange fora' in two Canadian cities that involved both domestic social workers and TSWs, employers, and representatives from the provincial regulatory bodies. Their study highlights the proposition that the adaptation of TSWs is never internal merely to the individual professional. Rather, it is the result of the interaction of those individual efforts with the work of 'employers, supervisors, colleagues and regulators ... because each position rests upon the others in the ultimate aim of expanding the possibilities of social workers finding their place in Canadian social work practice' (see p 198). The authors also remind us that in collaborating towards the profession's social justice aspirations, social work professionals and stakeholders can better resist the neoliberal policies and discourses that take such a toll on social work agencies and the communities with whom they work.

In Chapter Thirteen Karen Healy discusses government regulation of the health and human service professions in Australia, and the implications for social workers seeking to relocate to Australia. Healy explores the dynamics of professional self-regulation in the absence of the statutory registration of social workers. She addresses the challenges of self-regulation in achieving both professional standards and diversity within the social work profession, and the implications of the self-regulating environment for TSWs seeking to migrate and practise in Australia. Healy notes the potential for cooperation between jurisdictions in a discussion of how professional bodies in Australia and Aotearoa New Zealand are collaborating to strengthen professional standards and capacities.

In Chapter Fourteen, Angelika Papadopoulos uses those same social justice aspirations and the ethical principles that frame social work practice to critique the politics of credentialing in Australia. Presently, according to Papadopoulos, the processes for assessing and recognising the qualifications and experience of TSWs wishing to practise in Australia are situated in, and are products of, more narrow technocratic imperatives that are divorced from social work values. By foregrounding those values, Papadopoulos offers a discussion that is at once both familiar to social work professionals and challenging in its implications.

In Chapter Fifteen, Trish Walsh, George Wilson and Erna O'Connor present a European case study of social worker mobility in rapidly changing times. The authors draw on data from the Republic of Ireland from 2004 to 2013, capturing the years leading up to, and in the aftermath of, the global financial crisis of 2008. This is contrasted with the situation in Northern Ireland. Drawing on statistical and descriptive data provided by Irish social work registration bodies (National Social Work Qualifications Board [NSWQB] during 1997–2011, CORU established in 2011 and the Northern Ireland Social Care Council [NISCC] established in 2001) the authors illustrate the sensitivity of mobility patterns to rapidly changing economic and political factors. They note rapid changes in patterns of mobility and consider how much greater complexity in European social work mobility will present if the European project itself fractures, as is possible following the Brexit referendum vote in the UK.

Conclusion

It is evident that demand for social workers will persist in all the jurisdictions canvassed in this book and that in each of those countries, social workers will continue to practise in challenging contexts. Structural issues within the labour markets of each of the countries under discussion are such that TSWs will continue to be in demand for the foreseeable future. The profession's foundational commitments to human rights and social justice are especially relevant at this time when considering (and anticipating) the communities most at risk of disadvantage and marginalisation in each of the jurisdictions addressed in this book, particularly amid growing sensitivities regarding immigration and anti-migrant political rhetoric, and the flashpoints that these issues can – and have – become in populist discourses in the US, the UK, Australia, Ireland, Canada and Aotearoa New Zealand. The experiences of TSWs in this volume speak to the complexity of migration politics. Immigration policies are devised and exercised at a federal or national level, while the regulations that govern professionals are frequent devolved to the country (in the case of the UK), state or province level. While migration may often be characterised as driven by a 'market logic', this policy complexity amid the flurry of anti-migrant discourses creates contradictions impacting adversely on professional transnationals.

TSWs practising in these contexts may, in fact, face a dual impact: they may work with migrants, asylum seeks and refugees, and other marginalised communities, while simultaneously identifying as members of those communities and being equally subject to the alienating discourses currently gaining mainstream prominence. There can be no doubt that the social work profession occupies a critical space in this moment, although, as the contributions in this volume make clear, how the profession responds to the challenges and opportunities of transnationalism is far from resolved.

A note on conventions

As this is an international project, we as editors have tried to remain sensitive to local terminologies as far as possible. For instance, it is the Australian convention to capitalise 'Indigenous' when used as an adjective to describe the Indigenous populations in that country. Another indigenising influence is seen among the New Zealand contributions in the incorporation of Māori words and phrases (explained where appropriate), including the increasingly common practice of using both the Māori and English names when referring to the country – hence, Aotearoa New Zealand. At the same time, for the sake of consistency and in deference to our UK publisher, we have required all contributions to adhere to UK spelling conventions.

References

Bartley, A., Beddoe, L., Duke, J., Fouché, C., Harington, P.R.J. and Shah, R. (2011) 'Crossing borders: key features of migrant social workers in New Zealand', *Aotearoa New Zealand Social Work*, 23(3): 16–30.

Bartley, A., Fouché, C., Beddoe, L. and Harington, P. (2012) 'Transnational social workers: making the profession a transnational professional space', *International Journal of Population Research*, online: 1–11, doi:10.1155/2012/527510.

Beddoe, L. and Fouché, C.B. (2014) '"Kiwis on the move": New Zealand social workers' experience of practising abroad', *British Journal of Social Work*, 44(suppl 1): i193–i208.

Bolzman, C. (2015) 'Immigrant social workers and transnational practices: the example of Latin Americans in Switzerland', *Journal of Immigrant & Refugee Studies*, 13(30): 281–301.

Brown, M., Sansfaçon, A.P., Éthier, S. and Fulton, A. (2014) 'A complicated welcome: social workers navigate policy, organizational contexts and socio-cultural dynamics following migration to Canada', *International Journal of Social Science Studies*, 3(1): 58–68.

Faist, T. (2004) 'Towards a political sociology of transnationalisation: the state of the art in migration research', *European Journal of Sociology*, 45(3): 331–66.

Faulconbridge, J.R. and Muzio, D. (2011) 'Professions in a globalizing world: towards a transnational sociology of the professions', *International Sociology*, 27(1): 136–52.

Fouché, C., Beddoe, L., Bartley, A. and Brenton, N. (2013) 'Strengths and struggles: overseas qualified social workers' experiences in Aotearoa New Zealand', *Australian Social Work*, 67(4): 551–66.

Fouché, C., Beddoe, L., Bartley, A. and De Haan, I. (2014) 'Enduring professional dislocation: migrant social workers' perceptions of their professional roles', *British Journal of Social Work*, 44(7): 2004–22.

Fouché, C., Beddoe, L., Bartley, A. and Parkes, E. (2015) 'Are we ready for them? Overseas-qualified social workers' professional cultural transition', *European Journal of Social Work*, 19(1): 106–19.

Fulton, A.E., Pullen Sansfaçon, A., Brown, M., Éthier, S. and Graham, J.R. (2016) 'Migrant social workers, foreign credential recognition and securing employment in Canada: a qualitative analysis of pre-employment experiences', *Canadian Social Work Review/Revue Canadienne de Service Social*, 33(1): 65–86.

Glick Schiller, N., Basch, L. and Blanc-Szanton, C. (1992) 'Towards a definition of transnationalism: introductory remarks and research questions', *Annals of the New York Academy of Sciences*, 645: ix–xiv.

Hanna, S. and Lyons, K. (2014) 'Challenges facing international social workers: English managers' perceptions', *International Social Work*, 59(6): 722–33.

Harrison, G. (2013) '"Oh, you've got such a strong accent": language identity intersecting with professional identity in the human services in Australia', *International Migration*, 51(5): 192–204.

Hussein, S. (2014) 'Hierarchical challenges to transnational social workers' mobility: the United Kingdom as a destination within an expanding European Union', *British Journal of Social Work*, 44 (Issue suppl 1): i174–i192. doi:10.1093/bjsw/bcu050.

Hussein, S., Manthorpe, J. and Stevens, M. (2011) 'The experiences of migrant social work and social care practitioners in the UK: findings from an online survey', *European Journal of Social Work*, 14(4): 479–96.

Khan, P. and Dominelli, L. (2000) 'The impact of globalization on social work in the UK', *European Journal of Social Work*, 3(2): 95–108.

Levitt, P. and Jaworsky, B.N. (2007) 'Transnational migration studies: past developments and future trends', *Annual Review of Sociology*, 33: 129–56.

Lyons, K. and Hanna, S. (2011) 'European social workers in England: exploring international labour mobility', *Revista de Asistenţă Socială*, 10(3): 185–96.

Lyons, K. and Littlechild, B. (eds) (2006) *International labour mobility in social work*, Birmingham: Venture Press BASW.

Moriarty, J., Hussein, S., Manthorpe, J. and Stevens, M. (2012) 'International social workers in England: factors influencing supply and demand', *International Social Work*, 55(2): 169–84.

Nora Chiang, L.-H. (2008) '"Astronaut families": transnational lives of middle-class Taiwanese married women in Canada', *Social and Cultural Geography*, 9(5): 505–18.

Nuttman-Shwartz, O. (2017) 'Rethinking professional identity in a globalized world', *Clinical Social Work Journal*, 45(1): 1–9.

Papadopoulos, A. (2017) 'Migrating qualifications: the ethics of recognition', *British Journal of Social Work*, 47(1): 219–37. doi:10.1093/bjsw/bcw038.

Patterson, R. (2009) 'The migration–development model can serve two masters: the transnational capitalist class and national development', *Perspectives on Global Development and Technology*, 8: 211–29.

Portes, A. (2003) 'Conclusion: theoretical convergencies and empirical evidence in the study of immigrant transnationalism', *The International Migration Review*, 37(3): 874–92.

Portes, A., Guarnizo, L. and Landolt, P. (1999) 'The study of transnationalism: pitfalls and promise of an emergent research field', *Ethnic and Racial Studies*, 22(2): 217–36.

Portes, A., Escobar, C. and Radford, A.W. (2007) 'Immigrant transnational organizations and development: a comparative study', *The International Migration Review*, 41(1): 242–81.

Pugh, R. and Gould, N. (2000) 'Globalization, social work, and social welfare', *European Journal of Social Work*, 3(2): 123–38.

Pullen Sansfaçon, A., Brown, M., Graham, J. and Dumais Michaud, A.-A. (2014) 'Adaptation and acculturation: experiences of internationally educated social workers', *Journal of International Migration and Integration*, 15(6): 317–30.

Seabrooke, L. (2014) 'Epistemic arbitrage: transnational professional knowledge in action', *Journal of Professions and Organization*, 1: 49–64.

Simmons, H., Walsh-Tapiata, W., Litea, M.-S. and Umugwaneza, A. (2014) '"Cultural encounter": a framework of ethical practice for transnational social workers in Aotearoa', in J. Duke, M. Henrickson and L. Beddoe (eds) *Protecting the public – Enhancing the profession*, Wellington, NZ: Social Workers Registration Board, pp 66–78.

Verwiebe, R. and Eder, K. (2006) 'The positioning of transnationally mobile Europeans in the German labour market', *European Societies*, 8(1): 141–67.

Walsh, T., Wilson, G. and O'Connor, E. (2010) 'Local, European and global: an exploration of migration patterns of social workers into Ireland', *British Journal of Social Work*, 40(6): 1978–95.

Webb, S. (2003) 'Local orders and global chaos in social work', *European Journal of Social Work*, 6(2): 191–204.

Welbourne, P., Harrison, G. and Ford, D. (2007) 'Social work in the UK and the global labour market: recruitment, practice and ethical considerations', *International Social Work*, 50(1): 27–40.

White, R. (2006) 'Opportunities and challenges for social workers crossing borders', *International Social Work*, 49(5): 629–40.

Zubrzycki, J., Thomson, L. and Trevithick, P. (2008) 'International recruitment in child protection: the experiences of workers in the Australian Capital Territory', *Communities, Families and Children Australia*, 3(2): 30–8.

Part One:
Setting the transnational context

TWO

Opportunities and challenges of a global profession: an international perspective

Karen Lyons

Introduction

Social work is generally understood to be an essentially 'local' activity, rooted in the socio-economic conditions and political and legal systems of a particular country. Social workers generally intervene when problems occur at the interface between individuals, families and communities, and their environments. Some aspects of human functioning (including relationships) might be regarded as universal, but behaviours are likely to be affected by the cultural traditions of a whole society or by the norms of subgroups within it. Thus, there is an expectation that social workers 'understand' the local context and are 'able to communicate with' people in a particular locality.

However, over the past century, social work has been increasingly accepted as also having an international dimension and is, on occasion, even transnational in some of its practices. This has become more pronounced with the recognition of globalisation as a process that pervades all aspects of life in all societies (to a greater or lesser extent) and of the interdependency that ensues. Many social problems can now be understood as being global in scope – and perhaps having international origins – as well as having distinctive impacts on local populations (Healy and Link, 2012; Lyons et al, 2012; Lyons, 2015).

Migration, while not a new phenomenon, is a particular feature of contemporary life in relation to the scale of population mobility and the number of countries between which people now move. Distinctions are sometimes made between 'asylum seekers' (who may, in due course, qualify under United Nations [UN] definitions as refugees) and 'economic migrants', with the assumption that this is an unwanted move for the first group but a personal choice for the second, resulting in them being labelled as 'deserving' or 'undeserving' of official help. However, these are simplistic and unhelpful dichotomies as many people who leave their home countries can be regarded as being somewhere on a continuum of 'forced migration' from conflict, persecution and environmental causes through to crippling economic hardship. Migration, in turn, contributes to the interdependency of different countries, communities and families, while also persuading governments and international bodies to take steps to promote (or prevent) different forms of migration or the movement of particular groups or individuals (Fiddian-Qasmiyeh et al, 2014).

As mentioned, international labour mobility is one aspect of migration and is itself a diverse phenomenon, which has given rise to international conventions and policies, as well as bilateral and multilateral agreements. Workers in professional fields may be seen as having a privileged status in relation to the wider body of those migrating for work reasons since they are presumed to have desirable skills that are transferable, and there may be particular incentives for them to move to different countries. In the case of social work, the extent to which international labour mobility is a personal and/or professional choice, a response to a particular recruitment drive, or influenced by other 'push/pull' factors is variable and is not fully researched. However, like the social care workers included in a study by Christensen and Guldvik (2014), they are presumed to have agency, rather than being the victims of circumstance.

Over the last few decades, there has been some research (reported in English-language publications) into the motivations and experiences of internationally recruited doctors, teachers and nurses (and others in allied health and care professions), as well as social workers (Lyons and Littlechild, 2006; Walsh et al, 2010; Bartley et al, 2011). Indications from some of this literature are that transnational social workers may share similarities, in both motivation and experiences, with these other occupational groups (eg Winkleman Gleed, 2006; Williams and Balaz, 2008; Guo and Singh, 2009). However, the particular nature of social work, with its emphasis on relationships and communication (whether with individuals, groups or communities), and the need for knowledge of the national policy, economic and legal contexts, may make social work harder to 'transplant' to different countries and presents more challenges to transnational social workers.

This chapter: presents the factors that contribute to the idea of social work as a global profession and suggests that international perspectives are relevant even in local practice; discusses the range of problems typically addressed by social workers and the extent to which these have international as well as local dimensions; considers the strengths of, and challenges facing, transnational social workers; and presents a short concluding section about the particular contribution that this sector of the workforce makes to the internationalisation of social work.

Social work as a global profession with international perspectives

The beginnings of social work's recognition as an international profession occurred over a century ago, and were formally signified by a world conference in Paris in 1928 (Lyons and Lawrence, 2009). This, in turn, laid the basis for the three membership organisations that, today, represent social work globally. The International Association of Schools of Social Work (IASSW, 2016) has a membership of over 400 schools worldwide (as well as individual and associate members) and a primary focus on professional education, while the International Council on Social Welfare (ICSW, 2016) has organisational members from the not-for-profit sector/non-governmental organisations (NGOs) from over 70 countries, primarily concerned with activities and advocacy in the social welfare, social policy and social development fields. The International Federation of Social Workers (IFSW, 2016) has members (national associations) from 116 countries representing over 500,000 social workers. Recently, the three organisations, recognising their complementary strengths and the need to raise the international profile of social work and its role in contributing to social policy agendas, have produced a 'global agenda' and are in the process of establishing 'regional observatories' (Truell and Jones, 2014).

These three organisations are not the only international bodies in social work, but they are perhaps the best known and longest established. In addition, less formal, more fluid and sometimes time-limited transnational academic, practice and research networks have periodically (and certainly over the last few decades) also been significant in raising the profile of social work at regional and international levels and contributing to the sharing and development of knowledge, including about comparative welfare and social work organisation and practice. However, for the purposes of this chapter, the focus here is upon the role of the three international bodies in contributing to our understanding of social work as a global profession and their efforts to establish international definitions, standards and guidelines that help us to identify common concerns and goals.

Since 2000, the IASSW and IFSW have collaborated to produce three important international documents, the first of which was the 'International definition of social work': the initial definition was agreed in 2000 and has recently been revised as the 'Global definition of social work' (IFSW, 2014a). The 2000 definition became the basis for a 'Statement of ethical principles' and the 'Global standards for the education and training of the social work profession' (both were issued in 2004) (see IFSW, 2016), both of which, together with the global definition, have continuing relevance, including in the context of international labour mobility in social work.

The first two sentences of the 'Global definition' state that:

> social work is a practice-based profession and an academic discipline which promotes social change and development; social cohesion and the empowerment and liberation of people. Principles of social justice, human rights, collective responsibility and respect for diversities are central to social work. (IFSW, 2014a)

Having this global definition of social work suggests that there is a shared, international understanding about the nature of social work – and thus the roles that social workers undertake in different national jurisdictions – facilitating international mobility and transnational social work. The definition itself is very broadly framed in order to take into account the wide diversity of national (and sometimes more local) understandings, mandates and practices of social workers, and its authors suggest that the definition may be amplified at national and regional levels. However, the extent to which students at the qualifying stage are informed about this definition and have analysed its possible application in their own (national) situation – or considered its relevance to other jurisdictions – can be questioned, as can its inclusion in different forms of post-qualifying training. For example, the findings from a global survey of schools of social work carried out by the IASSW suggest that 'international social work' does not feature significantly (if at all) in the curricula of most qualifying programmes (Baretta Herman et al, 2016).

Similar concerns can be expressed about the 'Statement of ethical principles', while the universality (or otherwise) of particular values in social work has been considered by various authors (eg Healy, 2007; Hugman, 2013). As with the 'Global definition', the 'Statement of ethical values' is underpinned by a commitment to human rights and social justice, and while these may be uncritically accepted as common to social work internationally, the national conditions in which social workers operate may pose challenges in relation to respect for, and promotion of, both these values. At a general level, it has been suggested that the 'Statement of ethical principles' reflects a Western view that privileges the rights of individuals over the emphasis more often placed on family obligations and community interests reflected in the cultures of countries of the Global South. On another level, examples of value conflicts occur in relation to the treatment of some subgroups in society. For instance, freedom of expression about sexuality is now widely accepted (relating to social attitudes and legal and policy terms) in most Western countries, although there may be some people within national populations (including some social workers) who, perhaps for religious reasons, would still deny this freedom. In other countries, any deviation from heterosexuality is considered to be outside the accepted norms of human behaviour and might even be illegal, thus denying rights to people who would otherwise identify as part of the worldwide lesbian, gay, trans and bisexual (LGBT) community. While persecution (actual or feared) on grounds of sexuality may be a motivating factor for some people to leave particular jurisdictions, it is far from universally accepted by the governments of receiving countries as a legitimate basis for granting asylum to some migrants. There is anecdotal evidence to suggest that some LGBT social workers themselves choose to seek work in countries that they perceive as having more tolerant social attitudes, particularly if this is backed by legislation against discrimination on grounds of sexuality, though it is not known whether this proposition has been formally researched. However, it is also possible that some transnational social workers bring with them prejudices about, for example, homosexuality that would not have been challenged in social work training in their countries of origin, notwithstanding a policy statement by the IFSW (2014b) advocating for the inclusion of LGBT people and asserting the responsibility of social workers to protect and promote their rights and well-being.

Finally, regarding overarching statements framing social work at an international level, the document describing 'Global standards for social work education and training' sets out a range of standards in nine areas, including those related to the core curriculum, expectations regarding fieldwork and the qualifications of professional staff. The document is prefaced by a recognition of the 'context-specific realities' in which professional education for social work internationally takes place and an early commentary on the document described it as 'aspirational' rather than having a regulatory function (Sewpaul and Jones, 2004). Again, it is possible that having international standards might add weight to the efforts of professional educators to secure recognition and resources for social work programmes within their own higher education systems, but it cannot guarantee international conformity in the curricula and standards achieved by students on qualification. This can lead to a false sense of security about presumed similarities when considering how well equipped transnational social workers are to work in another jurisdiction, and, in fact, most countries with well-established professional education programmes also have regulatory bodies with the competence to assess the comparability of 'overseas qualifications' presented by aspiring transnational social workers.

Local and universal problems: different approaches and organisational issues

Notwithstanding the limitations of international statements about and aspirations for social work in the face of the wide diversity in socio-economic, political-legal and cultural conditions in which social work is practised, it is possible to identify a range of social issues that social workers are commonly expected to address. Poverty was the basis for the origins of social work in the West and is currently a characteristic of many of the people with whom social workers interact worldwide (Cox and Pawar, 2006; Desai and Solas, 2012). Even in the Global North, relative poverty is still an issue, although, for example, in the European Union, economic insecurity has more recently been labelled as part of a wider system of social exclusion and marginalisation of particular populations (Lyons and Huegler, 2012). People in such groups might be identified as members of a minority ethnic population or having a (particular kind of) disability and there are often related issues, such as poor living conditions, limited employment opportunities and health concerns. With regard to the latter, Bywaters and Napier (2008) authored a paper that formed the basis for a policy statement by the IFSW and an international network concerned with the significance of health issues and the role that social workers may play in contributing to policies and practices addressing the relevance of this issue for many aspects of social work practice, while Lyons et al (2006) had previously identified the international dimension of this issue.

In the West, social work strategies are frequently related to the assessed needs of individuals and families: workers have developed specialist skills (and sometimes have additional qualifications) and specialist agencies have often been established to address particular problems, such as child protection, elder abuse, substance misuse, homelessness or mental illness. In the Global South, policy concerns might focus on developing a social protection programme for a national population (Drolet, 2016) and a more community-oriented approach is represented in social development policies and projects. Social work 'specialisms', as individually tailored responses to the problems of particular population groups, are generally less in evidence, although they are sometimes addressed through the efforts of NGOs. The needs of vast populations in countries such as India or the Philippines have implications for the education and roles of social workers, as well as their expectations about living standards and social work practices if they migrate to a Western country.

There are substantial differences between the structural and cultural determinants of the environments within which social work is practised even among 'developed' (as opposed to 'developing') countries (Nielson, 2011; Payne, 2012). For instance, major differences are evident between Europe and the US in the organisation and funding of various aspects of health and social care, affecting the role of social workers in these sectors (Hoffler and Clark, 2012; Zavirsek and Lawrence, 2012). The entrenchment of neoliberal policies and the interests of capitalism have affected even the traditional 'welfare states', such as those long established in New Zealand, the Nordic countries and the UK, and the welfare systems of Canada and Australia have been similarly impacted (Teeple, 2000). The cultural aspect has been alluded to earlier and affects the extent to which societies expect family members or voluntary (including self-help and religious) organisations to address the needs of vulnerable people in the community. In addition, national populations often have minority groups, including indigenous people, with different expectations and experiences of welfare systems (see Baines, this volume). These factors affect the roles of social workers and the resources and recognition available to them in particular countries in ways that are, perhaps, at variance with those of social workers who train in one country and work in another.

Over the last few decades, the IFSW, in particular, has produced a number of policy statements covering a wide variety of topics of importance to social work policies and practices. These result from particular motions put forward at general meetings, reflecting issues that have gained international, as well as national, importance. So, for instance, in 2014, a statement was issued on the protection of children from all forms of sexual abuse. This not only recognised the previously nationally identified concerns about incest and other forms of child sexual abuse, but also highlighted the more recent concerns about the (international) trafficking of children and young people for commercial sexual exploitation. Earlier policy statements have addressed a wide range of issues, including 'globalisation and the environment', 'displaced people', 'poverty eradication', 'indigenous people', 'HIV/AIDS' and 'cross-border reproductive services', indicating that these issues have international dimensions as well as local relevance. (These and other papers were all uploaded to a revamped website in 2012 and can be accessed through the current IFSW website [see IFSW, 2016].)

One of these policy statements is perhaps of particular interest to transnational social workers since it concerns 'Effective and ethical working environments for social work: the responsibilities of employers of social workers' (IFSW, 2012). This document presents guidelines for: the provision of working environments that promote effective and ethical practice; the protection of service user interests; and the provision of (good-)quality services, where the objectives of the organisation are aligned with those of the practitioners. It specifically suggests that the values and principles of managers and social work practitioners should be consistent and mutually reinforcing. This suggests that the document is, in part, a response to the increased levels of managerialism experienced in what are often (in many Western countries) bureaucratic and/or budget-driven organisations.

The guidelines acknowledge that the context for social work practice varies according to local circumstances and recognises the variety of organisational contexts within which social workers are employed. These include: secondary settings (such as schools and hospitals); local government; NGOs; for-profit companies; and user-led organisations, including cooperatives. The statement refers to the three core statements (see earlier) and describes the responsibilities of social workers as being: to implement national policies; to safeguard human, social and economic rights; and to secure resources. Meanwhile, the document lists a number of agency responsibilities, including to ensure the provision of effective induction, supervision, workload management and opportunities for continuing professional development (CPD). With the possible exception of the latter, these are all factors mentioned in various studies as having a particular impact on the experiences (whether positive or negative) of transnational social workers (eg Fouché et al, 2015; Hanna and Lyons, 2017; see also the chapters in this volume by Beddoe et al, Brown et al and Walsh-Tapiata et al). The agency should also provide up-to-date written policies and guidelines and make appropriate use of research and regulatory frameworks.

While the agency needs to be 'consumer-facing' and have accessible procedures for complaints, it also has a 'duty of care' to its employees. As such, it should employ suitably qualified staff and have procedures in place to deal with dangerous, discriminatory or exploitative behaviour, including minimising the risk (and threat) of violence to social workers themselves. This suggests that the agencies in some countries

– and certainly their staff – are operating in 'hostile' environments, which can contribute to the professional culture shock sometimes experienced by transnational social workers. Some of them will be coming from countries where social workers have higher status or where the profession as a whole is subject to 'benign neglect', either condition seeming preferable to one where social workers feel, at best, undervalued and, at worst, scapegoated by the public and/or government for policy failings and/or organisational or individual shortcomings (Hussein et al, 2011; Fouché et al, 2014).

Transnational social workers: strengths and challenges

Transnational social work practice is now a recognised aspect of social work internationally (Negi and Furman, 2010), and social workers who have their own experience of 'transnationalism' have much to contribute to national workforces. However, being part of the transnational workforce is not without its challenges since, on one level, transnational social workers can simply be seen as part of a reserve army of labour, plugging the gaps in the labour force of particular countries. However, on more individual levels, transnational social workers bring with them a range of skills and expertise, although the extent to which social work agencies identify and build on these varies considerably. The lack of supportive environments and of policies for the induction, supervision and integration of transnational social workers has been commented on in several studies (as reported in this text) and undoubtedly contributes to the professional challenges facing transnational social workers.

As to their strengths, transnational social workers, by definition, bring with them important understandings of the processes of migration, resettlement and adaptation. It is assumed that only a relatively small proportion will have experienced the particular traumas of migration as asylum seekers but, nevertheless, they are likely to experience some of the feelings associated with loss, dislocation and culture shock (Casado et al, 2010). Their own experiences might particularly contribute to work with refugee or migrant populations, but having faced an unknown future, loss of familiar surroundings and support networks, and the uncertainties and stresses surrounding adapting to new situations, they might also have an empathetic understanding of the needs of any service users facing life-changing situations.

In addition, the different contexts, cultures and professional backgrounds from which transnational social workers come can bring fresh perspectives to the work of colleagues, teams and agencies – if acknowledged. Similar to local social workers transferring from one agency or sector to another, transnational social workers often have quite specific knowledge about social work skills and methods that can be transferred and/or adapted for use in another context. However, to some extent, this relies on the level of professional autonomy and openness to learning on the part of 'receiving organisations' and social workers in the host country. Like the doctors in the Williams and Balaz (2008) study, even experienced workers might be identified as only 'learners' and, as Dominelli (2010) has stated, the transfer of knowledge should not be assumed. This positioning of transnational social workers as 'incomers' and learners might prevent social work agencies from recognising and utilising new perspectives and alternative approaches to assessing problematic situations and ways of responding to them (see, eg, Brown et al, 2014; Fouché et al, 2014). An example (from the UK) might be a reliance on individually based assessments and interventions at the expense of group- or community-based initiatives, with which some transnational social workers would be very familiar.

The undervaluing of the possible contribution of transnational social workers is one of the particular challenges to this group of workers, who can consequently feel quite 'deskilled' and unsure about their professional identity. These feelings are accentuated when faced with highly bureaucratised and/or legally based forms of social work, where the 'new' social worker is on a steep learning curve regarding the policies, provisions and even rules of practice in particular agencies. While some aspects of human need and behaviour can be assumed to be universal – and international agencies might draw up conventions and guidelines relevant to social work values and practices – the particular situations facing transnational social workers and the expectations of the agencies employing them can require high levels of adaptability and resilience or can even prove to be overwhelming for some transnational social workers.

One of the specific challenges facing transnational social workers relates to language. This operates on two levels. In the case of someone whose first language is not the same as the country to which they move, there is the specific challenge of learning the national language; this would not be 'from scratch' since people who have learned a new language to a standard acceptable for 'employment overseas' usually have skills in reading and writing. However, for a profession that is heavily dependent on verbal communication, there are often challenges for transnational social workers in understanding (and becoming fluent in) local vocabulary usage, dialects and colloquialisms (Lyons and Littlechild, 2006; Harrison, 2013). On another level, even people who apparently speak the same language as the social workers in their new country face a confusing barrage of new terms, acronyms and professional jargon, some of which would seem to belie the fact that social work is a global profession. This is apparent to anyone who has been involved in cross-national research projects, where an international team usually has both the need and the opportunity to debate and 'translate' professional terms into words or even concepts that will be understood by social work respondents in different countries. In the case of transnational social workers, this 'translation work' is often a solitary pursuit, but one that must be accomplished quickly in order to make sense of written directives, team discussions and so on.

It is suggested that some of the challenges faced by transnational social workers arise from the assumptions that they and/or others make about the similarities between national education and training programmes, as well as about the organisation of welfare and the role of social workers within the wider system. This applies particularly across English-speaking countries and when specific countries have a shared history. It is the case that due to historical colonisation – and perhaps even the profession's more current international aspirations – particular approaches to the organisation of welfare and the training of social workers have been 'transplanted' from one jurisdiction to another. However, such homogenising influences often took place decades (even up to a century) ago, and despite the more recent spread of neoliberal political ideas and economic austerity measures, individual countries have asserted their own paths to the development of welfare systems (including social services), as well as to the education and training of social workers. Thus, notwithstanding superficial similarities, some common policy trends and the possible influence of international professional understandings, values and standards, individual countries have established different arrangements for delivering welfare and social services, and social work education itself is generally moulded to suit the particularities of a national context (eg Pullen Sansfaçon et al, 2012; Noble et al, 2014), usually with scant regard for international perspectives (as mentioned earlier).

Much of the literature about the challenges facing transnational social workers – and, indeed, about the challenges to an international professional labour force more generally – concentrates on the stresses associated with adaptations and learning in the workplace. However, there are also personal and sometimes family-based pressures of adapting to life in a new society and a different culture, some of which have been identified in studies about expatriate workers in multinational companies (eg EIU, 2010). It can be argued that in an occupation such as social work, where individual values and resources make an important contribution to professional performance, attention needs to be paid to the personal challenges being experienced in addition to those in the workplace, and thought needs to be given to wider support possibilities.

Concluding comments

Notwithstanding the harsh climate prevailing at the time of writing with regard to immigration to many Western countries, it is likely that labour mobility will continue to be a feature of the global economy, including the transnational movement of qualified social workers. Such mobility raises important questions about the extent to which initial professional education and subsequent training include international perspectives and comparative dimensions as a way of orienting social workers to the varied forms that social work takes and the particular opportunities and challenges open to social workers in different national jurisdictions.

An important role of social workers in many countries and occupational positions is helping individuals and groups to obtain resources; transnational social workers may question what resources are needed and have different ideas about how best to access them. More importantly, transnational social workers are a resource in themselves, not just in the sense of 'plugging the gaps' in understaffed organisations, but also regarding the particular attributes that they bring to this workforce.

Significant among these is their experience of the decisions and adaptations involved in migration itself. However, like other professional groups, there are usually major areas of difference regarding the cultures of various populations and organisations, as well as professional 'ways of doing things'. Specific challenges highlighted by various national studies include: attaining the right to work (including professional registration); securing a permanent post (with chances of advancement if their move is permanent); having their needs recognised as (usually) experienced workers who are also learners; and receiving appropriate support with regard to induction, supervision and ongoing professional development. These professional challenges are often experienced alongside the wider issues of adapting to the cultures and norms of a different country, sometimes also with responsibility for the local resettlement of other family members – or ongoing responsibilities to family members 'back home'.

However, as also recounted in some of the research studies, most transnational social workers demonstrate both adventurous and resourceful qualities and a strong desire to learn and succeed in their profession. Although there is now some literature in the migration field about 'circulatory migration' (eg Flavell, 2008), there is, as yet, little research evidence, globally, to indicate what proportion of transnational social workers seek work in another country as a temporary opportunity, relative to those who see it as a more permanent life change for themselves (and sometimes also family members) – or those who relocate more than once and perhaps have work experience in more than two countries. In any case, transnational social workers are part of wider migration and settlement patterns that vary according to international and national events and policies, as well as individual circumstances. However, it is clear that some transnational social workers will sometimes settle long-term, enriching the skills base and outlook of the profession in their 'new country', while others will return to their countries of origin – or move on elsewhere – having questioned both old and new ways of working. All such social workers help us to develop a wider view of social work as a global profession.

References

Baretta Herman, A., Leung, P. and Littlechild, B. (2016) 'The changing status and growth of social work education worldwide: process, findings and implications of the IASSW 2010 Census', *International Social Work*, 59(4): 459–78, doi:10.1177/0020872814547437.

Bartley, A., Beddoe, L., Duke, J., Fouché, C., Harington, P.R.J. and Shah, R. (2011) 'Crossing borders: key features of migrant social workers in New Zealand', *Aotearoa New Zealand Social Work*, 23(3): 16–30.

Brown, M., Sansfaçon, A.P., Ethier, S. and Fulton, A. (2014) 'A complicated welcome: social workers navigate policy, organizational contexts and socio-cultural dynamics following migration to Canada', *International Journal of Social Science Studies*, 3(1): 58–68.

Bywaters, P. and Napier, L. (2008) 'IFSW policy statement on health'. Available at: http://ifsw.org/policies/health/

Casado, B., Hong, M. and Harrington, D. (2010) 'Measuring migratory grief and loss associated with the experience of immigration', *Research on Social Work Practice*, 20(6): 611–20, doi:10.1177/1049731506360840

Christensen, K. and Guldvik, I. (2014) *Migrant care workers: Searching for new horizons*, Farnham: Ashgate.

Cox, D. and Pawar, M. (2006) *International social work: Issues, strategies and programs*, London: Sage.

Desai, M. and Solas, J. (2012) 'Poverty, development and social justice', in K. Lyons, T. Hokenstad, M. Pawaret and N. Huegler (eds) *SAGE handbook of international social work*, London: Sage, pp 55–9.

Dominelli, L. (2010) *Social work in a globalising world*, Cambridge: Polity Press.

Drolet, J.L. (ed) (2016) *Social development and social work perspectives on social protection*, London: Routledge.

EIU (Economist Intelligence Unit) (2010) 'Up or out: next moves for the modern expatriate', a report from the Economist Intelligence Unit Ltd. Available at: http://graphics.eiu.com/upload/eb/lon_pl_regus_web2.pdf

Fiddian-Qasmiyeh, E., Loescher, G., Long, K. and Sigona, N. (eds) (2014) *The Oxford handbook of refugees and forced migration*, Oxford: Oxford University Press.

Flavell, A. (2008) 'The new face of East–West migration', *Journal of Ethnic and Migration Studies*, 34(5): 701–16.

Fouché, C., Beddoe, L., Bartley, A. and De Haan, I. (2014) 'Enduring professional dislocation: migrant social workers' perceptions of their professional roles', *British Journal of Social Work*, 44(7): 2004–22.

Fouché, C., Beddoe, L., Bartley, A. and Parkes, E. (2015) 'Are we ready for them? Overseas-qualified social workers' professional cultural transition', *European Journal of Social Work*, 19(1): 106–19.

Guo, W. and Singh, M. (2009) 'Overseas trained teachers in Australia: a study of barriers, skills and qualifications'. Available at: https://www.aare.edu.au/publications-database.php/5882/overseas-trained-teachers-in-australia-a-study-of-barriers-skills-and-qualifications

Hanna, S. and Lyons, K. (2017) '"London calling": the experiences of international social work recruits working in London', *British Journal of Social Work*, 47(3): 719–36, doi.10.1093/bjsw/bcwo27

Harrison, G. (2013) '"Oh, you've got such a strong accent": language identity intersecting with professional identity in the human services in Australia', *International Migration*, 51(5): 192–204.

Healy, L. (2007) 'Universalism and cultural relativism in social work ethics', *International Social Work*, 50(1): 11–26.

Healy, L. and Link, R. (2012) *Handbook of international social work: Human rights, development and the global profession*, New York, NY: Oxford University Press.

Hoffler, E.F. and Clark, E.J. (2012) *Social work matters: The power of linking policy and practice*, Washington, DC: NASW Press.

Hugman, R. (2013) *Culture, values and ethics in social work: Embracing diversity*, London: Routledge.

Hussein, S., Manthorpe, J. and Stevens, M. (2011) 'The experiences of migrant social work and social care practitioners in the UK: findings from an online survey', *European Journal of Social Work*, 14(4): 479–96.

IASSW (International Association of Schools of Social Workers) (2016) 'International Association of Schools of Social Workers website'. Available at: www.iassw-aiets.org

ICSW (International Council on Social Welfare) (2016) 'International Council on Social Welfare website'. Available at: http://icsw.org

IFSW (International Federation of Social Workers) (2012) 'Effective and ethical working environments for social work: the responsibilities of employers of social workers'. Available at: http://ifsw.org/

IFSW (2014a) 'Global definition of social work'. Available at: http://ifsw.org/policies/definition-of-social-work

IFSW (2014b) 'Sexual orientation and gender expression'. Available at: http://cdn.ifsw.org/assets/ifsw_102638-5.pdf

IFSW (2016) 'International Federation of Social Workers website'. Available at: http://ifsw.org

Lyons, K. (2015) 'Globalization, welfare and social work', in J.D. Wright (ed) *International encyclopedia of social and behavioural sciences* (2nd edn), Oxford: Elsevier, pp 262–67.

Lyons, K. and Huegler, N. (2012) 'Social exclusion and inclusion', in L.M. Healy and R.J. Link (eds) *Handbook of international social work: Human rights, development, and the global profession*, Oxford: Oxford University Press, pp 37–43.

Lyons, K. and Lawrence, S. (2009) 'Social work as an international profession: origins, organisations and networks', in S. Lawrence, K. Lyons, G. Simpson and N. Huegler (eds) *Introducing international social work*, London: Learning Matters/Sage, pp 108–21.

Lyons, K. and Littlechild, B. (eds) (2006) *International labour mobility in social work*, Birmingham: BASW/Venture Press.

Lyons, K., Manion, K. and Carlsen, M. (2006) *International perspectives on social work: Global conditions and local practice*, Basingstoke: Palgrave Macmillan.

Lyons, K., Hokenstad, T., Pawar, M. and Huegler, N. (eds) (2012) *SAGE handbook of international social work*, London: Sage.

Negi, N.J. and Furman, R. (eds) (2010) *Transnational social work practice*, New York, NY: Columbia University Press.

Nielsen, L. (2011) 'Classifications of countries based on their levels of development: how it is done and how it could be done', IMF Working Paper (WP/11/31). Available at: http://www.imf.org/~/media/Websites/IMF/imported-full-text-pdf/external/pubs/ft/wp/2011/_wp1131.ashx

Noble, C., Strauss, H. and Littlechild, B. (eds) (2014) *Global social work education: Crossing borders and blurring boundaries*, Sydney: University of Sydney/IASSW.

Payne, M. (2012) 'Political and organisational contexts of social work internationally', in K. Lyons, T. Hokenstad, M. Pawaret and N. Huegler (eds) *SAGE handbook of international social work*, London: Sage, pp 121–35.

Pullen Sansfaçon, A., Spolander, G. and Engelbrecht, L. (2012) 'Migration of professional social workers: reflections, challenges and strategies for education', *Social Work Education*, 31(8): 1032–45.

Sewpaul, V. and Jones, D. (2004) 'Global standards for social work education and training', *Social Work Education*, 23(5): 493–513.

Teeple, G. (2000) *Globalization and the decline of social reform: Into the 21st century* (2nd edn), Aurora, Ontario: Garamond Press.

Truell, R. and Jones, D. (2014) 'The global agenda for social work and social development: extending the influence of social work'. Available at: http://cdn.ifsw.org/assets/ifsw_24848-10.pdf (accessed 24 April 2016).

Walsh, T., Wilson, G. and O'Connor, E. (2010) 'Local, European and global: an exploration of migration patterns of social workers into Ireland', *British Journal of Social Work*, 40(6): 1978–95.

Williams, A. and Balaz, V. (2008) 'International return mobility, learning and knowledge transfer: a case study of Slovac doctors', *Social Science & Medicine*, 67(19): 24–33.

Winkleman Gleed, A. (2006) *Migrant nurses, motivation and contribution*, Milton Keynes: Radcliffe Publishing.

Zavirsek, D. and Lawrence, S. (2012) 'Social work in Europe', in K. Lyons, T. Hokenstad, M. Pawar and N. Huegler (eds) *SAGE handbook of international social work*, London: Sage.

THREE

New Public Management, migrant professionals and labour mobility: possibilities for social justice social work?

Donna Baines

Introduction

As noted earlier in this volume, social work is practised mainly at the local level and is highly context-specific, despite increasingly global movements of capital and more privileged, 'skilled' labour forces. As Lyons (Chapter Two, this volume) asserts, in addition to the global mobility of 'professionals', including social workers, the forced migration of increasingly large groups of people is changing the face of many regions and impacting on local and international social work. As long-standing immigrant nations established during the height of European colonialism, Australia, Canada and New Zealand continue to struggle with the contradictions of wealthy, although increasingly polarised, societies, flourishing on land originally confiscated from local indigenous populations, who remain, for the most part, uncompensated, marginalised and struggling. As the major source of original waves of immigration to these three countries, the UK (then England) now faces its own crisis in relation to growing racism and xenophobia over immigration and asylum seeking.

Contemporary austerity policies in all four countries and the widespread adoption of New Public Management (NPM) models within social services do little to address long-standing inequities, racism and colonialism. Instead, evidence confirms a growing gap between indigenous and non-indigenous citizens (Vinson et al, 2015), and immigrants and non-immigrants (Dominelli, 2008; Ife, 2012; Robinson, 2014). NPM has been introduced into social service organisations across most of the industrialised world, meaning that most employers feel compelled to hire social workers who can 'perform' well within its high demand for documentation, heavy workloads, fast pace and work intensity (McDonald, 2006; Carey, 2008; Baines, 2017). Common across the countries studied in this collection, this performance of social work often restricts or removes possibilities for social justice practice.

Dovetailing with NPM's restrictiveness, questions have been raised as to whether transnational social work can be a social justice project or if it is predisposed to replicate global patterns of dominance and undermine local strengths and practices. Although presented as united and cohesive, social work is a highly contested field in which both the Left and the Right claim to do social justice. As Reynolds (1963) argued decades ago, unless social work is grounded in the struggles for justice of oppressed people, its purpose becomes corrupt and cannot advance its practice or theory. In today's context, social work that is not grounded in critical theory is similarly vulnerable to agendas that do little to dislodge the inequity inherent in global capitalism. This lack of critique undermines social work's capacity to advance theoretically or in socially engaged, social-justice-oriented practice. For the purposes of this chapter, critical perspectives will be understood as those in the structural tradition that view full and equitable access to fairness, resources and affirming identities as the basis for a just world, as achieved through democratic and participatory means (Fraser, 2010; for social work critical theory, see Mullaly, 2010; Lundy, 2011; Gray and Webb, 2013; Pease et al, 2016; Baines, 2017).

Drawing on the literature and qualitative case-study data collected in Canada, Australia, the UK and New Zealand, this chapter: (1) briefly sketches the history of colonialism and immigration that shaped these four countries; (2) discusses the global and standardising influence of NPM and managerialism on social work practice possibilities in the four countries, analysing, in particular, the increasing use of immigrant 'volunteer' labour and other forms of unpaid labour, including student placements and internships, as a response to the ongoing underfunding of social services and policies of 'permanent' austerity; and (3) explores associated implications for practice and possibilities for liberatory social work practice. This chapter will contribute to our understanding of social work in the context of labour force mobility, transnational practice, the ongoing challenges of social inequality and the need for social-justice-directed social work practice.

Social work, immigration and colonialism: part of the project

As noted earlier, as white settler countries, Canada, Australia and New Zealand came into existence as part of European colonial projects from the 15th century onwards, with Britain as the main source country for early waves of immigration. The benefits of colonialism to Britain are well documented. The notion of *terra nullius* (uninhabited land), and the colonists' right to claim the territories of others, dominated this era, resulting in the dispossession of indigenous lands and the undertaking of aggressive measures to dismantle indigenous societies and cultures (Gray et al, 2008; Smith, 2012). In addition to ensuring access to the land, the dismantling project was aimed at reordering indigenous societies, many of which were democracies, in some cases, matriarchal or matrilineal, with strong roles for women, and almost all of which were highly collectivist (Noel, 2006; Krull and Sempruch, 2011). The colonial project remade these societies in its own image: feudal, patrilineal, patriarchal and hierarchical. Indigenous families were restructured, with males at the head of small, immediate family units as opposed to complex networks of extended kinship and reciprocal support (Pohatu, 2003; Baines and Freeman, 2011). Indigenous societies were cast as dissipated, backward and in need of discipline and control rather than vibrant, multifaceted societies that had acted as custodians and stewards of the land for centuries (Hart, 2009). An additional aspect of this dismantling project was aimed at ensuring a supply of low-wage agrarian and domestic labour for the newly established colonies in the form of indigenous people barred from their regular productive activity (hunting, gathering, collective farming) and with no other means of support (Shewell, 2004). In Australia, Canada and New Zealand, these remaking projects were difficult to accomplish, extended over generations and involved strategies such as starvation and genocide to initially remove indigenous populations; they involved treaties that were largely not honoured and generally enshrined unequal rights and responsibilities, residential schools and assimilation projects, and ongoing widespread racism and oppression (Bennett et al, 2011; Smith, 2012).

The catastrophic conditions endured and resisted by indigenous people since European contact, not surprisingly, generated intergenerational trauma in which the psychological and emotional harms perpetrated on one generation were unintentionally transferred to subsequent generations (Gray et al, 2008; Freeman, 2017). While indigenous people struggled with inhuman conditions, colonial and racist ideologies legitimised and normalised the theft of land and the marginalisation of indigenous peoples, folding early versions of colonial exploitation seamlessly into modern, global capitalism (Shewell, 2004; Hart, 2009). Although access to clean water, health care, education and sanitation are a commonplace expectation of contemporary non-indigenous citizens living in Australia, Canada, New Zealand and the UK, many indigenous communities exist without these basic social rights and with little in the way of effective remedies or supports from governments and mainstream society (Vinson et al, 2015; Carniol et al, 2017). The resilience and self-organisation of indigenous communities is well-documented but their struggles remain an uphill battle against an increasingly strong, neoliberal global tide of inequity and growing economic polarisation (Gray et al, 2008; Smith, 2012; Carniol et al, 2017).

Although not yet in existence during the first waves of colonialism, social work as a profession played an active role in assimilationist policies, assisting local police in removing indigenous children from their families and placing them in residential schools aimed at 'taking the Indian out' of the children and training them as docile, low-wage workers (Gray et al, 2008; Baines and Freeman, 2011). Social workers were (and are) heavily involved in child welfare initiatives putatively aimed at protecting children from 'abuse and neglect' but, in the process, generations of indigenous children were harmed by separation from their communities, fostering or adopting them out to white families and reinforcing notions of the pathology and criminality of indigenous families and communities (Sinclair, 2007; Green and Baldry, 2008). By not explicitly challenging these practices, non-indigenous social workers have often uncritically replicated neo-colonial practices of normalising the privilege and benefit of non-indigenous people and, in the process, leaving racist practices and policies unexamined and unaddressed (Department of Social Welfare, 1986; Carniol et al, 2017).

Indigenous social work researchers and their allies have documented these injustices and developed interventions aimed at healing intergenerational trauma and strengthening the resilience of indigenous people while simultaneously demanding greater social justice, self-determination and equity (Brave Heart, 2003; Quinn, 2007; Ruwhiu, 2013; Freeman, 2017). Optimally, child welfare and all social services should be returned to indigenous communities, thus supporting processes of self-determination (Hart, 2009; Sinclair, 2009). Reflecting an overlap of neoliberalism and racism, non-indigenous governments have been reluctant to fund these services at levels where they can be successful (Hart, 2009; Carniol et al, 2017). As a result, services often struggle to serve indigenous communities in ways that empower individuals and communities rather than unintentionally reproducing the oppression underlying most non-indigenous services.

In Australia, Canada and New Zealand, it is common for social workers to work with indigenous people in most services in urban environments, even though in some rural and remote locations, indigenous peoples make up the majority of the population. In social work with indigenous and immigrant peoples, there are two proven strategies with strong social justice potential. The first of these is the adoption of an approach often referred to as 'ally-ship' (Bishop, 2002; Carniol et al, 2017) or 'working alongside' (Bennett et al, 2011). As Bishop (2002, p 1) argues, '[a]llies are people who recognize the unearned privilege they receive from society's patterns of injustice and take responsibility for changing these patterns'. Both of these approaches position the non-indigenous, non-immigrant worker as a skilled, humble and supportive companion to indigenous and immigrant people in a journey to uncover concrete and psychosocial resources that permit individuals and communities self-determination and empowerment (Bennett et al, 2011).

The second strategy involves the adoption of a critical, intersectional, anti-colonial and anti-racist analysis (Jefferey, 2005; Mullaly, 2010; Ife, 2012). A critical social analysis is a pivotal aspect of this work as it enables the worker to see beyond the immediate concerns and problems to larger social structures harming and restraining individuals (Mullaly, 2010; Lundy, 2011). Examples of intersecting oppressive social systems and relations include race, class, gender, colonialism, sexual orientation and gender identity, (dis)ability, and so on (Lundy, 2011; Gray and Webb, 2013; Baines, 2017). Sharing this analysis with service users and communities can be reassuring and energising as it clearly suggests that social problems have shared solutions and responsibilities, rather than individual blame and pathology (Mullaly, 2010; O'Neill, 2017). Fouché et al (2013) found that only 40% of transnational social workers were acquainted with the cultural and socio-political context in which they would be practising before they migrated to New Zealand and only 52% received any information from employers upon arrival. This means that social-justice-directed social workers will need to take responsibility for acquiring local and indigenous knowledges and cultural practices as part of their commitment to socially just and ethical practice.

Although international social workers can bring a critical analysis with them to a new country and might have skills in building ally-ships (Bishop, 2002), the effective application of these skills takes on a distinctly local and long-term aspect as trust-based, reciprocal, respectful relationships take time to develop and sustain (Bennett et al, 2011). These relationships and skills are not something that can be developed in the short term as they rely on a social worker's consistent and respectful engagement with individuals, communities and networks, as well as a record of dependable, consistent, social-justice-based work and commitment. Indigenous academics have noted the damage perpetrated by well-meaning social work practitioners who move in to, and then out of, work with indigenous people, failing to build ongoing, respectful relationships and the dependability necessary for social work practice that is equitable and mutually liberatory (Bennett et al, 2011; see also Bishop, 2002; Gray et al, 2008; Simmons et al, 2014). Thus, this work is not well suited to highly mobile transnational social workers, although it may suit those with a critical, community-engaged approach who intend to settle long-term in a new country.

While the UK (then England) was the original source of most of the colonialism discussed earlier (French and Spanish colonialism also played roles in Canada and elsewhere), the oppression of indigenous peoples and enslaved people forcibly brought in from Africa and subsequent waves of immigrants brought different kinds of challenges to the countries noted in this volume. Ending slavery in tandem with their colonial parent, Australia and Canada folded emancipated people into unequal and exploited positions within unreflectively white supremacist societies (Hochschild, 2006; Fidden-Qasmiyeh et al, 2014). Keeping the societies largely white, with some exceptions (eg the exclusion of Jews during the Second World War), immigration from the UK and Europe was encouraged during periods of high labour demand and discouraged when unemployment soared (Ongley and Pearson, 1995; Boyd and Vickers, 2000). Eventually, non-European sources of immigration were encouraged, though recently almost exclusively from privileged backgrounds, challenging the racism and colonialism of white settler societies in new ways (Ongley and Pearson, 1995; Carniol et al, 2017).

In early times, with the exception of New Zealand, where social work developed later as a profession (see Nash, 1998), social workers in the countries analysed in this collection were involved in the settlement house movement, in which they lived in the same or similar conditions to those they served and pursued social policy and community development strategies alongside interventions aimed at relieving immediate problems and individual pain (Benjamin, 2017). In all four countries, social workers continue to play largely progressive roles in immigrant settlement services, recently adding their names to calls for enhanced rights for refugees and asylum seekers and the closing of Australia's offshore detention centres in Manus and Nauru, and challenging the notions of borders and social exclusions of any form (Baines and Sharma, 2002; Dominelli, 2008; Robinson, 2013).

In the contemporary context, waves of involuntary immigration have been generated since 2001, resulting largely from wars in the Middle East and Northern Africa, and the aggressive and ineffectual strategies of developed countries who were willing to participate in wars in Iraq, Afghanistan, Libya and Syria (among others). These wealthy countries were not interested in remedying the causes of those wars (which often lay in the after-effects of the colonial division of the world), or in fully assisting those displaced by ongoing and seemingly irresolvable conflicts. Internationally, social workers have been involved in international aid organisations in conflict zones and adjacent countries, including Médecins Sans Frontières (Doctors Without Borders), Oxfam and the Red Cross/Red Crescent. In their local jurisdictions, social workers have been working in paid and unpaid capacities with social movements and organisations supporting refugee claimants, as well as with government welfare programmes and non-government settlement services.

Although some of the specific skills of working with refugees, such as trauma counselling, the reunification of families, advocacy and translation, may be transferrable between countries (Casado et al, 2010), policies framing work with refugees and other immigrants are national, state and municipal, rather than international. Knowledge of services and supports is highly local, as are effective advocacy strategies, links with government representatives, legal allies, social movements, minority ethnic communities and other groups and organisations that might assist in the resettlement and reunification of families. Similar to the discussion earlier, skills such as a critical social justice analysis along with a willingness to act as an ally are vital for effective social work practice with these groups, but knowledge of and links with local organisations are central to successful social work interventions. These skills generally take extensive time and persistence to develop. Transnational social workers newly employed in local services are at a disadvantage in terms of sensitivity to local issues, networks and services. In addition, they have not had the time to build up practices or the trust-based, reciprocal relationships that underlie social justice, community-engaged social work practice.

The waves of refugees and asylum seekers noted earlier have challenged the immigration policies and practices of the European Union and other industrialised countries, exposing the embarrassingly low numbers of refugees that they accept compared to poor countries, as well as the racism that is active within the ideologically divided populations within the UK, Australia, Canada and New Zealand. Although the free movement of trade and labour is often asserted to be a positive benefit of globalisation, the free movement of labour has been tolerated within these countries as long as it largely comprised people who could quickly assimilate and who posed no cultural or social threat to the larger society. This further advantaged more privileged and well-educated refugees and immigrants, and further disadvantaged those in dire circumstances but without the cultural or financial capital to move easily into middle- and upper-class life in anglophone countries.

Although some countries emphasise relationship-based, open-ended, community- engaged social work practice, the countries discussed in this volume have a growing emphasis on high-tech (computer-based), individual practice. It is to these aspects that the next section turns.

New Public Management as a standardising form of neoliberal governance under globalisation: our little piece of 'global'

Although social work in all four countries originated with the charitable organisations on the right-wing end of the political, organisational scale and the settlement house movement on the social policy, community-engaged left-wing (Carniol et al, 2017), social services since the 1980s reflect the dismantling of the welfare state through contracting out and the implementation of NPM. NPM is a form of governance and management model embedded within the requirements of government funding contracts that requires funded agencies to adopt outcome metrics, targets and competitive performance management (Carey, 2008; Davies, 2011).

Some authors have argued that NPM is not a uniform phenomenon, although it has been rolled out internationally. Instead, it varies significantly according to local cultures, policy strengths and the resistance of employees, policymakers and local populations (Clarke, 2004; Bach and Bordogna, 2011). While this may be true at the level of policy, at the level of conditions of employment, work process and the experience of front-line workers, a significant convergence has been confirmed (Cunningham, 2008; Charlesworth, 2010; Lundy, 2011).

It is well established in the literature that NPM and competitive performance management tend to standardise practice, removing or reducing practices that are difficult to quantify, such as: open-ended, trustful relationship building; community empowerment and mobilisation; and policy analysis and development (Cunningham, 2008; Baines et al, 2013; Ross, 2017). These changing conditions made critical, social justice approaches increasingly difficult to enact (Jefferey, 2005; Smith, 2017) and put growing pressure on managers to hire social workers who performed well within NPM's high demand for documentation, heavy workloads, high stress and work intensity (Baines, 2017). Labour 'flexibility' has also been emphasised, with a growing use of precarious forms of employment, including contract, part-time, temporary, casual and on-call staff (Davies, 2011).

The rest of this section draws on qualitative case-study data collected in the UK, Canada, Australia and New Zealand between 2010 and 2016 on restructuring in the social services. Exemplar quotes from qualitative interviews with social workers are provided to deepen the analysis provided by the relevant literature, though many more data exist to confirm findings. However, while, as qualitative insights, the findings are not generalisable, they might be highly transferrable to the other countries discussed in this collection.

In addition to removing more open-ended, social-justice-based practices, the standardisation of social services work makes it easier to replace higher-paid, higher-credentialed staff with lower-paid, lower-credentialed staff (Baines and Freeman, 2011). Faced with cutbacks and increasingly constrained resources, some employers have also developed a growing reliance on unpaid work in a number of forms, including: the unpaid overtime of paid staff, particularly precarious employees; volunteers; and placement students and interns. Unpaid work, in its various forms, is epidemic in the social work sector. Managers openly make use of the unpaid labour of their paid staff to extend increasingly overstretched resources. As one executive director told us, "We all work more than our hours and we [the organisation] couldn't survive if we didn't". Part-time workers are particularly vulnerable to expectations of unpaid work. A mid-level manager told us, "The trend in non-profit work is when there are three days a week half-time positions, really, you're doing full time. You're totally doing a full-time job, there's just no resources for it".

While clearly exploitation, unpaid work can simultaneously be a source of meaning, as one long-time, full-time worker explained, she and her co-workers do unpaid work in order "to give back". Sometimes, unpaid overtime is also used to undertake duties that have been reduced or removed within the rushed, high-intensity, NPM-organised workday. For example, one social worker told us that she undertakes advocacy for service users during her unpaid overtime, noting that "We have to be their voice because they quite frankly don't have one".

The use of volunteers, placement students and interns has long been a practice in social services to extend services. However, volunteers are often unreliable (Frumkin, 2009) and may not have the needed skill sets. Unpaid employees, placement students and interns have the appropriate skills and can be disciplined if they fail to show up or perform poorly in their unpaid work, thus neatly solving the problem of unreliability and incomplete skill sets. Providing an example of the use of many kinds of unpaid work, one non-profit social service agency recently studied in Canada made widespread use of placement students and interns for their core functions – their counselling programme would not have been functional without it. The counselling programme was run almost entirely by postgraduate-level social work and psychology placement students, while crisis counselling and intake were provided almost entirely by undergraduate social work and pastoral students. Front-line workers worried about the ethics of this situation, and as one young social worker told us, "we joke all the time about whether it is even legal" (Baines et al, no date).

In Canada, agencies in immigrant communities also made extensive use of volunteers who had originally approached the organisation as service users. Composed of economic immigrants and refugees, many of these volunteers were highly educated and had worked in human services in their countries of origin but, lacking Canadian credentials and experience, were unable to find employment. Similar experiences have been reported by migrant social workers in New Zealand (Fouché et al, 2013). Although the agencies provided references for volunteers who performed well and sometimes hired them into precarious paid employment positions, this global social service labour force was exploited and exploitable because of the xenophobia of the Canadian labour market and system for accreditation of foreign credentials. An additional xenophobic barrier is that Canadian organisations are unlikely to hire people who do not have Canadian experience, which leaves people with no way to gain Canadian experience. These systems favour those educated in industrial countries and disadvantage those from the same nations from which refugees and economic immigrants are like to originate. This dynamic suggests that the mobility of the social service labour force reinforces the privilege of those from privileged backgrounds and countries, and reinforces the disadvantages of those from difficult circumstance and regions – in effect, reproducing global patterns of dominance and injustice. Similar dynamics of racism and xenophobia in labour markets and credentialing systems can be seen to operate in the UK, New Zealand and Australia, ensuring the existence of a highly skilled and highly exploited unpaid volunteer social services labour force (see, eg, Fouché et al, 2013; Papadopoulos, 2017).

Reliance on volunteers and unpaid workers in social services shows no sign of abating in the countries analysed in this volume. For example, volunteering and 'charity work' has recently been strongly encouraged in the UK and New Zealand, with the UK's then Prime Minister David Cameron offering inducements of up to three days' paid leave for private and public sector workers to engage in charity work, with the claim that it will 'build the big society' and 'strengthen communities and the bonds between us' (*The Telegraph*, 2015). Similarly, while strictly adhering to an austerity budget of constraint and cutbacks, New Zealand's Minister of the Community and Voluntary Sector, Jo Goodhew, has been encouraging citizens to volunteer on national holidays. Goodhew asserts that this 'is a fantastic way of connecting neighbours, communities, and the nation through service' (New Zealand Government, 2016). The idea that volunteers can pop into a social service agency for a day or three and make a meaningful difference undermines the notion that social work is a highly skilled profession with a distinct body of knowledge requiring formal, university-based training. Instead, it feeds into the notion that absolutely anyone can undertake social service work at any point in their lives.

Implications for practice and possibilities for liberatory social work practice

In today's social work context (austerity, managerialism, growing inequity and the continued harms of colonialism), resistance and critical thought are desperately needed, in part, to counter the notion of 'impossiblism … that is, that nothing can be done about global suffering' (Morrall, 2008, p 215). Critical thought and theorising ensure that social work practice continues to move forward based on the lived experiences of workers, service users and communities, and with a focus on social justice. Larger, mass-resistance practices, such as advocacy, social organising, mobilising communities and working in coalition with social movements, are ways to sustain social workers' sense of integrity and foster their awareness that their best interests and the best interests of services users and communities do not always dovetail with the policies of employers and governments. Resistance practices are also a way in which social workers' and service users' concerns can be brought to the attention of those with the power to make changes in a workplace or at the level of policy. How does transnational social work fit with these challenges?

The International Federation of Social Workers' 'Global standards for the education and training of the social work profession' (IFSW, 2014) state that:

> social work is a practice-based profession and an academic discipline which promotes social change and development; social cohesion and the empowerment and liberation of people. Principles of social justice, human rights, collective responsibility and respect for diversities are central to social work.

While struggles at the level of the workplace necessarily have a local focus and require local connections and carefully nurtured relationships and networks, other struggles have global connections and implications – such as a given agency recognising the right of indigenous people to develop their own culturally enhancing practices within or alongside a given mainstream social work programme. Although the immediate effects are experienced in a local environment, these kinds of bold initiatives can have global implications for those working to right the wrongs of colonialism and white privilege.

This chapter has shown that social work in Australia, Canada and New Zealand continues to operate in the context of colonialism and the continued oppression of indigenous peoples. While international social work may helpfully theorise and study these issues, transnational social workers themselves require a commitment to rapidly acquainting themselves with the local struggles of indigenous peoples and the strategies that have been or could helpfully be used in solidarity with these struggles (Simmons et al, 2014). As noted earlier in the chapter, these practices include working alongside (Bennett et al, 2011) indigenous people in their struggles for resources, affirming identities and policies that expand both these attributes of a fairer and more socially just society. Without a critical analysis and willingness to learn about local contexts, indigenous knowledge and cultural practices (Simmons et al, 2014), transnational social workers are likely to reproduce the unquestioned and normalised relations of dominance characteristic of the mainstream culture and social services in these societies (Lundy, 2011; Simmons et al, 2014; Baines, 2017).

The context of colonialism and notions of cultural and racial superiority also extend to the forced global migration of peoples, particularly in recent times when Western powers intervened in armed conflicts with no improvement in local or global relations, and there is no end in sight to these conflicts. Although international social work theorises the struggles of asylum seekers and refugees, and international social workers often work in NGOs in refugee camps or regions of conflict, the local knowledges and ties needed to be effective in settlement work in local contexts are other aspects of practice that need to be framed by a critical theory lens and a recognition that networks and community-engagement relationships are nurtured slowly and carefully over long periods of time.

Although NPM has narrowed the field of practice in many social work organisations in the countries studied and has encouraged standardised, high-tech practice rather than the community-engaged holistic practice that would make international and local social work more liberatory, social workers resist in ways, big and small, that are creative and persistent.

Smaller, everyday efforts to sustain the dignity of service users and extend their social and human rights are essential to building a culture and ethics of social work resistance and challenging the power of global capitalism and continued colonialism (Mullaly, 2010; Ross, 2017). Similarly, working with social movements, advocacy groups and unions representing social and human service workers can provide resources and a broader analysis to resistance in social work arenas locally and internationally (Lundy, 2011; Carniol et al, 2017). These resistance practices help to position social work as a moral project of challenging global and local injustices and inequities (Baines, 2016). This sense of a moral project is one of the main reasons why most social workers and managers are drawn to social work, why they stay with the job and why some might seek to emigrate in search of learning opportunities, employment and new ways to contribute to the global project of social justice.

References

Bach, S. and Bordogna, L. (2011) 'Varieties of New Public Management or alternative models? The reform of public service employment relations in industrialized democracies', *International Journal of Human Resource Management*, 22(11): 2281–94.

Baines, D. (2016) 'Moral projects and compromise resistance: resisting uncaring in nonprofit care work', *Studies in Political Economy*, online, 19 August. Available at: http://dx.doi.org/10.1080/07078552.201 6.1208793

Baines, D. (2017) 'An overview of anti-oppressive practice', in D. Baines (ed) *Doing anti-oppressive practice* (3rd edn), Halifax: Fernwood Books.

Baines, D. and Freeman, B. (2011) 'Work, care, resistance and mothering: an indigenous perspective', in C. Krull and J. Sempruch (eds) *A life in balance. Reopening the family–work debate*, Vancouver: University of British Columbia Press, pp 67–80.

Baines, D. and Sharma, N. (2002) 'Migrant workers as non-citizens: the case against citizenship as a social policy concept', *Studies in Political Economy*, 69(1): 75–107.

Baines, D., Cunningham, I., Shields, J. and Lewchuk, W. (no date) 'Filling the gaps with unpaid, formal and coerced work in the nonprofit sector'.

Baines, D., Charlesworth, S. and Cunningham, I. (2013) 'Fragmented outcomes: international comparisons of gender, managerialism and union strategies in the nonprofit sector', *Journal of Industrial Relations*, 56(1): 24–42.

Benjamin, A. (2017) 'Afterword: resistance and social work', in D. Baines (ed) *Doing anti-oppressive practice: Social justice social work* (3rd edn), Halifax: Fernwood, pp 317–29.

Bennett, B., Zubrzycki, J. and Bacon, V. (2011) 'What do we know? The experiences of social workers working alongside Aboriginal people', *Australian Social Work*, 64(1): 20–37.

Bishop, A. (2002) *Becoming an ally: Breaking the cycle of oppression in people*, New York, NY: Zed Books.

Boyd, M. and Vickers, M. (2000) '100 years of immigration in Canada', *Canadian Social Trends*, 58(2): 13–20.

Brave Heart, M. (2003) 'The historical trauma response among natives and its relationship with substance abuse: a Lakota illustration', *Journal of Psychoactive Drugs*, 35(1): 7–13.

Carey, M. (2008) 'Everything must go? The privatization of state social work', *British Journal of Social Work*, 38(5): 918–35.

Carniol, B., Baines, D., Kennedy, B. and Sinclair, R. (2017) *Case critical*, Toronto: Between the Lines.

Casado, B., Hong, M. and Harrington, D. (2010) 'Measuring migratory grief and loss associated with the experience of migration', *Research on Social Work Practice*, 20(6): 611–20.

Charlesworth, S. (2010) 'The regulation of paid care workers' wages and conditions in the non-profit sector: a Toronto case study', *Relations Industrielles/Industrial Relations*, 65(3): 380–99.

Clarke, J. (2004) 'Dissolving the public realm? The logics and limits of neo-liberalism', *Journal of Social Policy*, 33(1): 27–48.

Cunningham, I. (2008) *Employment relations in the voluntary sector* (vol 10), London: Routledge.

Davies, S. (2011) 'Outsourcing and the voluntary sector: a review of the evolving landscape', in I. Cunningham and P. James (eds) *Voluntary organisations and public service delivery*, London: Routledge, pp 15–36.

Department of Social Welfare (1986) *Puao-Te-Ata-Tu (daybreak) report of a ministerial advisory committee on a Māori perspective for the department of social welfare*, Wellington: Department of Social Welfare. Available at: https://www.msd.govt.nz/documents/about-msd-and-our-work/publications-resources/archive/1988-puaoteatatu.pdf

Dominelli, L. (2008) *Anti-racist social work*, London: Palgrave Macmillan.

Fiddian-Qasmiyeh, E., Loescher, G., Long, K. and Sigona, N. (eds) (2014) *The Oxford handbook of refugee and forced migration studies*, Oxford: OUP.

Fouché, C., Beddoe, L., Bartley, A. and Brenton, N. (2013) 'Strengths and struggles: overseas qualified social workers' experiences in Aotearoa New Zealand', *Australian Social Work*, 67(4): 551–66.

Fraser, N. (2010) *Scales of justice*, New York, NY: Columbia University Press.

Freeman, B. (2017) 'Indigenous pathways to anti-oppressive practice', in D. Baines (ed) *Doing anti-oppressive practice* (3rd edn), Halifax: Fernwood Publishing.

Frumkin, P. (2009) *On being nonprofit: A conceptual and policy primer*, Cambridge: Harvard University Press.

Gray, M. and Webb, S. (2013) *The new politics of social work*, London: Palgrave.

Gray, M., Coates, J. and Yellow Bird, M. (2008) *Indigenous social work around the world*, Williston: Ashgate.

Green, S. and Baldry, E. (2008) 'Building Indigenous Australian social work', *Australian Social Work*, 61(4): 389–402.

Hart, M. (2009) 'Anti-colonial indigenous social work: reflections on an aboriginal approach', in R. Sinclair, M.A. Hart and G. Bruyere (eds) *Wicihitowin: Aboriginal social work in Canada*, Halifax: Fernwood Publishing, pp 25–41.

Hochschild, A. (2006) *Bury the chains: The British struggle to abolish slavery*, London: Pan Macmillan.

Ife, J. (2012) *Human rights and social work: Towards rights-based practice*, Cambridge: Cambridge University Press.

IFSW (International Federation of Social Work) (2014) 'Global definition of social work'. Available at: http://ifsw.org/policies/definition-of-social-work

Jeffery, D. (2005) '"What good is anti-racist social work if you can't master it?": exploring a paradox in anti-racist social work education', *Race, Ethnicity and Education*, 8(4): 409–25.

Krull, C. and Sempruch, J. (2011) *Destabilizing the nuclear family ideal: Thinking beyond essentialisms. A life in balance? Reopening the family–work debate*, Vancouver: University of British Columbia Press.

Lundy, C. (2011) *Social work and social justice: A structural approach to practice*, Toronto: University of Toronto Press.

McDonald, C. (2006) *Challenging social work: The institutional context of practice*, London: Palgrave Macmillan.

Morrall, P. (2008) *The trouble with therapy: Sociology and psychotherapy*, Berkshire: Open University Press.

Mullaly, B. (2010) *Challenging oppression and confronting privilege*, Ontario: Oxford University Press.

Nash, E. (1998) 'People, policies and practice: social work education in Aotearoa/New Zealand from 1949–1995', unpublished thesis, Massey University, New Zealand.

New Zealand Government (2016) 'Kiwis encouraged to serve New Zealand this Anzac Day'. Available at: https://www.beehive.govt.nz/release/kiwis-encouraged-serve-new-zealand-anzac-day

Noel, J. (2006) 'Power mothering: the Haudenosaunee model', in D. Luvell-Harvard and J. Corbiere Lavell (eds) *Until our hearts are on the ground: Aboriginal mothering, oppression, resistance and rebirth*, Toronto: Demeter Press, pp 76–93.

O'Neill, L. (2017) 'Cognitive behavioural therapy and anti-oppressive practice: compatible or irreconcilable differences', in D. Baines (ed) *Doing anti-oppressive practice. Social justice social work*, Halifax: Fernwood Books.

Ongley, P. and Pearson, D. (1995) 'Post-1945 international migration: New Zealand, Australia and Canada compared', *International Migration Review*, 29(3): 765–93.

Papadopoulos, A. (2017) 'Migrating qualifications: the ethics of recognition', *British Journal of Social Work*, 47(1): 219–37, doi:10.1093/bjsw/bcw038.

Pease, B., Goldingay, S., Hosken, N. and Nipperess, S. (2016) *Doing critical social work: Transformative practices for social justice*, Melbourne: Allen and Unwin.

Pohatu, T.W. (2003) 'Maori world-views: source of innovative social work choices', *Social Work Review*, 15(3): 16–24.

Quinn, A. (2007) 'Reflections on intergenerational trauma: healing as a critical intervention', *First Peoples Child & Family Review*, 3(4): 72–82.

Robinson, K. (2014) 'Voices from the front line: social work with refugees and asylum seekers in Australia and the UK', *British Journal of Social Work*, 6(1): 1602–20, doi:1093/bjsw/bct040

Ross, M. (2017) 'Social work activism amidst neoliberalism: a big, broad tent of activism', in D. Baines (ed) *Doing anti-oppressive practice* (3rd edn), Halifax: Fernwood Publishing.

Ruwhiu, L.A. (2013) 'Making sense of Indigenous issues in Aotearoa New Zealand', in M. Connolly and L. Harms (eds) *Social work: Contexts and practice* (3rd edn), Melbourne: OUP, pp 124–37.

Shewell, H. (2004) *Enough to keep them alive: Indian welfare in Canada, 1873–1965*, Toronto: University of Toronto Press.

Simmons, H., Walsh-Tapiata, W., Litea, M.-S. and Umugwaneza, A. (2014) '"Cultural encounter": a framework of ethical practice for transnational social workers in Aotearoa', in J. Duke, M. Henrickson and L. Beddoe (eds) *Protecting the public –Enhancing the profession*, Wellington, NZ: Social Workers Registration Board, pp 66–78.

Sinclair, R. (2007) 'Identity lost and found: lessons from the sixties scoop', *First Peoples Child & Family Review*, 3(1): 65–82.

Sinclair, R. (2009) 'Identity or racism? Aboriginal transracial adoption', in R. Sinclair, M.A. Hart and G. Bruyere (eds) *Wicihitowin: Aboriginal social work in Canada*, Halifax: Fernwood Publishing, pp 89–113.

Smith, K. (2017) 'Occupied spaces: unmapping standardized assessments in health and social service organizations', in D. Baines (ed) *Doing anti-oppressive practice: Social justice social work* (3rd edn), Halifax: Fernwood, pp 197–213.

Smith, L. (2012) *Decolonizing methodologies: Research and indigenous peoples*, London: Zed Books.

The Telegraph (2015) 'David Cameron: 15 million workers to get three days' paid volunteering leave each year'. Available at: http://www.telegraph.co.uk/news/general-election-2015/11526478/David-Cameron-15-million-workers-to-get-three-days-paid-volunteering-leave-each-year.html

Vinson, T., Rawsthorne, M., Beavis, A. and Ericson, M. (2015) *Dropping off the edge 2015: Persistent communal disadvantage in Australia*, Curtin, Australia: Jesuit Social Services/Catholic Social Services Australia. Available at: http://www.dote.org.au

Part Two:
Practitioner perspectives

The four chapters that comprise Part Two each draw on research conducted to examine, in turn, the experiences of transnational social workers in Canada, England, Australia, and Aotearoa New Zealand. While the different studies varied in their designs, the numbers of participants involved, and the methods of analysis used to interpret the data, the stories told in each chapter reveal some fundamental consistencies across the four countries. Transnational social workers have been, and continue to be, drawn from across the world to fill social work positions in these jurisdictions. This is the 'opportunities' side of the equation. Each of the chapters alludes to the fact that governments in the four countries have aligned their immigration and labour market policies to capitalise on the increased transnational mobility of professional labour, to make it easier for employers to attract transnational professionals and for the transnationals themselves migrate into these nations. It is noteworthy that this has produced a certain degree of 'churn' amongst social workers across the four jurisdictions: each of the four national studies includes transnational social workers from the other three countries, in addition to those from many other countries as well. In Chapter Four, Marion Brown, Annie Pullen Sansfaçon, Stephanie Éthier and Amy Fulton describe the 'pull' factor to Canada as 'a discourse of possibility and opportunity': this is a discourse that is actively mobilised in each of the four countries under discussion in the four chapters in this Part.

The equation has another side however: as well as the possibilities and opportunities offered to transnational social workers, there are also challenges. The four chapters share many of these as well: there tends to be an enduring disjuncture between immigration regimes that recognise and credit prospective migrants with foreign social work qualifications and practice experience, and professional regimes that are often less prepared to do so. That disjuncture is often manifest as an open door into the country, and (for some more than for others) a closed door – or at least a stubborn one – into the social work profession. Just as is the case with economic currency, there is a kind of variable exchange rate that impacts on the cultural capital of transnational professionals: receiving countries may value the qualifications and professional experience, as well as language proficiencies, from some jurisdictions more highly than from others. All the chapters in this Part of the book suggest that, depending on both the sending and receiving countries, as well as the impact of 'race' and class, the impact of such exchange rates benefit some TSWs and disadvantage others.

Each of the four chapters also highlights the challenges confronting TSWs in translating familiar social work values, so often understood to be universal, into practice contexts in an unfamiliar country. Social work is so deeply embedded in social-cultural dynamics, rooted in specific histories, that must be understood critically for social workers to practise competently in each context. Marion Brown and her collaborators illustrate in the Canadian context transnational social workers' struggle to interpret what is required to 'fit in' so as to adapt to their new professional context. In Chapter Five, Sue Hanna and Karen Lyons describe the specific context of the statutory child protection regime in England as being far more regulated, and indeed de-professionalising, than most TSWs anticipate. In the Australian context, this challenge is framed by Allen Bartley in Chapter Six as the need to clarify the expectations held both by TSWs and by their employers of how ready they actually are to practice in their new context, and whose responsibility it is to help them transition effectively. It is noteworthy that three of the countries addressed in these chapters have histories of colonisation by the fourth; some of the particular cultural, political and socio-economic conditions – particularly of these countries' Indigenous populations – cannot be understood without a deep appreciation of the on-going impact on these populations of colonisation, and of nation-states' variable attempts to address those problematic histories. Liz Beddoe addresses this in detail in the context of Aotearoa New Zealand, in the final chapter in this Part.

Finally, it is important to note that amidst the range of cultural, linguistic, political, institutional, and professional challenges that confront the transnational practitioners whose perspectives are presented in these chapters, the authors also offer to readers an insight into these practitioners' resilience. Amidst their frustration and struggles, their experiences of misunderstanding and unfulfilled expectations, are stories of determination to succeed; to translate their skills, dispositions, and expertise into meaningful and competent social work practice in their new settings. These are professionals who have crossed international borders not merely to pursue their own rational self-interest, but to contribute their skills, their dedicated commitment to the enhancement of human rights and social justice, to the societies that have welcomed them – even when that welcome is, as stated so succinctly in one of the chapters that follow, a complicated one.

FOUR

A complicated welcome: social workers navigate policy, organisational contexts and sociocultural dynamics following migration to Canada[1]

Marion Brown, Annie Pullen Sansfaçon, Stephanie Éthier and Amy Fulton

The context of immigration to Canada

Canada prides itself on a reputation for being a welcoming and inclusive country, promoting collective pride in a multicultural mosaic wherein a diversity of ethnicities, cultures and religions coexist. It is a country that often enjoys positive international assessment, with its reported comfortable standard of living, solid social programmes, mix of urban and rural lifestyles, vast and spectacular natural beauty, and people often considered polite and consensus-driven. It is also a country with a growing density divide between urban growth and rural out-migration, an ageing demographic, and regional variability in population growth (Statistics Canada, 2012). This scenic land of opportunity has evident appeal to immigrants leaving their countries of origin for a variety of social, economic and political reasons.

The Canadian government, reciprocally, views the newcomer to Canada as providing an answer to sustaining the country's demographic and economic growth. Under both Liberal and Conservative Party leadership, the Canadian government has sought to liberalise its labour and trade markets through policies including the North America Free Trade Agreement and programmes such as those designated for

[1] Excerpted and reprinted with permission. First published as: Brown, M., Sansfaçon, A.P., Éthier, S. and Fulton, A. (2014) 'A complicated welcome: social workers navigate policy, organizational contexts and socio-cultural dynamics following migration to Canada', *International Journal of Social Science Studies*, 3(1): 58–68.

temporary foreign workers, skilled trade workers and professional immigrants (Citizenship and Immigration Canada, 2014). These efforts are considered to have been successful. For example, the Migrant Integration Policy Index determined that Canadian immigrant workers and their families benefit from the third-best integration policies in the 31 countries considered, citing specific government efforts towards improving equal access in education and labour (Migrant Integration Policy Index III, 2011). The International Migration Outlook, published in 2013 by the Organisation for Economic Cooperation and Development (OECD), cites immigration as accounting for two thirds of Canada's population growth of 1.2%, primarily in the age bracket of 20–44 years, which is otherwise in decline. It is this cohort that contributes significantly to the labour force, grows families, buys homes and forms the basis of taxation revenue (OECD, 2013). Canada reached a record high of 281,000 new permanent residents to Canada in 2010, followed by 249,000 new permanent residents to Canada in 2011 (OECD, 2013). Further, employment for foreign-born Canadians in 2012 earned Canada the ranking of third-highest in the OECD (OECD, 2013). This government priority continues.

Internationally educated social workers are included in these trends, through both federal and provincial initiatives. For example, the social work profession is included as one of the 29 eligible occupations on the 'Federal Skilled Worker' recruitment policy list (Healy and Huegler, 2012), and Chapter 7 of the Agreement on Internal Trade – 'Mutual recognition agreement on labour mobility for social workers in Canada' – has been implemented (Canadian Information Centre for International Credentials, 2007). Further, the government of Quebec has enacted a Mutual Recognition Agreement between Quebec and France for the qualifications of social workers in professional employment (Canadian Information Centre for International Credentials, 2007). These policies and entities support the mobility of social workers both from overseas to Canada and across the country's provinces and territories.

Given the reach of globalisation and the development of policies and multilateral agreements, labour mobility in social work, both at national and international levels, is increasingly popular. Indeed, this cluster of considerations seems perfect: the idealised Canadian landscape and welcome + a declining and ageing population + the need for demographic and economic input + favourable immigration policies + social worker-specific labour mobility policies + an internationally endorsed set of global standards for the profession. Alluring though this picture may be, research examining the experiences of 44 migrant social workers who undertook their social work education outside Canada and currently practise social work within Canada suggest significant barriers on the levels of policy, organisational context and sociocultural dynamics. Analyses of findings regarding personal and professional adaptation across borders suggest that the idealised Canadian welcome is a complicated one. From the level of policy, to organisational context, to sociocultural dynamics, migrant social workers experience a tension between a discourse of possibility and opportunity surrounding life and work in Canada, and material constraints in bureaucratic processes and finding a fit in the social work profession in Canada.

Methodology

This chapter presents findings from a qualitative study with 44 participants who had completed their social work degrees in Australia, India, Philippines, Colombia, Spain, Liberia, New Zealand, Finland, France, Venezuela, Germany, UK, Romania, USA, Israel, Nigeria, Lebanon, South Africa, Netherlands and Ukraine since 2002. Grounded theory methods guided the analysis of the individual interviews given that this is a largely under-theorised field of study: with the exception of a team of researchers in the UK (see Hussein et al, 2010, 2011) and in New Zealand (see Bartley et al, 2012; Fouché et al, 2014), the experiences of social workers who migrate, their professional adaptation processes and the many changes in perception that they undergo while adapting to new cultural and organisational contexts have not been well conceptualised and theorised in the literature (Pullen Sansfaçon et al, 2012).

Participants were recruited through social work networks, including professional association newsletters, regulatory body list serves and posters in agencies. Three urban sites – Calgary, Montreal and Halifax – were selected, each for their distinct regional trends in the attraction of newcomers; as the study progressed, the pool of potential participants proved limited in Calgary and Halifax, thus the catchment area was extended to Southern Alberta in the west and Nova Scotia and Prince Edward Island in the east. Consistent with grounded theory methods, no extant concepts were taken from the literature; the coding structure and team analysis were generated 'from the ground up', directly from the data.

Findings

Canadian immigration policies

The first set of policies with which newcomer social workers grapple are Canadian immigration policies, often researching them from abroad while planning for their move. While detailed with regard to purpose and process on the federal government website (Citizenship and Immigration Canada, 2013), frustrations remain regarding their clarity and user-friendliness. It is clear from these data that finding one's way through the immigration process takes fortitude, self-advocacy, perseverance and patience. This combination is captured in a summary statement by a participant from England, who says: "My experience has been if you come into Canada ... then you need to put your helmet on and fasten your seatbelt.... It's not for the faint heart, the process, and you gotta stick with it" (England-2).

Detailing specific aspects of the process, the following participant highlights accessibility:

> "The process of immigration is extremely difficult. The Department of Immigration has a website and an email address. They do not have a phone number, so you can't call anyone and ask questions. Everything you need to know you need to find out off the Internet. And when you email a question to them, it may be several days before you get a response. And then it says, 'Look at the website'." (Australia-1)

Some wonder if the cumbersome process is intended to dissuade newcomers from seeking residence in Canada, like the participant from Spain who said: "Do they even ever want us here?". Indeed, there is a paradox in the approach of the federal government in that a coexisting policy of Citizenship and Immigration Canada (CIC) is clear that employers are required to undertake recruitment efforts to hire Canadian citizens and permanent residents before offering a job to 'foreign workers' (Citizenship and Immigration Canada, 2014). The priorities of the federal government appear to be at a crossroads: trying to manage the tension of hiring Canadian citizens first, which is important in a country where average unemployment is at 6.9%, yet ranges across the provinces from 4.5% in Saskatchewan to 11.8% in Prince Edward Island (Statistics Canada, 2014); and also building its population and economic base through the attraction of skilled professionals to the country.

Recognition of foreign credentials

Recognition of foreign credentials is the next level of policy navigation for newcomer social workers, a process through which assessment is made regarding the degree of equivalence between an international social work degree and a Canadian one. Given that social work is a regulated profession in Canada, this is required in order to be licensed by the regulatory body for each province. While the recognition of foreign credentials is not under the federal government's mandate, either by law or by the policy of the CIC, the Foreign Credentials Referrals Office was established by the CIC to provide information to immigrants (Citizenship and Immigration Canada, 2013).

The Canadian Association of Social Workers (CASW) is the mediating body for the provincial regulatory bodies that do not facilitate the recognition of foreign credentials; only British Columbia and Quebec undertake their own assessment (Pullen Sansfaçon, 2010). Findings from our study suggest that there are inconsistent criteria, lengthy time delays and general frustration with the process of evaluation of one's credentials earned at a university or college outside Canada:

> "I didn't really know where to start. I tried to figure it out, I tried to contact them and figure out what I needed then, if I'd missed something in my education.... But they wouldn't give me any information on what I missed and the message I got at that point ... was to register into a BSW [Bachelor of Social Work] program and then see what credits I would get, like that I already have, that I didn't have to retake and then just take whatever was left, kind of thing. And so I tried that. I tried to register at the [university] and they said I couldn't register because I already had a BSW." (Netherlands-1)

These difficulties in getting foreign credentials recognised are also echoed by participants from France. While the unique France–Quebec agreement should 'facilitate and accelerate the acquisition by people in France and Québec of a permit to practise a profession' (Gouvernement du Québec, 2013), several participants who established themselves in Montreal after moving from France experienced delays and challenges in getting their credentials recognised. A participant from France who immigrated to Montreal illustrates this:

> "I did not expect to have to wait six months because I had checked on the [Quebec] professional association of social workers' website and they did not explain at all the way to proceed or that it could take as long. I thought it would be much simpler. I was a little disappointed when I arrived here as I had to work as a [not qualified] social care practitioner." (France)

In addition, frustration was reported when there was a lack of communication, or circularity, between the CASW and the provincial bodies:

> "I spoke with the [provincial body], who said to ... have [the degrees] accredited by the Canadian association, so I did that.... When I then applied to register with the [provincial body], they said 'Oh, we need the transcripts and everything' and I said, 'You know, it was really kind of just a bit messy trying to get them from England, could you not get them from the Canadian [Association]?' and they said 'We have no connection with them'. And I was like, 'Hang on, you just told me I couldn't register with you until I was approved by the Canadian [body] ... so surely you have, like, one call you could make!'." (England-3)

These data align with the challenges documented in several countries (White, 2006; Bartley et al, 2012; Fang, 2012) that the difficulties faced in obtaining degree recognition are among the first challenges that migrant social workers encounter in a new country. After working through immigration processes and assessing the equivalence of international social work education to Canadian social work education, next comes securing the licence to practise as a registered social worker.

Social work licensing

Securing a licence to practise social work is a rite of passage for social workers seeking to work in the field in Canada. This process is also experienced as cumbersome and lengthy, sometimes with mixed messages regarding what is required for the licence. Given that licensing is a central requirement for securing social work positions, there were concerns with the amount of time that the process took:

"I sent my registration package and I was told I would get an answer in five days – an official answer, letter format. Nobody called me so I kept calling after one month, after the second month. I was always told that the registrar was out of her office, she's in the workshop, she's on vacation, she's here and there. I did not hear from them at all so finally I contacted them again. I said if … they want me to do some extra things like courses or approve credentials then I am definitely willing to do whatever it takes. So finally they wrote me back an email saying that I will have to prove some of my courses from Romania, that I took ethics in social work and social organisation courses.… I managed to translate that, to notarise it and then to send it to the [regulatory body].… They finally came back to me after another long two-month wait. They told me that they would register me provisionally." (Romania)

Issues of clarity, process delays and additional practice hours constitute significant challenges to finding employment in the field of social work because in each province, the profession has been granted protected title under legislation. The findings of this study align with research undertaken in New Zealand that, in addition to the recognition of their skills, candidates need to demonstrate evidence of their qualifications for local practice (Beddoe et al, 2012). Further, studies in the UK substantiate that migrant social workers often need to complete additional unpaid practicum hours, or accept a less-qualified position, in order to acquire local experience (Hussein et al, 2011).

Taken together, these policy-based challenges – immigration, the recognition of foreign credentials and securing a licence to practise – are experienced as impediments to the movement, settlement and integration of migrant social workers. A heavy onus rests on the social worker to verify that they are a worthy new Canadian, that their social work education is rigorous enough for Canadian expectations and that they can be reliably granted the social work title in the country.

Through these accounts, we begin to see the internationally famed Canadian welcome begin to tarnish at the edges. Examining a little more closely, we learn that the percentage of immigrants in social work in 2006 was slightly lower than in all occupations: 9% compared with 12% (Service Canada, 2013). Unemployment rates for social work are also reportedly low; Service Canada notes that few positions will be filled by unemployed experienced social workers because the jobs are not likely to be available. Auder (2003, p 699) theorises that 'regulatory institutions actively exclude immigrants from the upper segments of the labour market. In particular, professional associations and employers give preference to Canadian born and educated workers and deny immigrants access to the most highly desired occupations'. Creese and Wiebe (2012, p 56) question Canadian immigration policies that 'prioritize the recruitment of well-educated immigrants without also addressing multiple barriers that exist in the work place'. Hence, we turn our attention to the organisational context, and, subsequently, socio-cultural dynamics, to begin to distinguish the discursive from the material in the experiences of migrant social workers.

Organisational context

After the immigration process, the recognition of international education and licensing with the provincial regulatory body, migrant social workers are in a position to secure employment in their professional field. Yet, organisations and agencies have their own layers of explicit and implicit assessment, providing shape to the experience of newcomer social workers seeking work. In the realm of organisational context, we move more into a discursive dimension, where there are as many systemic expectations conveyed through subtle interactions and interpretations as there are formally explicated through the official hiring practices and human resources procedures of particular agencies. The following participants articulate this issue:

> "How do I put forth my skills and tell [them] 'Hey, I'm available; I'm available to volunteer; I'm available to give my resources to you'. How do I do that? That is the biggest block I have." (India-1)

> "it was difficult to get into social work, even though I have social work experience and my degree is recognised. So after that, what did I do is, my wife and I chose, you know what, we need to go back [to the Netherlands] because this is not working in Canada, I can't get a job, proper job, on the level that I had." (Netherlands-2)

The tautological relationship between getting a Canadian job and needing Canadian experience is exemplified here:

"you end up in this vicious circle of you don't have a local experience, right? And you cannot get any experience here because you don't have a working experience here. Well, how can I get it if I don't have a chance?" (Ukraine)

Like the participant from the Netherlands cited earlier, for many of these social workers, migration is not a one-time, one-way move. Given the systemic and bureaucratic challenges to securing work, people move to, from and within Canada due to cumulative stressors. A participant from the US moved to one of the eastern provinces, returned to the US after six months of searching for a job, then took a one-year-term position in the Yukon, before settling in the eastern province to which he had originally come. Similarly, participants from Finland and Lebanon both went back and forth several times due to financial need, knowing that they could work in their home countries for short periods and earn enough money to then return to Canada again to try to secure long-term social work employment. Their stories align with the following participant, who kept moving to find work:

"We landed to Quebec City and, as we all know, it's a government city, so I would say all the good jobs were taken by the locals and, you know, although I look like them, I really, really had a hard time finding employment and I was already bilingual French and English at that time. So we moved to Calgary." (Romania)

The struggle to find work led many to theorise what was happening, questioning why they faced barriers. Some came up with concerns about a paradoxical welcome to this new land:

"Not to blow my own trumpet, but I think I have a really good background.... from age 20, I've worked in social arenas.... I've done a lot of jobs.... I'm quite surprised that I've never even had an interview, no feedback. And the only deduction I can make, which is obviously not a really good one, is that there is some prejudice against being qualified from another country." (England-3)

The following participant theorised the reasons for the challenges she faced in her first Canadian social work job:

"The first one is racism, the second one is fear. I have two masters' degrees and a bachelor's degree and then I have a boss who has a Certificate of Diplomatic Social Work [sic]. So you can imagine what it was like. So I literally lasted one month on that job and I was let go. Yes, because every report I was writing was critically analysed and scrutinised and someone told me they did not like it. I don't think I do anything wrong. I think I was just doing something according to my knowledge and my skills. And perhaps she did not understand and she felt threatened, you know, and so they let me go." (Nigeria)

Organisational contexts structure the realities of employment-seeking in the field of social work in Canada. In the new organisational context, migrant social workers are faced with different types of relations with stakeholders, supervisors, regulators and colleagues. The participants in this study experienced that they need to work harder than their local counterparts to obtain credibility and/or positioning within the organisational context. This has as much to do with unwritten expectations and understanding of the local context as it does with written procedures and site-specific policies and laws.

Sociocultural dynamics

Delving into the discursive domain more deeply, participants talked of the struggle to 'fit in' either while looking for social work employment or after they had secured it. Social relations among colleagues and with clients are a central means through which personal and professional adaptation occurs, not only through the translation of skills and knowledge from one's country of origin, but also through figuring out the spoken and unspoken ways of being that are acceptable in the new setting. The following participant begins with a global statement about Canadians, which she stated "comes out in a lots of ways": "The Canadian lifestyle, it's completely different than German … they're more laid back I would say in Canada. In Germany, we're really strict" (Germany).

Proficiency in the primary language of Canada, English, is another area of focus for both personal and professional adaptation, on the professional side, likely because social work's central method for intervention relies on the spoken word:

"It was a real, real challenge because my language skills were very poor.... I didn't feel confident to even start the process of applying for a real job because I was so afraid that I wouldn't be able to communicate.... I think it took two years to feel that I can really apply for a job with confidence, applying for a job." (Israel)

For others, proficiency in the language was reportedly fine; however, use or tone of the language, or its delivery, was a notable area for attention:

"in my culture, we talk fast and loud and here if you do that, people find you aggressive and I try to watch how I talk, how I behave. Sometimes maybe my humour is different. I notice sometimes they don't really understand my jokes, so I was like, 'OK, that is not the way how you do it with your co-workers!'." (Romania)

In the complexity of adapting the practice of social work to new local contexts, the matter of racism bears particular mention. In this study, social workers of colour face discrimination and Caucasian social workers experience the white privilege that upholds discrimination:

"I have to say, just as a comment, and I know it's very sad that I'm saying that, but ... I was lucky that I'm Caucasian. It's very sad for me to tell this. I know that that's a factor in the ability to get a job. It's unfortunate." (Israel)

"In Canada, discrimination is a huge challenge if you're black from another country." (India-3)

Following a difficult exchange with a co-worker, the following participant from Nigeria discussed her impressions with her manager: "I said, 'It's unfair. I feel unfairly treated. At this point I feel targeted and I feel discriminated against because I'm the only person of colour here and I don't think you're giving me the support'" (Nigeria).

A participant from Lebanon explains that while being from a foreign country may not have stopped her getting into a management job, she nevertheless felt that she had to go above and beyond to prove her competence. In a meeting, she explains that:

"People were asking tough questions, and were tough in the way they were asking questions. I felt my anxiety levels going up and at some point, I had to [tell] myself that I knew well my caseload, and that whatever questions they ask me, I knew my caseload.... At the end of the meeting, people were positively impressed by my level of preparation ... and it is like they were telling me, "This one, the Lebanese, she is not too bad" – like if people who come from elsewhere, they were not necessary, good or able, not necessarily competent ... and that we only employ them because we are trying to get a certain level of equity ... in the number of employees [from an minority ethnic group]." (Lebanon)

Findings of discrimination and racism have been substantiated elsewhere. In the UK, studies have shown that migrant social workers can be perceived as a less desirable option in recruitment (Simpson, 2009; Hussein et al, 2011). Further, a study conducted in New Zealand reported that more than half of the participants had experienced discrimination in the workplace. This discrimination took many forms, such as hostility, humiliation, verbal abuse, sabotage and devaluation. These realities and the ensuing feeling of exclusion can cause distress, and have been related to the inability to use skills acquired internationally (Fouché et al, 2014). Moreover, in her study about professional identity in overseas-born social workers in Australia, Harrison (2013, p 8) discovered that migrant social workers can perceive a 'glass ceiling effect', experiencing that they are 'confined to an "ethnic sector" due to their identity'.

Discussion

Qualitative analysis asks researchers to continuously ask the question 'What is happening here?', exploring the social processes in which the participants are engaged and striving to make meaning of these processes. In this chapter, we hone in on the material and discursive barriers experienced in the migration of social workers to Canada, which is an expression of the global movement of people and products, trade and technology. Thus, we continue to theorise, expanding upon the notion that processes of adaptation and acculturation can be explained 'as an interactional process among one's notions of identity, including professional identity, which involves one's experiences in various social work roles and interventions and the sociocultural and professional environments' (Pullen Sansfaçon et al, 2012, p 44).

Specifically, here, we develop our theorising to include Bourdieu's (1986) notion of cultural capital as a foundation of social life and the basis for one's station in the social order.

Bourdieu's conceptualisation of capital takes the definition beyond the economic to the cultural, differentiating institutionalised, embodied and objectified forms as the means and ends through which people have greater or lesser access to a particular social class and its privileges of membership (Bourdieu, 1986). In this study, we can see both institutionalised and embodied cultural capital at work. Institutionalised capital is accrued through immigration status, the recognition of academic credentials and being granted a licence to practise social work. These represent the formalised acknowledgement that one's citizenship, education and practice experience have value and accrue authority in the social order, and they reflect the neoliberal priority on optimising personal productivity in the marketplace. Embodied capital is the cluster of less tangible aspects required to gain entry to the desired social class of the social work practitioner: one's dress, accent, skills, mannerisms and the more subtle ways in which people demonstrate that they have the resources to meet the expectations to practise in the field. These forms of capital facilitate mobility by enabling access to the opportunities and tools to acquire status and entry to a particular class, that of the social work practitioner in Canada, and thus contribute equally in the construction of the neoliberal subject who is ready – and responsible – to maximise competitive advantage.

Like economic capital, cultural capital requires an investment and, through a complicated calculation, may promise a profit on that investment (Bourdieu, 1986). This is the negotiation that we hear the participants in this study detailing: the ways in which they have invested their time, energy and intellect in their educational pursuits, in their migration and in their efforts to practise social work in Canada, and are seeking a return on that investment. Just as financial markets fluctuate based on the decisions of worldwide economic agreements and agents, so, too, does value in the *social* market vary and shift based on similarly constructed measures of worth. In other words, there is no inherent and static value system to cultural capital, just as there is not for economic capital: the dominant actors of the (social or financial) market assign the worth of currency, and material and discursive processes scaffold this deliberate decision-making. Through the processes of social construction and the hierarchising of worth, there is differential value placed on some investments and resources more than others, and inequalities in access and opportunity are experienced as a result. Participants in this study are thoroughly concerned about access and opportunity, questioning systems and processes that are promoted as available yet experienced as rife with impediments.

The concept of cultural capital helps explain what is happening for the social workers in this study in a way that simultaneously focuses on individuals while holding to account the social and cultural systems in place that differentially advantage individuals. Thus, it has an embedded critique of neoliberalism's full weight of responsibility resting upon individual success and triumph: what is experienced as an individualised, personalised and barrier-ridden journey can be unpacked to its socially constructed roots, and avenues for advocacy and change emerge. This is important analysis to bring to the current data and the literature on adaptation and acculturation, so often conveyed in individualised ways.

Given this analysis, for example, nation-based standards of accreditation for social work degree programmes can be questioned. Specifically, built upon the partnership of the International Association of Schools of Social Work and International Federation of Social Work, and the jointly developed 'Global standards' document (International Association of Social Work, 2012), could educational accreditation be pursued at the international level, thus eliminating the need for each country to undertake credential recognition? Further, taken from the model of collaboration among these two bodies, perhaps the CASW and provincial regulators could design a single-stop service that would both recognise credentials and grant social work licensing. This possibility seems all the more likely in light of Canadian government policy designed to reduce the barriers to interprovincial labour mobility; it could be an extension to international mobility of that intent. On the level of sociocultural and organisational dynamics, we have tools within the profession of social work – analyses of privilege, oppression, exclusion and domination embedded in systems and visited upon individuals, along with a focus on inherent strengths, resilience and capacity for change – on which to draw in the effort to strive for congruence between the personal, professional and political. These are future directions illuminated by the analyses of this research.

Conclusion

This chapter has reported on the experiences of 44 social workers who undertook their social work education outside Canada and migrated to Canada intent on continuing to practise social work. Data from this study suggest that migrant social workers are reflecting upon the cultural capital of their ethnic background, social work education and experience, and personal and professional identity, and comparing it with those desirable in the Canadian market, both economic and social. Their experiences tell stories of a complicated welcome to Canada, challenging the construction upheld by Canadians and others across the world that this is an unequivocal land of opportunity and possibility. Ultimately, these data substantiate the inextricable relationship among personal and professional adaptation, and the ascribed value in institutional and embodied capital, as articulated well by this participant:

> "When I start working, I start feeling that I am starting to adapt and to adjust only when I start working. Up until then, I was ... I knew I didn't want to go back to Israel, but I never felt that Canada is the place for me. So I was really unhappy. But when I start working and being engaged in intellectual aspects of life and with work and being able to perform my skills and to feel valued, I guess, that's where I said 'Okay, yeah, Canada is the place I can stay'. So, really, getting the job in social work, that's what made the difference and just helped me settle in. And I started building my life." (Israel)

References

Auder, H. (2003) 'Brain abuse, or the devaluation of immigrant labour in Canada', *Antipode*, 35(4): 699–717.

Bartley, A., Beddoe, L., Fouché, C. and Harington, P. (2012) 'Transnational social workers: making the profession a transnational professional space', *International Journal of Population Research*, 1: 1–11.

Beddoe, L., Fouché, C., Bartley, A. and Harington, P. (2012) 'Migrant social workers' experience in New Zealand: education and supervision issues', *Social Work Education*, 31(8): 1012–31.

Bourdieu, P. (1986) 'The forms of capital', in J. Richardson (ed) *Handbook of theory and research for the sociology of education*, New York, NY: Greenwood, pp 241–58.

Canadian Information Centre for International Credentials (2007) 'Mutual recognition agreement on labour mobility for social workers in Canada'. Available at: http://www.cicdi.ca/docs/mra/social-workers.en.pdf

Citizenship and Immigration Canada (2013) 'Foreign Credentials Referral Office'. Available at: http://www.cic.gc.ca/english/department/fcro/index.asp

Citizenship and Immigration Canada (2014) 'The employer's roadmap to hiring and retaining internationally trained workers'. Available at: http://www.statcan.gc.ca/pub/11-402-x/2012000/chap/pop/pop-eng.htm

Creese, G. and Wiebe, B. (2012) 'Survival employment: gender and deskilling among African immigrants in Canada', *International Migration*, 50(5): 56–76.

Fang, C. (2012) 'Foreign credential assessment and social work in Canada'. Available at: http://sasw.in1touch.org/uploaded/web/council/FQR-Report2012-Final.pdf

Fouché, C., Beddoe, L., Bartley, A. and De Haan, I. (2014) 'Enduring professional dislocation: migrant social workers' perceptions of their professional roles', *British Journal of Social Work*, 44(7): 2004–22, doi:10.1093/bjsw/bct054

Gouvernement du Québec (2013) 'Québec–France agreement on the mutual recognition of professional qualifications'. Available at: http://www.mrif.gouv.qc.ca/en/ententes-et-engagements/ententes-internationales/reconnaissance-qualifications/entente-quebec-france

Harrison, G. (2013) '"Oh, you've got such a strong accent": language identity intersecting with professional identity in the human services in Australia', *International Migration*, 51(5): 192–204.

Healy, K. and Huegler, N. (2012) 'International mobility in social work', in K. Healy and R. Link (eds) *Handbook of international social work*, New York, NY: Oxford University Press, pp 487–92.

Hussein, S., Manthorpe, J. and Stevens, M. (2010) 'People in places: a qualitative exploration of recruitment agencies' perspectives on the employment of international social workers in the UK', *British Journal of Social Work*, 40(1): 1000–16.

Hussein, S., Manthorpe, J. and Stevens, M. (2011) 'The experiences of migrant social work and social care practitioners in the UK: findings from an online survey', *European Journal of Social Work*, 14(4): 479–96.

International Association of Schools of Social Work (2012) 'Global standards'. Available at: http://ifsw.org/policies/global-standards

Migrant Integration Policy Index (2011) Migrant Integration Policy Index III. Available at: http://old.mipex.eu/canada

OECD (Organisation for Economic Cooperation and Development) (2013) 'International migration outlook'. Available at: http://dx.doi.org/10.1787/migr_outlook-2013-en

Pullen Sansfaçon, A. (2010) 'La migration internationale des travailleurs sociaux: Un survol du contexte et des enjeux pour la formation en service social au Québec' ['The international migration of social workers: an overview of the context and issues for social work training in Quebec'], *Intervention Numéro Spécial: La Formation en Travail Social*, 132(1): 64–74.

Pullen Sansfaçon, A., Brown, M. and Graham, J. (2012) 'International migration of professional social workers: toward a theoretical framework for understanding professional adaptation processes', *Social Development Issues*, 34(2): 37–50.

Service Canada (2013) 'Job Futures Quebec: social workers'. Available at: http://www.servicecanada.gc.ca/eng/qc/job_futures/statistics/4152.shtml [page no longer available, but updated 'Job Futures' information for 2015–19 may be found at: https://www.jobbank.gc.ca/content_pieces-eng.do?cid=10813].

Simpson, G. (2009) 'Global and local issues in the training of "overseas" social workers', *Social Work Education: The International Journal*, 28(6): 655–67.

Statistics Canada (2012) 'Population and demography'. Available at: http://www.statcan.gc.ca/pub/11-402-x/2012000/chap/pop/pop-eng.htm

Statistics Canada (2014) 'Labour Force Survey estimates (LFS), by sex and age group, seasonally adjusted and unadjusted, monthly'. Available at: http://www.statcan.gc.ca

White, R. (2006) 'Opportunities and challenges for social workers crossing borders', *International Social Work*, 49(5): 629–40.

FIVE

The experience of transnational social workers in England: some findings from research

Sue Hanna and Karen Lyons

Introduction

The notion of the transnational social worker (TSW) is not uncommon as international labour mobility has become a feature of social work just as it has in many other occupations. The experiences of this group of workers, until recently under-theorised, has lately received attention as a result of virtually simultaneous research projects examining this aspect of social work experience in England, Australia, Canada and New Zealand (see, eg, Hanna and Lyons [2016], Harrison [2013] and Bartley et al [2012], respectively).

England has been a receiving country for TSWs for many years, and as a dominant economy, it has managed the immigration of this group to suit its own local labour supply needs. Over the past decade or so, this workforce has been used primarily as reserve labour to fill gaps in local child protection services.

The findings forming the basis of this chapter derive from a qualitative study exploring the experiences of TSWs in South-East England. Interviews conducted from 2011 to 2012 focused on the post-arrival, integration, professional practice and development of 28 TSWs from six countries working in statutory child and family services in London and the Home Counties who had been in the UK for five years or less.

The results from this study demonstrate that while social work may now be a global profession with a common definition and set of professional social work standards (IFSW, 2016), it is far from a common professional project (Weiss-Gal and Welbourne, 2008). The local character of social work, rooted in the historical developments and current manifestations of national welfare systems and the cultural norms of a given society, remains a commonly accepted conception of social work practice. Previously published findings from this study have demonstrated that transnational experience presents social workers with a challenging emotional and cultural transition on both professional and personal levels (Hanna and Lyons, 2016). Using the theoretical framework of professional adaptation, understood as 'the changes that occur in social workers in response to the new cultural and organisational environments in which they undertake their work' (Pullen Sansfaçon et al, 2013, p 3), allows this chapter to explore other views of the data, showing that English conceptions of social work significantly challenge fundamental understandings of the professional values and practice held by many TSWs who work in England.

Despite the much-acclaimed rhetoric about 'relationship-based practice', the lens that TSWs provide on front-line statutory social work practice offers more evidence of the extent to which social work in England remains governed (indeed, captured) by professional regulation, statutory and practice guidance, and inspection regimes that have led to an 'explosion of different ways of measuring and controlling social work and social care' (Cree, 2008, p 25). For TSWs, it seems that this is social work, but not as we know it.

In 2015, a report by the regulatory body (the Health and Care Professions Council [HCPC][1]) indicated that there are about 92,000 registered social workers in the English workforce, of which TSWs form less than 1.25% (HCPC, 2016).[2] However, this small proportion, as well as having their own strengths and needs, have served to highlight some of the issues common to the wider professional workforce and have been the subject of research by those concerned with improving standards and curtailing costs, as well as by those interested in social work as a global profession and in international labour mobility. After a brief review of the literature describing the English context, this chapter reports, then discusses findings and draws some conclusions.

The English context

Between 2012 and mid-2016, 2,029 applicants from 53 countries applied to the HCPC for registration and 1,069 people from 43 countries were registered to work in England.[3] The majority of applicants were from within the European region (1,054), of whom 497 have been registered; 399 applicants from the Australasia Pacific region have obtained registration; 129 from the Americas and Caribbean region; and 63 from Africa. The largest number of recent registrants has come from Australia (207), with between 49 and 94 registrants coming from Poland, Spain, Portugal, Ireland, India, the US and Romania. Smaller numbers have been registered from countries such as Canada, Lithuania and New Zealand (HCPC, 2016). TSWs have, therefore, come from various 'home countries' with different national social concerns, forms of social work (organisation and approaches) and traditions of education and training – different both from English social workers and from each other.

There is no guarantee that registered TSWs are currently employed in social work posts in the UK – nor is there centrally collated information about the type or location of agencies employing them. However, there are strong indications that the majority of these TSWs are employed in children and family services, based particularly in London and the South-East. They may have joined longer-established TSWs previously recruited to London boroughs but also working in locations as diverse as Birmingham and the West Midlands (an urban and industrial region with high levels of black and minority ethnic groups in local populations) and Lincolnshire (a large rural county with a mainly indigenous British population) (Lyons and Littlechild, 2006). So, what are the likely conditions facing TSWs and the characteristics of social work in England?[4]

The UK might be regarded as a tolerant and wealthy country, where various forms of inequalities have been addressed and social work is a well-established profession. However, the class system persists and there are concerns that: the income gap between a minority of rich people relative to those living in poverty has increased; gains made with regard to gender equality and multicultural policies have not been sustained; and trust has been lost in politicians, public institutions and professionals (Wilkinson and Pickett, 2009). There is a marked North–South divide in relation to employment opportunities and quality-of-life indicators. More specifically, wealth and employment opportunities tend to be concentrated in London and the South-East, with concomitant social tensions, higher crime rates and practical consequences, including pressures on housing, transport stock, health services and education services, as well as personal social services. These factors have direct implications for all social workers, not least those coming from other international jurisdictions.

These divisions manifested starkly in June 2016 when the referendum was held concerning Britain's membership of the European Union (EU). Those voting to leave won by a narrow margin (52% to 48%), increasing economic and employment uncertainties, prompting chaos in both main political parties, intensifying already bitter debates about 'national sovereignty' and immigration, and revealing latent racism, Muslimophobia and Europhobia, surfacing in verbal and actual aggression against those identified as different (Sherwood, 2016). It is debatable whether the source of Britain's woes really lay with EU membership or could more appropriately have been attributed to global economic forces (including the power of multinational corporations) (Brown, 2016), together with the national government's determination to pursue austerity measures and the privatisation of many of the functions and provisions of centrally and locally provided services. All aspects of Britain's long-established welfare state – income maintenance, housing for eligible groups, universal health and education provisions, and personal social services for vulnerable adults and children – have experienced funding cuts and organisational changes impacting directly on the most vulnerable members of society.

Social work is now a fragmented profession in England, with authority to define the central elements of practice now in the hands of those – mostly government agents – outside the profession. Although it had disparate roots in various fields developed over nearly a century, efforts were made in the late 1960s to recognise the common core of various specialisms, culminating in the establishment of generic social service departments (in England and Wales), the establishment of the British Association of Social Workers and the setting up of a council to regulate professional education. In the ensuing 30 years, a number of factors combined to lead to a demoralisation of the profession. For example, given that the majority of social workers were employed by local authorities, they joined a public sector union (at the expense of the professional association), and in the public mind, social work became equated with poor decisions regarding keeping children at home or taking them into care. From 1975 on, calls for better training, multi-agency working and more accountability, as well as the imposition of increasingly prescriptive 'guidelines', followed the deaths of children known to social services at the hands of their parents or carers.[5] Changing ideas about the role and nature of social work – as well as external pressures – saw professionals shift from providing group and community-based services with ambitions to include and empower clients, to being risk-averse 'agents of the state', increasingly expected to control people on the margins of society and to ration the scarce resources available to vulnerable individuals (Garrett, 2014).

Meanwhile, personal social services felt the impact of public sector management and computer-based systems as much as other public services, as well as being subject to a broader political agenda to weaken the power of the professionals (Henkel, 1994; Evans, 2010). One response in the face of these pressures, in social work education, has been the inclusion of service users in the training of social workers and efforts to instil not just knowledge and skills or competencies, but also the value base of the profession – the protection and promotion of 'human rights and social justice'[6] (IFSW, 2016) – in the context of an increasingly suspicious, unsympathetic or even hostile public and political climate. However, the Human Rights Act 1998, which might have supported efforts to challenge central and local governments in the interests of service users, has not received universal support and has tended to result in defensive social work practices. Apart from this Act, there have been frequent changes in legislation and organisation pertaining specifically to personal social services, notably, the splitting of social services between 'adults' (under the central direction of the Department of Health) and 'children and families' (now the responsibility of the Department for Education).

At a local level, social work services might be available from the local authority or from specialist agencies (such as the National Society for the Prevention of Cruelty to Children [NSPCC]) on a contractual basis. Social work with children and families covers a broader field than only child protection and includes, for instance, specialist teams or agencies working in relation to fostering and adoption or services for young people leaving care. However, it is largely in the field of child protection, one of the most challenging areas of social work practice (Welbourne et al, 2007), that TSWs are employed, certainly initially. High vacancy rates and rapid staff turnover, as well as high rates of referral (Bilson and Martin, 2016), have contributed to high caseloads and stress among the remaining workers. Periodic child deaths, each leading to new reports and recommendations, have cumulatively led to low morale and ever-greater efforts by the government to 'fix' social work.

Child deaths have, therefore, sometimes led to specific changes. For example, a fundamental shift in policy and practice to placing the emphasis on promoting child welfare as well as protecting children (following the death of Victoria Climbié) was signalled in the Children Act 2004 and the publication in 2006 of 'Working together to safeguard children' (Department for Education and Skills, 2006). These statutory guidelines have been revised and reissued several times, most recently in 2015, and Ferguson (2016) considers that these codify many areas of good social work practice, including the interviewing of children alone when abuse or neglect is suspected. However, Featherstone et al (2014a) have offered a more broadly based critique of the existing child welfare/child protection paradigm. The 2015 (ie the sixth) version includes supplementary guidance on children affected by gangs, female genital mutilation and forced marriage, as well as child victims of trafficking, suggesting a more sophisticated understanding of what constitutes abuse of a wider age range of children and young people, thus explicitly extending the remit of social workers (Jackson, 2016).

It is into this unsettled and insecure environment that TSWs redeploy. Following a three-year review (2012–15), the HCPC reported that social work 'generates more interest and involvement from stakeholders from outside of the profession' than other professions in its remit (HCPC, 2016, p 40). It is understood that a new regulator will take over the current HCPC responsibilities by 2018 but the government has not yet issued proposals for this change. We presume that the registration of TSWs will continue to be part of any new regulatory body established.

The experience of transnational social workers in England

This section presents our findings on the characteristics of TSWs, their motivations for working in England, the factors that constrain and support their professional adaptation, and the extent to which TSWs felt that their previous professional knowledge and experience was capitalised on, and sought by, English colleagues to facilitate a dialogue about practice.

London calling – who answered?

Table 5.1 provides details of the age and country of origin of the TSWs participating in the study.

Motivations and reasons for coming to the UK

People chose to live and work as TSWs in England for a variety of reasons. Many younger social workers came for a finite period to travel, broaden their practice experience and build their CVs. A minority, usually older participants, were primarily motivated by economic reasons, the reality of poor remuneration and diminishing work opportunities in their home countries, and the desire to build a better life for themselves and their families in the UK.

Table 5.1: Participating transnational social workers by age and country of origin

Age	USA	Romania	India	New Zealand	Southern Europe	Total
26–30	7 (25%)	4 (14.3%)	3 (10.7%)	1 (3.6%)	1 (3.6%)	16 (57%)
31–35	3 (10.7%)	1 (3.6%)	1 (3.6%)	1 (3.6%)		6 (21.4%)
36–40	1 (3.6%)	2 (7.1%)	1 (3.6%)			4 (14.3%)
41–46				1 (3.6%)		1 (3.6%)
50–60	1 (3.6%)					1 (3.6%)
Total	12 (42.9%)	7 (25%)	5 (17.9%)	3 (10.7%)	1 (3.6%)	28 (100%)

Source: Hanna and Lyons (2016, p 8), available at: http://bjsw.oxfordjournals.org/ (accessed 2 August 2016).

Factors complicating professional adaptation

The way in which statutory child protection social work is practised in England presented a variety of challenges to TSWs' understandings of social work. Their understandings were informed by the way in which social work was structured and understood at home as well as their length of practice, type of previous practice experience and the economic and social issues prevailing in the TSWs' countries of origin. The process of professional adaptation was initially a steep learning curve lasting between six months to a year, with a number of challenges being commonly experienced by the overwhelming majority of the TSWs interviewed.

Values and models of practice

TSWs had various reactions to the values underlying the day-to-day practice of statutory social work in England. Respondents from India and Romania thought that the dominant model of social work in their countries was more grounded in a 'befriending' and community-based approach to social work. American social workers believed that the English child protection system favoured parents' rights over children's rights (despite 'welfare of the child' principles) and that children were left too long in unacceptable home situations; this was particularly the case for participants who came from a US child protection background, where the emphasis is on 'child rescue' (removing children from an 'at risk' home situation). Conversely, social workers from New Zealand felt that there was insufficient focus on working with extended families to find solutions for children. The American social workers expressed further frustration that they had skills sets (eg counselling skills) that they could not utilise because children and young people needing counselling would be referred to specialist National Health Service (NHS) mental health services or other specialist voluntary agencies. Respondents specifically commented that it was difficult to advocate for social work as a profession in England and that there was a tendency for social workers to be risk-averse and unwilling 'to put their head above the parapet'. The public antipathy and negative views of social work shocked many TSWs where social work as a profession was viewed with more respect 'back home'.

Bureaucracy and paperwork

The English child protection system was experienced as driven by organisational rather than professional values, and as large and fragmented, highly structured and formal, over-regulated, and governed by a large amount of legislation. It was initially difficult to understand, not least because of reliance on acronyms to communicate what was required of social workers and, for many, 'procedures' were seen as the main driver of practice, with TSWs from virtually all the countries commenting on the excessive amount of paperwork involved in the practice of protecting children. This was felt to exacerbate the stressful nature of the work and gave rise to a belief that the balance in English social work was wrong, with the emphasis on paperwork coming at the expense of direct work engaging with, and responding to, the needs of children and families.

Factors supporting professional adaptation

The ability of the TSWs in this sample to adapt was evident as many had had their contracts extended from two to three years and felt that they had developed the ability to work competently within the English statutory child protection system. Factors identified as facilitating adaptation included: the support and constancy of managers in supervisory positions; positive relationships with team members and colleagues; and developing confidence and a sense of competence over time – usually beyond the first year. After an initial period in child protection assessment and intervention, participants often tried to move to other areas, such as adoption and fostering services, where they felt that they could use skills more commensurate with their previous experience and training.

Sadly, given the opportunities and potential that TSWs could provide for a cross-fertilisation of knowledge, values and skills with local approaches to social work, the experience of TSWs in the sample was that there was little sense of the organisation or senior colleagues being willing to learn from front-line practitioners if their expertise had been gained in other countries.

Discussion

The number of participants in this qualitative study was small and not representative of the wide range of countries from which TSWs come, or of the proportions that come from different countries and regions. In the wider context of labour mobility, immigration laws and rules exert external constraints on social workers seeking work in the UK, favouring applicants from some countries while making it more difficult for others to get work permits (see Hussein, this volume). Applicants from other EU countries have been at an advantage in this respect since the free movement of labour is one of the tenets of the single market. This accounted for a trend over the past decade away from recruiting workers from anglophone countries to an increased proportion of registrations from the EU (Lyons and Hanna, 2011). However, the result of the recent (June 2016) referendum (in which immigration was 'an issue') has set Britain on a path to exiting the EU, with as yet unknown consequences for the recruitment of workers from abroad, including in professional fields such as social work.

Looking more specifically at what this study has to tell us about the experiences of TSWs, their responses highlight some of the challenges faced by TSWs. Some of these are also issues perceived as problematic by English social workers but with the added dimension of the cultural and professional adaptation required of social workers from other countries. They also throw into sharp relief the variations in professional understandings and practices in social work globally and the particularities of regional concerns and national organisational and practice models.

The findings from this study suggest that the motivations of TSWs for seeking work 'abroad' are as varied as in other sectors of the migrant workforce. We can speculate that their reasons for migrating – and for coming to England specifically – are partly related to their countries of origin. For example, there are only limited opportunities for the employment of qualified social workers in Romania (despite the pressing social problems of that country) and EU funding enabled British social workers to assist Romanians to establish social work education and develop services for children in the 1990s and into this century (Sorescu, 2015). Other factors, including more personal ones, may predominate in the decision to join the transnational workforce on the part of social workers, for example, from the US or New Zealand (Lyons and Huegler, 2012).

With regard to the values and models of practice, this study reinforces the perception that social work in England has little (if any) professional autonomy and is heavily influenced (in both its organisation and its practice) by political priorities and ideologies, with both service users and social workers themselves feeling disempowered. This is at variance with the situation in some of the countries from which TSWs come, where the position of social work ranges from a profession that has distinct and respected skills and powers in a variety of fields, for example, in the US, to one that is understood to be part of a wider range of personnel working for social development, for example, India (Pawar, with Tsui, 2012; Watkins et al, 2012). Although the educational backgrounds of the participants were not probed in detail, we can presume that these have a significant bearing on both the expectations of the TSWs' professional role and the skills and values that they bring to social work practice in England. Evidence of equivalence in education standards and competencies are the touchstone of the HCPC's assessment of applications for registration and, by definition, the participants in this study had been judged as meeting English requirements. It seems clear that their qualifications often exceeded the minimum requirement of a three-year degree, leading to a sense of frustration about their undervalued, and even unused, skills. In some cases, it also led to criticism of English co-workers as lacking in certain skills.

Notwithstanding the possibly superior qualifications of some TSWs, the reluctance of English social workers to be curious about and draw on their different experience may simply reflect a hard-pressed workforce unable to look beyond individual caseloads, or it may illustrate a phenomenon noted elsewhere. This locates migrant workers as 'learners' in an organisation: Williams and Balaz (2008) and Dominelli (2010), among others, have commented on the resultant wasted opportunity for the cross-fertilisation of ideas – including about the remit and possibilities of social work – which might be open to English social workers.

The issue of bureaucracy and excessive paperwork commented on by TSWs is one that resonates strongly with English social workers themselves. Managerialism, targets and overreliance on inappropriate computerised systems have been the subject of critical research (Wastell et al, 2010). Around the time that these research interviews were being conducted, the government commissioned an independent review of child protection services, resulting in recommendations for a child-centred system (Munro, 2011), though more recent literature suggests that in a period of cuts to local authority funding and ongoing issues in staffing, these ambitions have not yet been fully realised (Featherstone et al, 2014b).

Finally, TSWs' perceptions of the factors that support professional adaptation also chime with the findings of a succession of reports in the child protection field (including Munro, 2011) which state that the quality of the supervision and management of staff is important for a number of reasons. Monitoring and enabling of good social work practices in the interests of child protection is the overriding priority but closely aligned to this is the matter of the morale and development of front-line staff who need to deliver consistently appropriate responses to complex cases in a highly pressured environment. If this is important for local social workers, then how much more so is it for TSWs? Some organisations have good systems of senior staff supervising front-line workers but others have a managerialist culture that fails to support new or less experienced staff. Also, as other research has indicated, there is little specific training for the senior staff who should provide good supervision, and they may feel that they lack both the skills and time to identify and respond to the particular needs of TSWs (Hanna and Lyons, 2014).

Conclusion

The political and economic climate in England has been fractured over the past decade and both children's services and education for social work have been in a state of flux, with a succession of reviews and changes in governance and requirements. The key characteristics of English social work in the second decade of the 21st century, not least in the child protection field, are that it is highly regulated, bureaucratised and rule-bound, fragmented, and technocratic. Concerns about accountability have driven out most elements of professional discretion to the point where deprofessionalisation seems practically a reality. The sense of professional identity (including its value base) is not strong, and the profession seems unable to resist political, managerial, inspectorial and financial drivers. Accordingly, TSWs have been required to adapt to legislative and organisational changes at the same time as adapting to a different cultural context and to different models of social work and procedures in relation to child protection in particular.

Not surprisingly, this has proved to be a challenging situation for many of the TSWs interviewed, although, given the criteria for selection, the participants in this study had proved themselves to be flexible and resilient. While some of their perceptions and experiences were specific to individual participants (and perhaps to others from the same national background), others were more widely shared. Among these were the concerns about bureaucracy and the need for good supervision, which have both been identified as serious issues for the profession as a whole, not least those involved in child protection work.

International labour mobility in the field of social work offers important opportunities to individuals for expanding their understanding and repertoire of skills. However, it seems to be more difficult to translate these individual experiences into a fuller appreciation of social work as a transnational profession and activity that has a contribution to make at international levels as well as in relation to regional and national concerns.

Notes

[1]   The HCPC is a UK-wide regulator for 16 occupational groups in the health and social care fields. It regulates educational standards and the registration of newly qualified entrants, with the primary goal of protection of the public (service users). The HCPC took over responsibility for the regulation of social work *in England only* from 1 August 2012. It assesses standards on 221 social work education programmes in England and had registered 92,000 social workers by late 2015 (20% of all professional courses and 25% of professionals for which the HCPC is responsible). It did not assume responsibility for post-qualifying education and training in social work (HCPC, 2016). It has responsibility for the assessment of the qualifications of applicants who have qualified outside the UK and are seeking employment in professional posts (HCPC, 2016).

[2]   Authors' own calculations based on data supplied by the HCPC up to May 2016 following an email request under the Freedom of Information Act 2000.

[3]   The annual registration figures for this group of social workers were the responsibility of a previous body, the General Social Care Council (England) (2000–12). While some figures were obtained and interrogated by the authors in 2011, a trend analysis was not undertaken at that time. However, general concern about workforce issues was signalled by the establishment of the Social Care Workforce Research Unit (SCWRU) (at Kings College, London) in 2002, core-funded by the Department of Health. More specifically, the International Sub-committee of the Joint University Council Social Work Education Committee (JUC SWEC) held a seminar on the topic of 'international social workers in the UK' in 2005 (Lyons and Littlechild, 2006), and in 2010, the SCWRU published the first research-based article in this field (Hussein et al, 2010).

[4]   Social work has developed differently in the four constituent 'countries' of the UK: England, Northern Ireland, Scotland and Wales. Social work in Northern Ireland shares some similarities in terms of scale and organisation with its counterpart in the Republic of Ireland; Scotland has had distinctive legislation in a number of areas for many years and social work has also been differently organised there since 1970; Wales has largely the same legislation and administrative systems as England,

though it has obtained a measure of devolution more recently and has distinctive characteristics, including in social work. This chapter is solely concerned with social work in England.

[5] There has been a series of reports (serious case reviews) since the Maria Colwell case in 1975 investigating the causes of the deaths of children known to social services at the hands of their parents or carers. Most of these have found a lack of inter-professional communication and coordinated interventions but also 'blamed' individual social workers (and sometimes their line managers) as well as education and training inadequacies – there was some evidence of scapegoating. Recommendations have been used to support changes to the structures that should support inter-professional work, to social work training and to the organisation of social services, as well as the development and imposition of yet more prescribed ways of working.

[6] The phrase 'human rights and social work' appears in the commentary on the 'Global definition of social work'. The original (international) definition was jointly agreed by the International Federation of Social Work (IFSW) and the International Association of Schools of Social Work (IASSW) in 2000. The revised version, agreed in 2014, appears on both organisations' websites.

References

Bartley, A., Beddoe, L., Fouché, C. and Harington, P. (2012) 'Transnational social workers: making the profession a transnational space', *International Journal of Population Research*, doi:10.1155/2012/527510

Bilson, A. and Martin, K. (2016) 'Referrals and child protection in England: one in five children referred to children's services and one in nineteen investigated before the age of five', *British Journal of Social Work* (online): 1–19, doi: 10.1093/bjsw/bcw054.

Brown, G. (2016) 'It's now clear, globalisation must work for all of Britain', *The Guardian*, 29 June, p 35.

Cree, V. (2008) 'The changing nature of social work', in R. Adams, L. Dominelli and M. Payne (eds) *Social work, themes, issues and critical debates* (3rd edn), Basingstoke: Palgrave, pp 20–9.

Department for Education and Skills (2006) 'Working together to safeguard children', UK Govt.

Dominelli, L. (2010) *Social work in a globalising world*, Cambridge: Polity Press.

Evans, T. (2010) *Professional discretion in welfare services: Beyond street-level bureaucracy*, Farnham: Ashgate.

Featherstone, B., Morris, K. and White, S. (2014a) 'A marriage made in hell: early intervention meets child protection', *British Journal of Social Work*, 44(7): 1735–49.

Featherstone, B., White, S. and Morris, K. (2014b) *Reimagining child protection: Towards humane social work with families*, Bristol: The Policy Press.

Ferguson, H. (2016) 'How children become invisible in child protection work: findings from research into day-to-day social work practice', *British Journal of Social Work*, online: 1–17, doi:10.1093/bjsw/bcw065.

Garrett, P.M. (2014) *Critical and radical debates in social work: Children and families*, Bristol: The Policy Press.

Hanna, S. and Lyons, K. (2014) 'Challenges facing international social workers: English managers' perceptions', *International Social Work*, online, doi:10.1177/0020872814537851.

Hanna, S. and Lyons, K. (2016) '"London calling": the experiences of international social work recruits working in London', *British Journal of Social Work*, online, doi:10,1093/bjsw.bcw.027.

Harrison, G. (2013) '"Oh, you've got such a strong accent": language identity intersecting with professional identity in the human services in Australia', *International Migration*, 51(5): 192–204.

HCPC (Health and Care Professions Council) (2016) 'Social work education in England: review of approval process 2012–15'. Available at: http://hcpc-uk.org/assets/documents/10004ED2Socialwork inEnglandreport-FINAL.pdf

Henkel, M. (1994) 'Social work: an incorrigibly marginal profession', in T. Becher (ed) *Governments and professional education*, Buckingham: SRHE/OUP, pp 86–103.

Hussein, S., Manthorpe, J., and Stevens, M. (2010) 'People in places: a qualitative exploration of recruitment agencies' perspectives on the employment of international social workers in the UK', *British Journal of Social Work*, 40(3): 1000–16.

IFSW (International Federation of Social Work) (2016) 'Global definition of social work'. Available at: http://ifsw.org/get-involved/global-definition-of-social-work

Jackson, L. (2016) 'A profession that keeps on learning', *The Guardian Supplement*, 16 March, p 6.

Lyons, K. and Hanna, S. (2011) 'European social workers in England: exploring international labour mobility', *Revista de Asistență Socială*, 10(3): 185–96.

Lyons, K. and Huegler, N. (2012) 'International labor mobility in social work', in L. Healy and R. Link (eds) *Handbook of international social work: Human rights, development and the global profession*, New York, NY: Oxford University Press, pp 487–92.

Lyons, K. and Littlechild, B. (2006) *International labour mobility in social work*, Birmingham: BASW/Venture Press.

Munro, E. (2011) 'Munro review of child protection: Final report – A child-centred system'. Available at: https://www.gov.uk/government/collections/munro-review

Pawar, M., with Tsui, M.-S. (2012) 'Social work in Southern and Eastern Asia', in K. Lyons, T. Hokenstad, M. Pawar, N. Huegler and N. Hall (eds) *The Sage handbook of international social work*, London: Sage, pp 407–20.

Pullen Sansfaçon, A., Brown, M., Graham, J. and Dumais Michaud, A. (2013) 'Adaptation and acculturation: experiences of internationally educated social workers', *Journal of International Immigration and Integration*, 15(2): 317–30.

Sherwood, H. (2016) 'Faith leaders condemn people of "evil will"', *The Guardian*, 29 June, p 10.

Sorescu, E.-M. (2015) 'Romanian social work education – history, standards and perspectives', *Revista de Asistenţă Socială [Social Work Review]*, 1. Available at: http://www.swreview.ro/index.pl/numar-1-2015-ro

Wastel, D., White, S., Broadhurst, K., Hall, C., Peckover, S. and Pithouse, A. (2010) 'Children's services in the image of performance management: street level bureaucracy and the spectre of Svejkism', *International Journal of Social Welfare*, 19: 310–20.

Watkins, J., Jennison, T. and Lunday, C. (2012) 'Social work in North America', in L. Healy and R. Link (eds) *Handbook of international social work: Human rights, development and the global profession*, New York, NY: Oxford University Press, pp 400–10.

Weiss-Gal, I. and Welbourne, P. (2008) 'The professionalization of social work: cross national approach', *International Journal of Social Welfare*, 17: 281–90.

Welbourne, P., Harrison, G. and Forde, D. (2007) 'Social work in the UK and the global labour market: recruitment, practice and ethical considerations', *International Social Work*, 50(1): 27–40.

Wilkinson, R. and Pickett, K. (2009) *The spirit level: Why more equal societies always do better*, London: Penguin.

Williams, A. and Balaz, V. (2008) 'International return mobility, learning and knowledge transfer: a case study of Slovac doctors', *Social Science & Medicine*, 67: 1924–33.

SIX

Transnational social workers in Australia: naivety in the transnational professional space

Allen Bartley

Introduction

Transnational professional spaces are shaped by several key actors: governments, employers, relevant professional bodies and the transnational professionals themselves. Such spaces are created as labour market pressures motivate governments to modify immigration and selection policies to target needed foreign professionals with relevant qualifications and experience. Employers advertise widely to fill critical skills shortages and, at times, actively recruit in foreign markets. Professionals respond to these signals and pursue opportunities in foreign jurisdictions, and professional bodies are confronted with the pressures and politics of recognising and accrediting the qualifications, skills and professional experience of foreigners aspiring to enter the local labour market (Boyd, 2013; Hussein, 2014; Koumenta et al, 2014). All the actors in such a transnational professional space might reasonably be expected to embody a level of intentionality. It would be naive, after all, for an actor (whether employer or prospective employee) to enter the transnational arena without recognising and appreciating significant differences in the cultural, legal and political contexts in which a given profession is embedded in far-flung foreign fields, and the implications of these for day-to-day practice. The risks posed by such naivety are significant: the non-recognition of qualifications, the mismatch of skills and roles, the underutilisation of imported expertise, discrimination against culturally diverse workers, and labour market churn all work against the realisation of the benefits of skilled migration (Hugo, 2014). Thus, a key element of our analysis of Australian social work as a transnational professional space concerns the preparedness with which the relevant actors – the transnational social workers (TSWs) themselves, their employers, the Australian Association of Social

Workers (AASW) and government policymakers – operate in respect of fitting professionals with overseas qualifications and experience into Australian social work practice.

This chapter reports on an exploratory study undertaken in 2014–15 to investigate the experiences of transnationally mobile social workers in Australia, and to assess the preparedness, or naivety, of the various actors in this increasingly transnational environment. Social work is not alone in engaging with significant transnational labour market mobility: similar dynamics have been explored by others in nursing and other medical professions (Martineau and Willetts, 2006; Humphries et al, 2012; Boese et al, 2013), teaching (Han, 2004; Bense, 2014), and higher education (Pherali, 2012). As argued by Sansfaçon and colleagues (2014) and Lyons (this volume), the unique nature of social work practice – including the intensely interpersonal nature of the work and the central role played by culture and other forms of social identity in the context of professional interactions – makes direct comparisons with other professions difficult, and provides unique contours to this particular transnational professional space. On the other hand, some of those professions – such as teaching and nursing – have begun to develop systematic, profession-wide responses to the transnationalisation of their professional spaces (Peter et al, 2017). The response in those professions has been to widen questions of the preparedness of transnational professionals for local practice away from a restricted employer–employee proposition to include active measures established by professional bodies, which both assert the role of the profession and the professional identities of transnational professionals, and help to facilitate good transitions to the local environment, thus improving retention rates (McCluskey et al, 2011). Measures undertaken in teaching and nursing include requiring formal systems of induction, mentoring and supervision during initial periods of provisional registration. As discussed elsewhere in this book, the debate over a professional registration regime for Australian social work continues.

Details about the growing transnationalism of Australian social work appear in other chapters in this volume (see the chapters by Barnes, Papadopoulos and Healy). However, it is useful to set the issue within the recent policy context to illustrate the extent to which the Australian government is one of the key actors in the transnationalisation of the profession. Like most Organisation for Economic Co-operation and Development (OECD) countries, Australia's immigration policies and targets are tied directly to the labour market. The emphasis in Australia's immigration policy is on skilled migrants, and on employers identifying immigrants with expertise in areas of skills shortages. Policy has recently shifted to favour the temporary migration of skilled workers, and then creating pathways for these temporary migrants to become permanent residents (Khoo et al, 2007; Hugo, 2014). As social work is regularly identified as experiencing a skills shortage, the pathway is available for social work professionals in other countries to read those policy signals and to recognise the opportunities presented in Australia. As in many other employment fields, Australian social work employers have moulded their hiring practices to those policy changes: many of the TSWs who participated in the study described here first migrated to Australia on temporary skilled migrant work visas. Such changes make it easier for employers to respond quickly to 'market' pressures – though even using such language with regard to social work illustrates the ideological basis for the impetus to liberalise immigration policy for highly skilled workers (Wright, 2015). Thus, social work in Australia is transformed into a transnational professional space – even if the various actors in that space might not be as well prepared for it as they could be.

The current discussion is focused on the experiences of transnationally mobile social workers in Australia, with a particular emphasis on the preparedness of the profession to engage intentionally in a transnational professional space. Specifically, the discussion addresses the advance knowledge of the migrants themselves about the Australian social work environment, their engagement with the relevant professional bodies and the provision by Australian social work employers of specialised induction and continuing professional development for foreign-trained professionals. In particular, we examine the TSWs' experiences with their first Australian social work employer.

Methodology

The data for this chapter were gathered in 2014–15 through an online survey advertised via the AASW. Ethics approval was granted by the University of Auckland Human Participants Ethics Committee in October 2014, and formal support of the project was granted by the AASW. The survey was open to individuals living (or who had lived) in Australia who held an overseas social work qualification. It was designed to engage three different cohorts of TSWs in Australia (or in two cases, having lived in Australia and on-migrated to another country):

- those who were currently working in Australia as social workers;
- those who had previously worked in Australia as social workers but were not currently doing so; and
- those who had moved to Australia but had never worked in Australia as social workers.

While all participants were asked the same range of questions concerning their personal characteristics, educational backgrounds and migration experiences, additional questions elicited details specific to the experiences of each of these three cohorts. For example, those who had never practised social work in Australia were asked about the reasons for this, and were asked for details of their work/life experiences since moving to Australia. Participants who had practised in Australia but were not currently doing so were asked to detail their reasons and histories, as well as questions about their Australian social work experience.

Who came to Australia?

A total of 119 individuals took part in the survey. Reflecting the gendered nature of the profession, 70% of the participants identified as female (a further 11% declined to specify their sex). Their origins were diverse – from 26 different countries – including three Australian-born social workers who had qualified and practised overseas and had since returned to Australia. Twenty participants chose not to divulge their age; the average age of those who did was just over 46 years old, ranging from 30 to 81 (see Figure 6.1). They had been in Australia an average of just over six-and-a-half years.

The extent of their overseas experience was diverse: while 40% of the participants had practised social work for five or fewer years before moving to Australia, the average length of overseas practice experience was just over nine years, with seven participants each claiming more than 20 years' overseas experience (see Figure 6.2). That overseas clinical experience ranged across many fields of practice, including: child protection; clinical or community health and mental health services; drug and alcohol services; community development; work with victims of crime, homeless people, migrants or refugees, and people with disabilities; older people; school social work; social service management; youth work or youth justice; and social work education.

Most participants indicated that they had arrived in Australia directly from their country of birth. However, of the 119 participants, more than one in five (27 in total, or 23% of the sample) came to Australia

Figure 6.1: Participants' ages (*n* = 99)

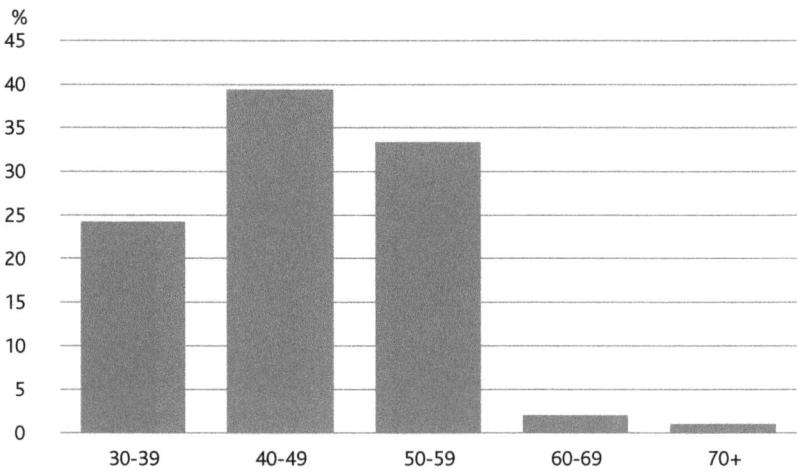

Figure 6.2: Participants' years of social work practice experience prior to moving to Australia (*n* = 91)

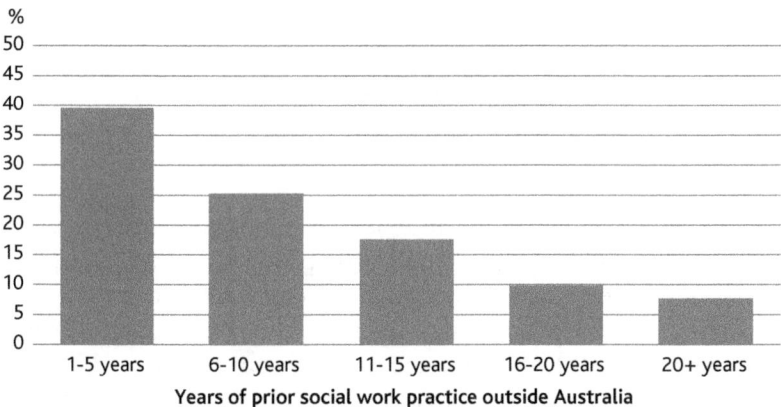

not from their birth country, but from another country in which they had also practised social work. These participants demonstrated a somewhat deeper level of transnationalism, having had migration and professional transition experiences in multiple countries. The most common transit countries – those non-native countries that participants left in coming to Australia – were New Zealand and the UK: eight participants had each migrated to those countries and then moved to Australia. Two other participants had migrated to, and then subsequently left, Canada and the US, respectively.

About two thirds of the survey participants came to Australia accompanied by immediate family members. Of those who indicated this, about 90% came with a partner, and half of those also came with children. Four participants indicated that they arrived in Australia only with children (see Figure 6.3).

Figure 6.3: Who accompanied the participant to Australia? (*n* = 69)

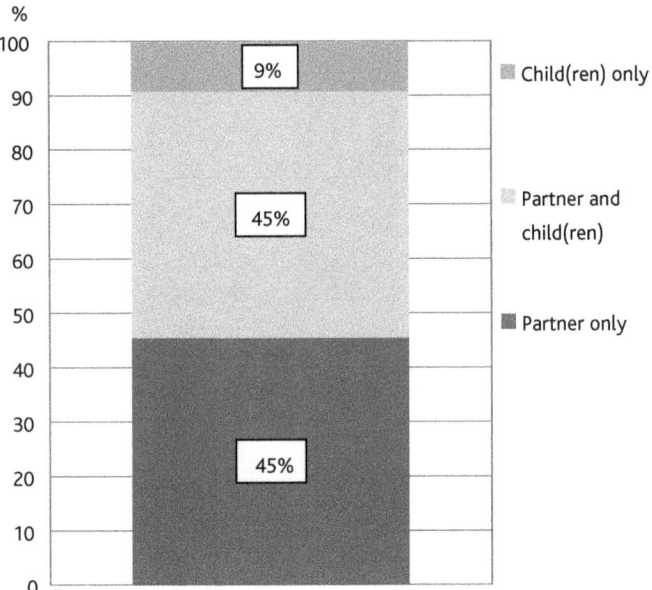

The reasons for individuals and families choosing to migrate – if, indeed, they *do* choose – are often complex and involve a range of motives, aspirations and 'push' and 'pull' factors. We asked participants to offer a primary reason for coming to Australia, and just over half the respondents (51.4%) indicated a family connection or obligation as their primary reason. One participant in eight (12.4%) arrived in Australia with a job in hand and/or a work permit for a specific job, and a further 10% moved to Australia to look for work. Just over 10% of respondents indicated 'quality of life' motives (safety, security or opportunity), which constitute 'push' factors as much as 'pull' factors (see Table 6.1).

Naivety in the transnational professional space

As to employment status, 102 of the 119 participants (86%) were working, or had worked, in Australia as social workers, though 15 of these were currently not doing so. Of these, five were working in roles that were related to social work but were not called 'social work' (including teaching in social work education), two were engaged as

Table 6.1: Primary reason for first coming to Australia (*n* = 105)

	n	%
Accompanying a family member/joining Australian partner/family reunification/other family or personal reason	54	51.4
Recruited from overseas/offered work permit for a specific job	13	12.4
Quality of life (safety, security, opportunity)	11	10.5
Looking for work in Australia	10	9.5
Holiday/short visit	9	8.6
An overseas student	7	6.7
Returning home (Australian born)	1	1.0
Total	**105**	**100.0**

primary family carers, two had left Australia and were now pursuing careers in other countries, and one had retired. Those currently employed indicated a wide diversity of specialisms and job titles: nearly half (46%) indicated that they were in senior roles – as senior social workers, managers, heads of departments, team leaders or principal consultants. More than a third (36%) identified themselves as social workers or case workers; one was practising as a psychotherapist, and two were university-based, as a social work lecturer and a post-doctoral researcher. A small number of the currently employed social work participants (22, or 18%) indicated that they were still working in their first Australian social work position. Most of these were relatively new in the job (fewer than three years). Some had longer tenure in the first Australian social work jobs, however: two were still working in their first Australian position after eight years, and one participant had been in post for 11 years (see Table 6.2).

Table 6.2: Tenure of current job (currently employed in first Australian social work job) (*n* = 22)

Years in current job	*n*	%	Cumulative %
0	6	27.3	27.3
1	5	22.7	50.0
2	5	22.7	72.7
3	1	4.5	77.3
5	1	4.5	81.8
6	1	4.5	86.4
8	2	9.1	95.5
11	1	4.5	100.0
Total	**22**	**100.0**	

Of the 17 participants who indicated that they had never worked in Australia as a social worker, six indicated that they *had* worked in related roles using their social work skills, and for which their social work qualifications were viewed by their employers as an asset – for example, as a case worker in an asylum-seekers' service, as a team leader in a non-governmental organisation (NGO) that provides crisis services to families or in community-based mental health services. When given the opportunity to comment on the difficulties they encountered in gaining a social work position in Australia, one Swedish participant noted that a number of jobs that would have been social work roles in Sweden were filled by other professions in Australia: "Social workers do not have a high status in this country. Employers often prefer other professional backgrounds. What is more important is other training [and] your work experience". Other participants highlighted the apparent reticence of some employers to consider those with only overseas qualifications and experience, as well as the specific policy of government employers to hire only Australian citizens and permanent residents. Several indicated that they perceived 'a stigma' and 'barriers' because of their non-Australian backgrounds, as summarised succinctly by a Papua New Guinean participant: "The recruiting agencies said I had not been in direct practices [sic] in Australia".

To explore the preparedness of the various actors to engage in the transnational professional space, we enquired about the survey participants' first Australian social work position experiences. Their responses concerning their employers' provision of induction and continuing professional development speak to not only how well prepared the TSWs were, but also their employers' transnational preparedness. How well did the TSWs anticipate and prepare themselves for Australia-specific professional practice? How well did their employers orient them to practise in the local context while maximising the TSWs' existing expertise? A number of chapters in this book discuss the way in which social work employers anticipate and accommodate the needs – and strengths – of TSWs and their integration into the local workforce; this is a strong indicator of the current state of the transnational professional space. When reflecting on their first Australian social work job, 22 of the participants were commenting on their current employers (they were still in their first Australian post), while most reflected back on that first job.

The survey design reflected five essential elements of practice requiring contextualised local knowledge that employers of TSWs could reasonably be expected to anticipate and those for which some induction should be provided. These elements of practice knowledge were:

- the Australian legal and policy context;
- working with Aboriginal and Torres Strait Islander clients;
- cultural diversity in Australia more generally;
- the nature of social work in Australia; and
- occupational health and safety.

We asked a series of questions about these, but only three respondents indicated that they had received any specific *transnational* induction. However, most TSWs had received some kind of induction in their first Australian social work job, though it was mostly the standard induction/training that employers offered any new employees. When asked to assess (using a five-point scale from 'Not at all' to 'Very well') how well that general induction prepared them to practise effectively, the median response was merely 'adequate' (see Figure 6.4). The results indicate that those currently still in their first Australian position were much more critical than those who were no longer in that first job and were reflecting on it retrospectively (see Figure 6.5). This suggests that current employers of TSWs may be no less naive as actors in the transnational professional space as employers from a number of years earlier, and, in fact, may be less effective at anticipating (predictable) knowledge gaps and helping TSWs to prepare for practice in the local context.

Figure 6.4: How well 'general' induction prepared respondents to practise effectively (*n* = 70)

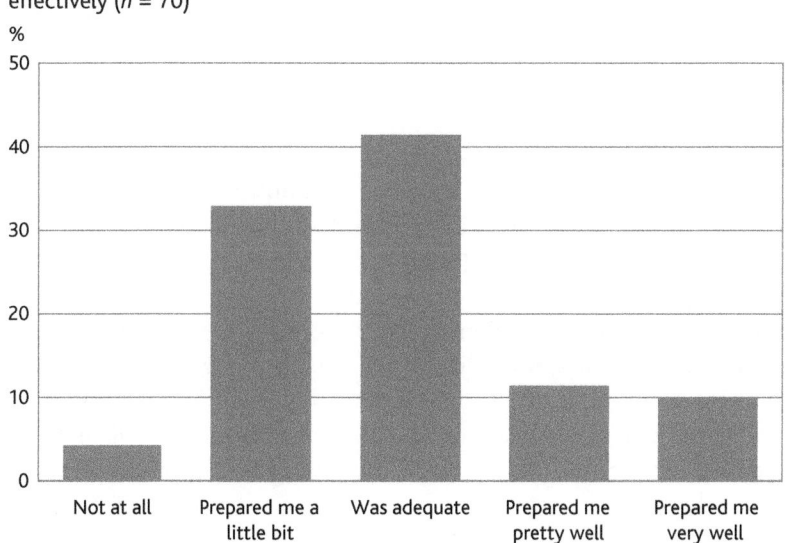

Figure 6.5: 'Overall, how well do you feel that your employer prepared you for your first Australian social work job?'

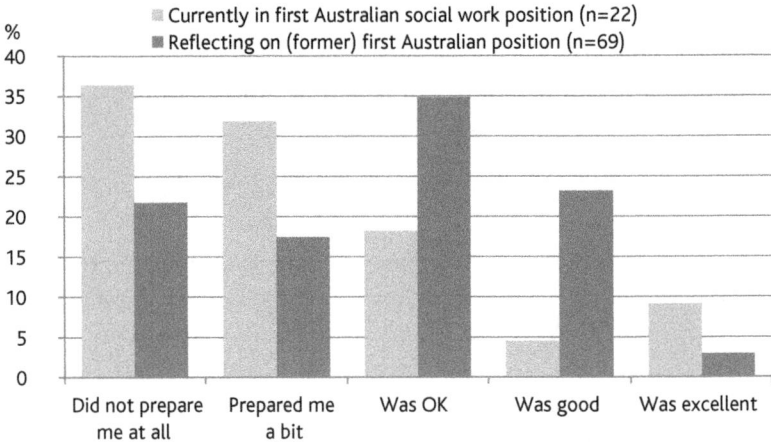

This is not to suggest that no respondents were positive: indeed, some were, as reflected in their comments:

> "Very supportive team. Good learning plan in place with opportunity to identify needs for professional development." (P21, prior NGO employer)

> "I worked for Queensland Health and the trainings were abundant and free. It was excellent." (P82, prior NGO employer)

> "Excellent state-wide training. Mental Health Social Work specific training also provided." (P84, prior statutory employer)

> "Most training was good and I was supported to travel to Adelaide for courses or [to] see other country social workers (quarterly) for networking and professional development." (P97, prior NGO employer)

Conversely, some respondents offered comments that were highly critical of their first Australian employers' training regimes. These came from both statutory and NGO sectors, across the many fields of practice in which social workers engage, and across all Australian states and territories. Some indicated that ongoing training and support were available, and might even be of good quality, but that opportunities to attend these were limited – either because most of the available training was at an inappropriate level or because they were required to self-fund. Some participants had opted to undertake the bulk of their own training expenses, even negotiating periods of unpaid leave to do so:

> "Any training that I have attended has been good but there is very little on offer … and it appears to be designed for non-qualified or undergraduate level, nothing … at postgraduate level." (P41, current statutory employer)

> "There is a lot available but the cost is high both for the courses and the loss of income as well as interstate travel." (P60, current NGO employer).

> "Fortunately, there are some [free or very low-cost] trainings. My employer gave consent for me to take … unpaid leave to attend a course I paid for and then one week of paid leave for me to complete it. For the AASW symposium, they paid for me to attend the dinner. I had to pay all other costs and they do not contribute to AASW membership." (P11, prior statutory employer)

While this may be the standard provision of professional development across the profession, it was apparent that most participants' first Australian employers had not prepared for the specific needs that TSWs might have for such training experiences.

Other critical comments focused on the quality of ongoing training, which they assessed as poor. A number of participants highlighted the value of professional colleagues and peers at their first jobs, on whom they relied to 'fill in the gaps' in their local knowledge. The following two participants reveal this (the first relates that her current position is her first Australian social work job; the second reflects that her first Australian position was a prior job):

> "The quality of the induction was very poor … and did little to prepare me for the role. However, I was informed by Australian colleagues that they have experienced worse! Informal support from colleagues … has been brilliant and much more helpful in preparing me for the role." (P91, UK, current employer)

"Felt like I learned on the go and from asking my peers."
(P2, USA, prior employer)

Several participants mentioned that their most valued support came informally from other members of their multidisciplinary teams. Two stated that the most supportive colleagues were professionals who were not themselves social workers: "There was a great clinical manager/ nurse and a social worker [who] provided me with invaluable care and planning so I could learn appropriately and apply my skills to the Australian rural context" (P114, USA, prior employer).

Other participants indicated that their first Australian social work employers did not prioritise new employee induction or ongoing training in any way – that the onus was completely on the TSWs themselves to identify knowledge gaps and fill them:

"I had no induction other than to read some health and safety information so had to hit the ground running and ask when I didn't know something." (P85, Welsh, current employer)

"It was general induction which any staff would get. I did my own work in acquiring knowledge of the state's Mental Health Act and other legislative requirements." (P36, Indian, prior employer)

"Induction wasn't great. I started as a senior social worker three days before my manager was taking unpaid leave…. I did not have a supervisor for the initial three weeks of my employment. As the role was significantly different to my previous roles in child protection, I found this very difficult." (P13, New Zealander, prior employer)

"The induction came three months after I had already started my work. There was no structured training or personal development plan. It was all ad hoc. Staff development was not viewed by my employer as an important aspect for continued excellence in service delivery, but … was viewed as a privilege." (P59, Filipino, prior employer)

Several participants suggested that their managers were dismissive, or even derisive, of the suggestion that employers should provide some structured, systematic training for newly employed TSWs, as exemplified by the following two participants (one reflecting on the experience from her current position; the other on a position that she had since left): "In-house training was extremely poor and external opportunities for training were not made available as I was told repeatedly I was there to work not "skive off to training"" (P42, Irish, prior employer); "I was told to read reports, that was the preparation!" (P49, New Zealander, current employer).

Many of these comments reflect the highly pressured and often short-staffed workplaces in which TSWs are (and have been) employed; they are often needed to fill critical shortages and appear generally expected to start immediately. On the other hand, one of the continuing themes of this book is that while social work values and imperatives – and many of the theories that inform practice – may be global, the actual engagement of these in everyday practice relationships is intensely local. Funding models, legislative requirements and restrictions, cultural values, and the customs of particular communities and workplaces all shape the work that social workers do, and the demand for competent and ethical practice requires that employers must ensure that those transnational professionals are equipped to grapple competently with these. The failure of employers to anticipate, or even enquire about, the gaps in knowledge of those critical local elements, and act intentionally and systematically with the TSWs they employ to meet those needs, is, at best, naive.

As surprising as it may be to imagine that managers employing TSWs in their first local social work role would not prioritise a systematic induction to operationalise the fit of the TSWs' prior knowledge and experience into the local professional, legal and cultural context, it is equally surprising that the TSWs entering those contexts do not appear to anticipate their need for these processes, and thus asking about induction packages is not part of their negotiation for the job. This often leads to disappointment and disillusion (largely avoidable had the TSWs entered the workplace having better prepared themselves to do so):

> "My experience here is resources for training are poor. The opportunities are rare and I am surprised that training is not adequately financed. I have had all my education paid for previously by my employers – eg my postgraduate training." (P68, Portuguese, current employer)

> "It would have helped to explain the Australian system[s] of care, rights and social opportunities for people with a

disability, as well as financial provisions and incentives rather than having to find out as you go.... I was not always aware how much the Dutch and Australian system[s] differ. I guess some rules and provisions you just take for granted as a social right and you don't question this presumption [until] you find out it simply doesn't exist or is done differently in Australia." (P47, Dutch, prior employer)

"I have been shocked at the difference between training and support available in my current team (very little) compared to that of my previous team in the UK (more structured development and training pathways and encouragement to take up opportunities, promotion of professional development to improve services to clients as well as for the benefit of practitioners). Supervision not provided in current team, whereas supervision acknowledged as crucial to practice in previous [UK] team." (P91, UK, current employer)

These comments suggest dimensions of naivety in the transnational professional space. Participant 91, with considerable practice experience in health and mental health social work in the UK, and who was first employed in Australia in a clinical role, did not research professional development opportunities before taking the job, although in another survey question, she claimed to know 'quite a lot' about the Australian cultural or socio-political context before moving there. Participant 47, from the Netherlands, had nearly 15 years' practice experience before moving to Australia but did not begin practising there for five years, and would have experienced an election cycle, the debates and public and political discourses about the very elements of welfare entitlements that became problematic when she took up her first Australian role. In that sense, most of the participants in the survey communicated a similar naivety. In summary, whatever the differences that these transnational professionals cognitively expected between the new environment and 'home' (wherever that was), they often expected the new professional context to be very similar to the previous context. Their professional frame of reference (about what *good* social work looks like, or what *good* social work management entails) tends to have been fixed, and most of the participants who offered comments demonstrated real shock, often outrage, that the reality of the practice context in their new country did not match expectations.

Conclusion

The combined naivety of employers and professionals in the transnational professional space combines to create real distress and hardship. One of the impacts on the TSWs has been described elsewhere as enduring professional dislocation: the 'profound, lasting sense of unease' experienced by TSWs, being produced by the disjuncture between their own professional identity and expectations of good practice, on the one hand, and the disconcerting reality of a completely unfamiliar practice environment in which they find themselves, on the other (Fouché et al, 2013, p 2006). That the TSWs arrive into completely unfamiliar environments can be attributed to naivety – both theirs and their employers'. The findings from this exploratory study suggest that few TSWs enquired deeply about the nature of their prospective practice environment. They were unaware of particular standards, professional development or expectations and practices, and even failed to make these elements of employment negotiations. On the other hand, their experiences indicate that employers expect a kind of 'plug-and-play' ease in inserting transnational professionals into local practice roles – many employers resist or reject outright any responsibility for bridging foreign expertise and local competence. An (avoidable) impact on the employer is often an antagonistic relationship with a disgruntled and disillusioned new employee, an underutilisation of imported professional skills and expertise, and unnecessary staff turnover. This naivety stems from the failure of all concerned to grasp the essential truth of the 'local' nature of social work practice. The impact of this naivety on service users and their communities remains underexplored.

In this context, a frequent refrain from social change movements takes on sharper meaning: 'think globally; *act locally*'. There is an obvious need for both transnational professionals and their local employers to better anticipate the differences between foreign and local practice contexts. Additionally, it may be that a more systemic, profession-wide response is needed. Employers, state and commonwealth government agencies, social work educators, and the AASW could cooperate to develop a robust and universally available package of resources to better prepare *all* the players in the transnational professional space. Such an initiative would reduce professional dislocation and help maximise the benefits that TSWs offer to Australian social work.

References

Bense, K. (2014) '"Languages aren't as important here": German migrant teachers' experiences in Australian language classes', *The Australian Educational Researcher*, 41: 485–97.

Boese, M., Campbell, I., Roberts, W. and Tham, J. (2013) 'Temporary migrant nurses in Australia: sites and sources of precariousness', *The Economic and Labour Relations Review*, 23(3): 316–39.

Boyd, M. (2013) 'Accreditation and the labor market integration of internationally trained engineers and physicians in Canada', in T. Triadafilopoulos (ed) *Wanted and welcome? Immigrants and minorities, politics and policy*, New York, NY: Springer.

Fouché, C., Beddoe, L., Bartley, A. and De Haan, I. (2013) 'Enduring professional dislocation: migrant social workers' perceptions of their professional roles', *British Journal of Social Work*, 44(7): 2004–22.

Han, J. (2004) 'Teacher shortages, bilingual teachers and the mobility of transnational knowledge workers', *Melbourne Studies in Education*, 45(2): 99–114.

Hugo, G. (2014) 'Skilled migration in Australia: policy and practice', *Asian and Pacific Migration Journal*, 23(4): 375–96.

Humphries, N., Brugha, R. and McGee, H. (2012) 'Nurse migration and health workforce planning: Ireland as illustrative of international challenges', *Health Policy*, 107: 44–53.

Hussein, S. (2014) 'Hierarchical challenges to transnational social workers' mobility: the United Kingdom as a destination within an expanding European Union', *British Journal of Social Work*, 44(Supplement 1): 174–92.

Khoo, S., McDonald, P., Voigt-Graf, C. and Hugo, G. (2007) 'A global labor market: factors motivating the sponsorship and temporary migration of skilled workers to Australia', *International Migration Review*, 41(2): 480–510.

Koumenta, M., Humphris, A., Kleiner, M.M. and Pagliero, M. (2014) *Occupational regulation in the EU and UK: Prevalence and labour market impacts*, London: Department for Business, Innovation and Skills.

Martineau, T. and Willetts, A. (2006) 'The health workforce: managing the crisis ethical international recruitment of health professionals: will codes of practice protect developing country health systems?', *Health Policy*, 75: 358–67.

McCluskey, K., Sim, C. and Johnson, G. (2011) 'Imagining a profession: a beginning teacher's story of isolation', *Teaching Education*, 22(1): 79–90.

Peter, S., Bartley, A. and Beddoe, L. (2017) 'Transnational social workers' transition into receiving countries: what lessons can be learned from nursing and teaching?', *European Journal of Social Work*, doi. 10.1080/13691457.2017.1366430

Pherali, T.J. (2012) 'Academic mobility, language, and cultural capital: the experience of transnational academics in British higher education institutions', *Journal of Studies in International Education*, 16(4): 313–33.

Sansfaçon, A.P., Brown, M., Graham, J. and Michaud, A.D. (2014) 'Adaptation and acculturation: experiences of internationally educated social workers', *Journal of International Migration and Integration*, 15(2): 317–30.

Wright, C.F. (2015) 'Why do states adopt liberal immigration policies? The policymaking dynamics of skilled visa reform in Australia', *Journal of Ethnic and Migration Studies*, 41(2): 306–28. Available at: http://dx.doi.org/10.1080/1369183X.2014.910446

SEVEN

Transnational social workers in Aotearoa New Zealand

Liz Beddoe

Introduction

The structure of immigration in Aotearoa New Zealand changed significantly in the late 1980s, with a shift from limiting cultural diversity by favouring migrants from the UK to an explicit policy that valued multiculturalism and identified 'desirable' migrants on the basis of their human (and economic) capital (Bartley and Spoonley, 2004). This chapter draws on research about the experiences of migrant social workers in Aotearoa New Zealand, where the cultural context brings particular challenges. It highlights this population's perceptions of the status of social work as a profession and their own professional identity. The study utilised a combination of qualitative and quantitative strategies in a three-phase project. The findings provide insights into the nature of the transitional experience for migrant professionals and new vantage points on views of social work as practised in different contexts. We identify perceptions reflecting what we term 'enduring professional dislocation', and argue that while maintaining a broad view of social work is the foundation for understanding the profession in a new country, transnationals need support and education. The often-cited argument that social work is a global profession is of limited utility when so much of what constitutes practice is shaped by the politics, policy and practice in national or even regional and local contexts. We advocate for strategies to facilitate migrant social workers' adjustment to a new setting, especially where some significant degree of social and cultural contextualisation in social work practice is required.

Context

Aotearoa New Zealand is a small island nation in the south-western Pacific, inhabited first by Māori most probably in the 13th century.

European explorers began to visit from the mid-1600s and large-scale colonisation by the British began in the 1840s with a treaty between the joint tribes of New Zealand and the British Crown signed in 1840 (Wilson, 2009). The Treaty of Waitangi is considered to be New Zealand's founding document and is of great significance in many aspects of public policy (Belgrave et al, 2005). Its meaning is often contested: two versions exist, one in English and one in the Māori language. The Treaty provided protection and governance but does not, according to the Māori version, cede sovereignty in exchange for British citizenship (Fleras and Spoonley, 1999). Barnes et al (2012, p 199) argue that in contemporary New Zealand society, 'the entrenchment of Pākehā [white Anglo Celt] culture as the obvious, unremarkable foundation of New Zealand society and nation' is generally an unquestioned assumption. Furthermore, there is an ideological consensus that sovereignty was ceded in the Treaty and that the impact of colonisation has been largely benign (Huygens, 2016). The illumination of these damaging assumptions and the negative historical and contemporary impact of colonisation on Māori people provide a starting point to consider the role of social work in Aotearoa New Zealand society.

The Treaty of Waitangi and social work in Aotearoa New Zealand

The key principles of the Treaty are partnership, protection and participation, and these feature in many Acts of Parliament; thus, it 'is central to New Zealand political life' (Fleras and Spoonley, 1999, p 13) in a modern democracy with a Westminster system of government. The partnership principle embeds biculturalism – that is, active recognition of the two Treaty partners' cultures – in government policy, especially health, education, welfare and justice (see Ruwhiu, 2013; Eketone and Walker, 2015). In the social work profession, this is reflected in the *Code of ethics and bicultural code of practice* of the Aotearoa New Zealand Association of Social Workers (ANZASW, 2008), which requires members to advocate for equal Māori participation in policy and decision-making, and equal access to resources. Social workers need an appreciation of Māori culture and protocols and aspire to support Māori social workers to work with their own communities (Ruwhiu, 2013).

Over the last three decades, Aotearoa New Zealand has become a more ethnically and culturally diverse country with the arrival of new migrant groups as a result of changing immigration policies. Narrow immigration policies had, up until the 1990s, reflected historical links to the British Empire (Bartley and Spoonley, 2005). Since the early 1990s, liberalised immigration policy has led to increased migration from Asia, with a view to developing trade and attracting investment. New Zealand's population is now 4.7 million, with roughly 74% of the population identifying their ethnicity as European, 15% as Māori, 12% as Asian, 7% as having Pacific Islands heritage and 2% as Middle Eastern, Latin American or African (Statistics New Zealand, 2015). While the Treaty of Waitangi's influence on policy is a fundamental acknowledgement of the 'indigeneity and original occupancy' of the Māori people (Fleras and Spoonley, 1999, p 248), greater population diversity also offers legitimation of migrants' status and contributions in Aotearoa New Zealand society via programmes of support and integration.

Ethnicity and culture within the social work profession in Aotearoa New Zealand

In most countries, professional bodies work alongside educational institutions and regulatory bodies to ensure the development and oversight of professional practice. Aotearoa New Zealand's largest professional association, the ANZASW, has approximately 3,000 members. In addition, the Tangata Whenua Social Workers Association (Māori Social Workers Association) was formed in 2009, with self-determination for Māori practitioners being a major goal, recognising that, over the last 20 years, '[b]y Māori for Māori services have grown and produced practice models, Māori frameworks, Māori fields of practice and iwi [tribes] and Māori social services. Together these models and services are all assertions of rangatiratanga [self-determination and governance]' (Tangata Whenua Social Workers Association, 2010, cited in Beddoe, 2016: 159).

Colonisation led to disproportionate inequalities for Māori, including children in state care, and for several decades, major steps were made towards the integration of the Māori concepts of child welfare and family well-being, which Bradley (1996, p 3) optimistically suggested had become 'the norm and were no longer seen as alternative'. In 2016, however, the outcomes for Māori children remain disproportionately poor, with their over-representation in care being a stubborn problem (Office of the Commissioner for Children, 2015).

The development of bicultural practice (Ruwhiu, 2013), intended to address and reduce inequalities and social injustice, has generated significant change in social service delivery. The particular needs of

Māori service users are often addressed through cultural advisors and specific services designed to ensure that Māori values and practices are central and respected. In social work, this commitment was codified in the *Bicultural code of practice* within its *Code of ethics* (ANZASW, 2008). Overseas-qualified social workers arrive in Aotearoa New Zealand to face practice in a complex context. Before they can settle and experience living in Aotearoa New Zealand society, they must address some formal requirements. The ANZASW *Code of ethics and bicultural code of practice* (ANZASW, 2008) makes a very clear commitment to bicultural practice for the profession.

Eketone and Walker (2015), however, note that 'biculturalism' is a contested term, its meaning being dependent on aspects of location and context. In Aotearoa New Zealand, they suggest that rather than being a description of a demographic profile, it rather 'encompasses the wide range of governmental, institutional and social policies and practices. It has grown out of recognition of New Zealand's past' (Eketone and Walker, 2015, p 104). In this context, biculturalism has, over time, been expanded to mean that Māori language, values and cultural practices should be reflected in society and its institutions (Durie, 1998).

In social work in Aotearoa New Zealand, this aspiration to biculturalism has come to be strongly reflected in professional codes and expectations. The expression of these aspirational statements is a *process*, rather than a line drawn in the sand where the profession takes a position and becomes bicultural. The process is, of course, steeped in complex political dynamics (see Fraser and Briggs, 2016). The Social Workers Registration Act 2003 (SWRA) was criticised, for example, as not including any mention of the Treaty of Waitangi (O'Donoghue, 2007), but it did embed in legislation a specific, required competency of working with Māori. The codification of bicultural aspirations is found in the ANZASW instruments, but becoming bicultural is one thing for Māori (who, by colonisation, have had no choice) and another for non-Māori, who often describe the process of growing bicultural awareness as a journey (Crawford, 2016).

In Aotearoa New Zealand, there are approximately 6,000 registered social workers, with the likely total reaching 8,000 with mandatory registration. Social work in Aotearoa New Zealand currently has a limited registration scheme, mainly applied to social workers working in government-funded services (mandatory child protection and youth justice services) and in public health services (Beddoe and Duke, 2009). Major legislative changes are currently in progress that will bring in protection of title and full mandatory registration in 2017.

Developments related to professional registration, scopes of practice and other forms of credentialing are also anticipated.

The educational qualification needed for registration as a social worker is a four-year Bachelor of Social Work degree, or a Master of Social Work degree that is designed to meet qualifying requirements. The programmes are assessed for recognition by the Social Workers Registration Board (SWRB) under current legislation (the SWRA). Graduate social workers are expected to possess (along with others) two highly significant competencies (see Table 7.1).

Table 7.1: Social Workers Registration Board cultural competencies

Competencies	Descriptions
1. Competence to practise social work with Māori	The social worker demonstrates this competence by: demonstrating knowledge of the Treaty of Waitangi, te reo Māori and tikanga Māori; articulating how the wider context of Aotearoa New Zealand, both historically and currently, can impact on practice; Te Rangatiratanga: maintaining relationships that are mana-enhancing, self-determining, respectful, mindful of cultural uniqueness and acknowledge cultural identity; Te Manaakitanga: utilising practice behaviours that ensure mauri ora by ensuring safe space, being mana-enhancing and respectful, acknowledging boundaries, and meeting obligations; and Te Whanaungatanga: engaging in practice that is culturally sustaining, strengthens relationships, is mutually contributing and connecting, and encourages warmth.
2. Competence to practise social work with different ethnic and cultural groups in Aotearoa New Zealand	The social worker: acknowledges and values a range of world views, including divergent views within and between ethnic and cultural groups; understands that culture is not static, but changes over time; demonstrates awareness and self-critique of their own cultural beliefs, values and historical positioning, and how this impacts on their social work practice with their clients from other cultural backgrounds; critically analyses how the culture and social work approaches and policies of their employing organisation may compromise culturally safe practice; demonstrates knowledge of culturally relevant assessments, intervention strategies and techniques; and engages with people, groups and communities in ways that respect family, language, cultural, spiritual and relational markers.

Source: SWRB (no date[b]).

For overseas-qualified social workers, the current Aotearoa New Zealand legislation enables the SWRB to assess applications for registration under an equivalency clause (SWRB, no date[a]). If an applicant is applying from overseas or if they have less than 12 months' social work practice in Aotearoa New Zealand, then they are provisionally registered with overseas competency and required to do specific continuing professional development in the first two years of registration to address competencies 1 and 2 (see Table 7.1). They then have to do a full competency assessment within the two years. If they have been in Aotearoa New Zealand and practising for longer than two years, they have to identify the courses that they have done that address competencies 1 and 2 (see Table 7.1) and address these in a full competency assessment to gain registration. The SWRB would like to be able to direct overseas-qualified social workers to specific courses to help transnational applicants to meet these requirements (private communication Dr Jan Duke, SWRB, November 2016).

Social work has come in for the criticism that despite the competency requirement, too many social workers lack the depth of competency needed to be effective in working with Māori *whānau* (family) (Office of the Commissioner for Children, 2015). The Social Services Committee (2016) report also recommends strengthening social work education in this regard and more stringent assessment of people with overseas social work qualifications. The SWRB is developing a more in-depth approach to the assessment of cultural competency, expected to be embedded in initial social worker education and continuing professional development. This will be assumed when a practitioner has an Aotearoa New Zealand social work qualification but will need to be assessed in overseas-qualified applicants, as will their abilities to communicate well in English (Social Services Committee, 2016, pp 17–18).

So, in anticipation of the intensified requirements signalled earlier, what might this strengthened cultural competency mean in practice? At the time of writing, a new Kaitiakitanga Framework, which will provide more in-depth guidance on expected standards, is in development.

First, any suggested practice frameworks must be understood within an understanding of history and context. This requires the social worker as learner to grapple with their own positioning in this history, for all in Aotearoa New Zealand, other than Māori, are players in a colonisation process. For contemporary arrivals from the UK, for example, there is a painful recognition that there is a history of colonisation by appropriation of land and resources by force, rather than by benign offers of bibles and blankets. For other arrivals, there may be a growing recognition that, as a late colonial society, Aotearoa New Zealand shares some of the oppressive relations and inequalities as their country of origin.

With these cautions in mind, what is written about what (non-Māori) social workers need to know? It is useful to distinguish knowledge from actual embodied practice while avoiding the trap when people 'essentialize social work practice with Māori down to a few cultural artefacts' (Eketone and Walker, 2015, p 111). What militates against such essentialism is an analysis of power in the relationships of social work.

Eketone and Walker (2015, p 111) argue that the aim in developing cultural competency here is 'to achieve ethnorelativism, which can also be described as showing cross-cultural literacy (having knowledge) and cross-cultural fluency (the ability to participate in that culture)'. Eketone and Walker (2015, p 111) advocate, as a minimum, the incorporation of the following practices: *mihimihi* (introduction of oneself); *waiata* (cultural songs for particular circumstances); *karakia* (prayers for opening and closing meetings and other occasions); and *pōwhiri* (welcoming).

Cultural practices are enacted in relationships in context. The two elements of understanding and physical practice come together very effectively in the work of Simmons et al (2014) and, in this volume, Walsh-Tapiata et al. As noted by Simmons et al (2014, p 67), 'any professional training is culturally encased and therefore transferring practice from one cultural context to another is not a straightforward transaction'. Simmons et al (2014, p 67) adopted a community development process to explore the professional responsibility 'to support transnational social workers to work competently with Māori and other ethnic groups, and to consider how transnational social workers are equipped for dealing with the cultural considerations peculiar to this context'. In Chapter Ten in this volume, *pōwhiri* is offered as a powerful process to assist transnational social workers to 'settle and feel at home in this new land and in their new area of work' (see p 158).

New migrants to any country will be negotiating many changes, and for practice in the professions, the concept of 'cultural safety' (Wepa, 2015) requires that they do find out about Māori culture and consequentially experience exposure to New Zealand's colonial past and present. New migrants may become aware that a decolonisation project (Huygens, 2016) is active, and *Pākehā* allies and others are involved in Treaty education that includes education specifically designed for migrants.

The 'Crossing borders – migrant professionals' studies

In 2009, we began our project after having all encountered migrant social workers (overseas-qualified) who were struggling to find employment in social work or, if employed, were struggling to make sense of organisational and professional cultures in Aotearoa New Zealand social services. Our first step was to discover the numbers of overseas-qualified social workers practising in Aotearoa New Zealand via an examination of the (anonymised) database from the SWRB, which considers overseas-qualified social workers for registration. From the SWRB data, we found that 9% of the registered social workers at that time had gained their social work qualification in another country, mostly in their country of birth and in English (Bartley et al, 2011).

Our next step was to carry out a sequential, mixed-methods study comprising four key informant group interviews with 18 migrant social work practitioners and a national online survey of 294 overseas-qualified social workers in Aotearoa New Zealand (Bartley et al, 2012). The interview schedule for the group interviews was developed from issues identified in a review of the international literature dealing with migrant social workers. The interview data were analysed both to give clarity and scope to the design of the survey questions, and to provide a rich data source for thematic analysis.

This study found that migrant social workers encountered two very significant issues: first, the limited provision and quality of their induction into the Aotearoa New Zealand social work context; and, second, the extent to which their employment in social work allowed them to make good use of the range of professional training and skills that they had gained before moving to Aotearoa New Zealand. These concerns can be thematically captured in the phrases 'professional cultural transition' (Fouché et al, 2015) and 'enduring professional dislocation', where adaption to the distinctive socio-political and organisational cultures in their new professional context can create disillusion, stress and challenges to professional identity (Fouché et al, 2013a, 2013b). These two themes are explored in the following.

Professional cultural transition: understanding cultural context

In terms of induction, our findings echoed Hussein et al (2011), who found that over 40% of the social workers and health professionals in their survey indicated that they had received no induction. Social workers in the survey were also the least likely to feel that their induction was good or excellent, if they had one at all (Hussein et al, 2011). Despite the significance of cultural competencies in the Aotearoa New Zealand profession, many focus group participants faced challenges in understanding the sociocultural context, and this led to many personal challenges (Fouché et al, 2013a). British settlers may still come to Aotearoa New Zealand expecting a British colonial outpost, as one of our focus group participants said he came in the mid-2000s with an assumption that 'it is one of England's forgotten back gardens and learning that it is very different' (Fouché et al, 2015, p 112), and was both surprised and enriched to find Māori culture.

Social work practice principles that may be assumed to be universal may be articulated quite differently within indigenous cultures. For example, the Māori term '*tino rangatiratanga*', often translated to 'self-determination', is one example of this. The Western concept of self-determination is generally one of individual self-determination, focusing on individual human rights as a paramount principle. In the Māori context, individual needs most often yield to the collective good. Without an understanding of the socio-political and sociocultural history, the nature of the social work profession may seem highly conflictual for social workers trained in a different tradition (Fouché et al, 2015). In our research, this was illustrated by one participant's response to being prevented from working with Māori in their workplace:

> if a person is identified as a New Zealand Māori, I'm not allowed to service them. I have to refer to the Māori social worker which is a completely different unit. I find that extremely frustrating because they are sometimes overworked and they don't get to the patients and I feel that coming from a background where I've been trained to be really open minded, I can work with people across cultural boundaries – I have no problem with that. (Fouché et al, 2015, p 114)

Without any adequate induction, such experiences can be interpreted as criticism of social workers' ability to work with people of other cultures. Rather, the practice is a result of Aotearoa New Zealand's social work agencies' endeavours to uphold *tino rangatiratanga*. The research participants were clear that induction should focus on biculturalism and on the rights of Māori and should:

incorporate aspirations for Māori and Pacific development in NZ [Aotearoa New Zealand] in practice frameworks. NZ is leading the way in relation to bicultural and indigenous social service delivery … [we need] workshops … to reflect the experiences of Māori, Pacific, Pākehā working relationships – the struggles and strengths that are uniquely NZ. (Fouché et al, 2015, p 114)

Enduring professional dislocation

Many of the study participants encountered a serious disjuncture between the professional identity as social workers that they had established via practice in overseas contexts and the practice environment that they experienced in Aotearoa New Zealand. Far from representing a merely transitory adjustment period, 'a profound, lasting sense of unease' (Fouché et al, 2013b, p 2006), produced by the uncertain professional status and unclear role in relation to the work of other professions, led some to experience what we have referred to as 'enduring professional dislocation'. Participants in our survey answered questions about the professional roles and public recognition of social work in Aotearoa New Zealand. They were asked to reflect on the comparative strength of elements such as: salary; scope to exercise clinical judgement; relationships between social work and other professions, state agencies and communities; and the professional association (Fouché et al, 2013b). One third of the 233 respondents found the item 'relationships between social work and other professions' worse than in their country of qualification. Relationships between social work and state agencies were perceived overall as about the same (39.6%) or better (19.8%), with only 20.3% reporting that they felt that these relationships were worse than where they qualified (Fouché et al, 2013b, p 2011).

Social work as valued by the public was a negative finding, with 37.5% finding this worse than in their country of qualification and only 10.1% believing this element of the professional experience to be better in Aotearoa New Zealand. The profession as valued by social workers themselves was similar, with 35% believing that it was worse, 25% feeling that it was better and the remainder being neutral. An open response to the survey highlighted persistent concerns:

Social workers need to stop doing the *underdog* role … it's not working. If this persists then social work will never be taken seriously and why should it with such an unprofessional approach.... workers rarely understand the political role of social work; they are voiceless in the political arena. (Fouché et al, 2013b, p 2011)

There was general agreement in both qualitative and quantitative data that 'professional recognition of social work per se is where the crux of the problem lies' and that, in Aotearoa New Zealand, 'the sense of profession is less owned by social workers' (Fouché et al, 2013b, p 2014). In a focus group, one participant explained that before she began work in Aotearoa New Zealand, she regarded social workers as on a par with other professions, but with meeting general agreement from other focus group participants, she saw the social work role as unclear to other professionals and with a lower status. Of particular concern was finding social workers doing work for which they were overqualified. Participants from North America, for example, had experienced practice in countries where social work routinely includes counselling and psychotherapy, a form of practice that they found reserved in Aotearoa New Zealand for people with the title 'counsellor' or 'therapist'. This low status was attributed to the lack of protection of the title 'social worker' in the registration legislation (the SWRA).

Hussein et al (2011) noted that the opportunity to use existing skills is highly significant in the satisfaction levels of migrants, but professionals may often feel that their skills are underutilised. In the Aotearoa New Zealand study, participants were asked: 'Are there valuable aspects of your training which you have not been able to use in practice in New Zealand?' (Fouché et al, 2013b, p 2015). We received 233 open responses to this question identifying underutilised skills, including: skilled assessment/interventions; counselling and therapeutic work; specialised work with children and families; community work/development with cultural communities; mental health; and leadership, training and practice teaching (Fouché et al, 2013b, p 2015). There was much discussion in both focus groups and survey responses about the lack of opportunity to use the full range of social work skills acquired and practised overseas, as highlighted by the following statement: 'There seems to me to be a tendency to treat foreign social workers as if they know nothing and their experience abroad is not valuable' (Fouché et al, 2013b, p 2015).

Conclusions

Social workers moving across borders may be heading north, south, east and west. They bring with them valuable experiences and aspirations to make a difference in their new context. Our research has given voice to the experiences of migrant social workers, and much more can be done to support transition and adaptation, without assuming deficits. There are, however, some challenges. Without support to develop their careers in the new social context, transnational social workers can face a sense of dislocation and going backwards, and can feel undervalued. It is thus important that induction to a new sociocultural and professional context is not overly didactic or essentialist (Eketeone and Walker, 2015), with lists of information to be absorbed. In some contexts, such as Aotearoa New Zealand, the dynamics of globalisation and transnational professional mobility create the positioning of transnational social workers as part of ongoing colonisation even though they may have left to escape oppressive conditions in their countries of origin. Migrant social workers can be drawn as victims of racism (and have experienced this) but they do have a responsibility to understand the local socio-political dynamics and become allies of oppressed people in their new country context. Supporting them to do so effectively is a professional imperative.

References

ANZASW (Aotearoa New Zealand Association of Social Workers) (2008) *Code of ethics and bicultural code of practice*, Christchurch, NZ: ANZASW. Available at: http://anzasw.nz/wp-content/uploads/Code-of-Ethics.pdf

Barnes, A.M., Borell, B., Taiapa, K., Rankine, J., Nairn, R. and McCreanor, T. (2012) 'Anti-Maori themes in New Zealand journalism – toward alternative practice', *Pacific Journalism Review*, 18(1): 195.

Bartley, A. and Spoonley, P. (2005) 'Constructing a workable multiculturalism in a bicultural society', in M. Belgrave, M. Kawharu and D. Williams (eds) *Waitangi revisited: Perspectives on the Treaty of Waitangi*, Melbourne: Oxford University Press, pp 136–50.

Bartley, A., Beddoe, L., Duke, J., Fouché, C., Harington, P.R.J. and Shah, R. (2011) 'Crossing borders: key features of migrant social workers in New Zealand', *Aotearoa New Zealand Social Work*, 23(3): 16–30.

Bartley, A., Beddoe, L., Fouché, C.B. and Harington, P. (2012) 'Transnational social workers: making the profession a transnational professional space', *International Journal of Population Research*, 11: Article ID 527510.

Beddoe, L. (2016) 'Supervision in social work in Aotearoa New Zealand: Challenges in changing contexts', *The Clinical Supervisor*, 35(2): 156-174, doi:10.1080/07325223.2016.1217497

Beddoe, L. and Duke, J. (2009) 'Registration in New Zealand social work: the challenge of change', *International Social Work*, 52(6): 785–97.

Belgrave, M., Kawharu, M. and Williams, D.V. (eds) (2005) *Waitangi revisited: Perspectives on the Treaty of Waitangi*, Melbourne: Oxford University Press.

Bradley, J. (1996) 'Iwi and cultural social services policy: the state's best kept secret', *Social Work Review Te Komako*, 8(4): 3–5.

Crawford, H.S. (2016) 'A Pākehā journey towards bicultural practice through guilt, shame, identity and hope', *Aotearoa New Zealand Social Work*, 28(4): 80–8.

Durie, M. (1998) *Whaiora: Māori health development* (2nd edn), Auckland, NZ: Oxford University Press.

Eketone, A. and Walker, S. (2015) 'Bicultural practice: beyond mere tokenism', in K. van Heugten and A. Gibbs (eds) *Social work for sociologists: Theory and practice*, New York, NY: Palgrave Macmillan, pp 103–19.

Fleras, A. and Spoonley, P. (1999) *Recalling Aotearoa: Indigenous politics and ethnic relations in New Zealand*, Auckland, NZ: Oxford University Press.

Fouché, C., Beddoe, L., Bartley, A. and Brenton, N. (2013a) 'Strengths and struggles: overseas qualified social workers' experiences in Aotearoa New Zealand', *Australian Social Work*, 67(4): 551–66.

Fouché, C., Beddoe, L., Bartley, A. and De Haan, I. (2013b) 'Enduring professional dislocation: migrant social workers' perceptions of their professional roles', *British Journal of Social Work*, 44(7): 2004–22.

Fouché, C., Beddoe, L., Bartley, A. and Parkes, E. (2015) 'Are we ready for them? Overseas-qualified social workers' professional cultural transition', *European Journal of Social Work*, 19(1): 106–19.

Fraser, S. and Briggs, L. (2016) 'Bi-culturalism and accountability: fundamental changes in social work practice in Aotearoa New Zealand 1984–1990', *Aotearoa New Zealand Social Work*, 28(1): 43–51. Available at: http://dx.doi.org/10.11157/anzswj-vol28iss1id118

Hussein, S., Stevens, M. and Manthorpe, J. (2011) 'What drives the recruitment of migrant workers to work in social care in England?', *Social Policy and Society*, 10: 285–98.

Huygens, I. (2016) 'Pākehā and Tauiwi Treaty education: an unrecognised decolonisation movement?', *Kotuitui: New Zealand Journal of Social Sciences Online*, 11(2): 146–58.

New Zealand Social Services Committee (2016) *Inquiry into the operation of the Social Workers Registration Act 2003: Report of the Social Services Committee*, 51st Parliament. Available at: https://www.parliament. nz/en/pb/sc/reports/document/51DBSCH_SCR71955_1/inquiry- into-the-operation-of-the-social-workers-registration

O'Donoghue, K. (2007) 'Re-imagining registration: dream a new dream!', *Social Work Review*, 19(1): 1–2.

Office of the Commissioner for Children (2015) *The state of care report 2016: What we learnt from monitoring child, youth and family*, Wellington, NZ: Office of the Commissioner for Children. Available at: http:// www.occ.org.nz/assets/Publications/OCC-State-of-Care-2015.pdf

Ruwhiu, L.A. (2013) 'Making sense of indigenous issues in Aotearoa New Zealand', in M. Connolly and L. Harms (eds) *Social work: Contexts and practice* (3rd edn), Melbourne: Oxford University Press, pp 124–37.

Simmons, H., Walsh-Tapiata, W., Litea, M.-S. and Umugwaneza, A. (2014) '"Cultural encounter": a framework of ethical practice for transnational social workers in Aotearoa', in J. Duke, M. Henrickson and L. Beddoe (eds) *Protecting the public – Enhancing the profession*, Wellington, NZ: Social Workers Registration Board, pp 66–78.

Statistics New Zealand. (2015) '2013 Census – Major ethnic groups in New Zealand', Statistics New Zealand, updated 29 January 2015. Available at http://www.stats.govt.nz/Census/2013-census/profile- and-summary-reports/infographic-culture-identity.aspx

SWRB (Social Workers Registration Board) (no date[a]) 'Overseas qualified applicants: policy guidance'. Available at: http://www.swrb. govt.nz/new-applicants/overseas-qualified-social-workers

SWRB (no date[b]) 'Core competence standards'. Available at: http:// www.swrb.govt.nz/competence-assessment/core-competence- standards

Wepa, D. (ed) (2015) *Cultural safety in Aotearoa New Zealand* (2nd edn), Melbourne: Cambridge University Press.

Wilson, J. (2009) 'History – Māori arrival and settlement', *Te Ara – The Encyclopedia of New Zealand*, updated 3 March. Available at: http:// www.TeAra.govt.nz/en/history/

Part Three:
Employer/stakeholder views

The stakeholders with an interest in transnational social worker mobility include professional bodies, employers and others, along with the social workers themselves and their colleagues. The chapters in Part Three were designed to capture examples of how social work employers and other key stakeholders encounter social work as a transnational professional space. The main idea for these chapters was to provide country-specific examples of the challenges and opportunities that are presented by the employment of transnational social workers in particular contexts. In doing so, we asked that authors would remain sensitive to opportunities to highlight the social work profession's commitment to human rights, the ongoing politics of 'race' and class in the communities we serve, and the ways in which these are played out in particular national contexts, with an examination of issues relating to access, equity and distribution of resources – including employment opportunities. Although these chapters are very different, each meets our brief well, illustrating how an understanding of the political and cultural dimensions of practice are crucial in the relocation of social workers to new employment contexts across the world. In 'In search of better opportunity: transnational social workers in the United Kingdom navigating the maze of global and social mobility', Shereen Hussein explores the transnational movements of social workers against a background of social policy and significant change in UK social work. She notes that there is a set of impact factors operating at different stages for migrating social workers, from the initial application, to qualifications recognition, to securing jobs and practising in a new environment. These factors involve the participation of multiple stakeholders, arising from the institutional dynamics of how social work practice connects to wider policies and national priorities. Others may relate to international agreements and processes of qualifications and experience recognition, issues that are explored further in Part Four of this collection. Hussein depicts these many aspects of the transnational space as 'layered challenges' impacting on transnational social workers themselves, both at individual and professional levels, as well as in relation to stakeholders in their destination countries. In England, in particular, an intense period of 'reform' of social work has meant many changes to the professional bodies who are stakeholders in social worker mobility.

In the Australian context Gai Harrison's chapter 'Transnational social workers and the Australian labour market' draws on the broader literature on skilled migration, diversity management and labour force trends to examine these dynamics. Harrison notes that over 2013–14 the number of incoming social workers to Australia was double the previous year and yet very little is known about how these newcomers fare in terms of employment opportunities and professional adaptation. Nor, Harrison avers, is there clarity about the nature of any shortage of social workers and where incoming professionals might find employment. She notes that migration agents promote a very rosy outlook to encourage overseas social workers to come to Australia via the independent skilled migrant route. Yet in reality many challenges may be faced by those who are successful in their application to migrate. Those who face language challenges or whose qualifications are not recognised in Australia and who are not in a position to upgrade their qualifications face limited employment opportunities. As in other jurisdictions migrants may seek employment where their skills are underutilized, resulting in 'skills atrophy which, in turn, further hinders chances of professional employment'. Harrison argues for more rigorous analysis of the job market for intending social work migrants, with much more accurate information on workforce demand.

In the context of Aotearoa New Zealand, where the profession of social work has made a commitment to bicultural practice, there are particular challenges for transnational social workers, as explored in Chapter Seven. In 'Pōwhiri: a safe space of cultural encounter to assist transnational social workers in the profession in Aotearoa New Zealand', Wheturangi Walsh-Tapiata, Helen Simmons, Litea Meo-Sewabu and Antoinette Umugwaneza provide a rich description of how the traditional Māori ritual of welcome, the **pōwhiri**, can be employed as a metaphor. Each element of this significant ritual of engagement can be experienced by transnational social workers in order to strengthen their understanding of their new practice context and develop their cultural competence to work with Māori people. A strong case is made that new migrant social workers should experience such a welcome on their arrival in a new employment setting. Such a practice would (and, for many, does) highlight the unique cultural context and underline in a lived experience, that this is living culture, needing respect and humility.

Finally, in this Part in 'Consistency and change: internationally educated social workers compare interpretations and approaches in

Canada and their countries of origin', Annie Pullen Sansfaçon, Marion Brown, and Stephanie Éthier draw on research to explore issues related to knowledge transfer in different practice contexts, and to further investigate how social workers really adapt to local variations. The authors employed an interesting design utilising in-depth interviews and the discussion of clinical vignettes. This approach allowed research participants to reflect concretely on their experiences and compare sites of practice.

The researchers identified the presence of foundational, common principles amongst their transnational social workers as well as context-specific applications to practice in Canada. There were however differences between Global North and Global South social workers. The way social workers analysed the needs of service users in the vignettes incorporated both the availability of resources and the potential interventions to meet needs. Exploring how transnational social workers from different countries looking at the same practice vignettes revealed the significant influence of the context.

EIGHT

In search of better opportunities: transnational social workers in the UK navigating the maze of global and social mobility

Shereen Hussein

Introduction

There is growing evidence that transnational social workers (TSWs) contribute significantly to the national workforce of many developed countries, including Canada (Pullen Sansfaçon et al, 2012), England (Hussein et al, 2011), Ireland (Walsh et al, 2010) and New Zealand (Bartley et al, 2012). These transnational movements occur within a set of constraints at different stages, from application, qualifications recognition and securing jobs, to practising in a new environment. Some of these difficulties might arise from how social work practice has evolved as a profession within different national and local contexts, as well as how it connects to wider policies and national priorities. Others may relate to international agreements and processes of qualifications and experience recognition. Thus, different TSWs are faced by a multitude of challenges and hurdles, some of which are similar to professionals from other domains, such as medicine or engineering; yet, others are specific to the nature of social work itself. These layered challenges are observed by, and impact on, TSWs themselves, both at individual and professional levels, as well as in relation to their new context of practice in the destination countries.

Aims and methods

This chapter aims to discuss, based on empirical research, the various challenges and opportunities when TSWs engage in British social work practice. These are identified through the perspective of different actors, including TSWs themselves, their managers and colleagues.

The analysis utilises data from different sources and studies. First, it explores trends in the levels and profile of non-UK-qualified social workers registered in England through interrogating data held by the previous and current social work regulators in England, the General Social Care Council (GSCC) and the Health and Care Professions Council (HCPC). It then draws on rich qualitative and quantitative data obtained through interviews, focus group discussions and national surveys with different stakeholders (see Hussein et al, 2013; Hussein, 2014). Data sources include: workforce records (GSCC 2003–12 and HCPC 2012–15); online surveys of non-UK-qualified TSWs ($n = 101$ in 2010 and $n = 32$ in 2014); interviews ($n = 18$) and two focus group discussions ($n = 7$) with TSWs; and interviews with British managers and social workers ($n = 6$) and service users ($n = 35$). Social worker interview participants were recruited through invitations distributed to a sample of employers; focus group discussions were held with newly recruited TSWs in two local authorities in England recruited via other participants who participated in the online survey; service users were recruited through older people's forums and carers' associations. It should be noted that while the policy framework addressed in this chapter (eg immigration and labour market policies) generally cover the whole of the UK, the practice context is focused specifically on England. In other words, the research in this chapter explores the impact of recent changes in UK immigration and labour market regulations on the social work profession, and the opportunities and challenges in England for TSWs.

Drivers for recruiting transnational social workers

The past two decades have seen a dynamic process of social work education and practice that has direct implications on TSWs. While recruitment issues have remained a particular concern, especially for child protection work, a number of attempts have been made to reform social work education and practice. Some of these include the transition of social work qualifications from a two-year diploma to a three-year degree in 2003 in an attempt to increase the status and portability of social work qualifications and to attract new recruits (Orme et al, 2009). More recently, there has been a number of 'fast-track' social work training programmes, some of which target graduates from other disciplines to enter social work practice after relatively short and 'condensed' university and practice-based training schemes. The latter usually have some financial support attached to them. The rationale behind such schemes is to address chronic shortages in certain social work areas, such as mental health, and to widen the pool of students. However, these have attracted some controversy. Figure 8.1 shows some social work reforms and policy developments from 2009 to 2015, where recruitment needs and policy reactions to public 'scandals', such as the infamous 'Baby P' case, featured strongly.

Figure 8.1: Selected policy and practice developments in the English social work system (2009–15)

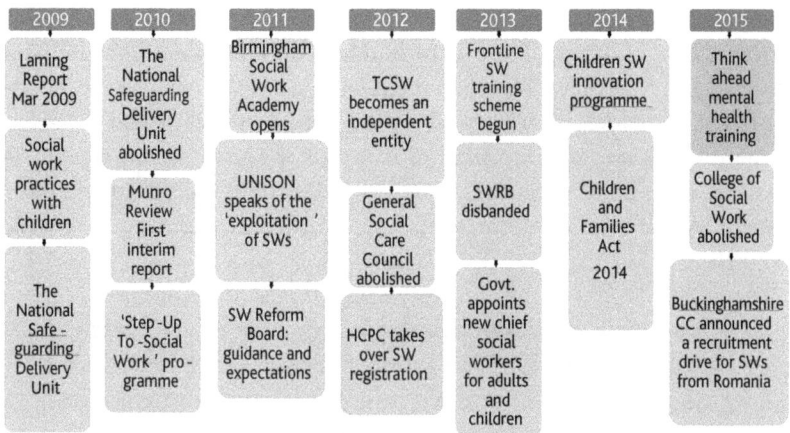

Notes: UNISON is one of the UK's largest trade unions, representing staff involved in public services.
SW / SWs – social work / social workers
TCSW – The College of Social Workers
HCPC – Health and Care Professions Council
SWRB – Social Workers Registration Board
Govt. – Government
CC – City Council

Social work in England has faced a number of recruitment crises over the past few decades. The reasons behind the inability of the sector to recruit enough social workers are multiple and include the intrinsic nature of social work and subsequent emotional burden (Hussein et al, 2014), the poor public image of social work, and the tight pool of traditional social work students.

For employers, the short supply of UK-qualified and experienced social workers is a key driver in resorting to recruiting TSWs, especially from outside the UK (Hussein, 2014). The higher stress level observed among children's social workers and continued recruitment shortages partly explain overseas recruitment campaigns undertaken by local authorities for children and families social workers since the late 1990s. For example, between 2001 and 2002, overseas social workers accounted for approximately one quarter of all new recruits (Tandeka, 2011). Interviews with employers in the UK confirmed that the main reasons behind the active recruitment of TSWs related to shortages and high caseloads. However, many employers also highlighted other positive outcomes from recruiting TSWs, including their work ethic and how TSWs value their employment in the UK. In some situations, these attributes were subconsciously assigned to some groups of migrants more than others: for example, there was a tendency to profile TSWs from Eastern Europe as hard-working but, at the same time, as groups that can pose retention challenges because of a perception that they can easily change jobs. On the other hand, there was some preference for social workers from Australia and Canada, where there are more similarities in terms of social work practice, as well as a common language. Employers also highlighted other values that TSWs bring, including their willingness to accept high caseloads and to work in 'challenging' situations:

> "The actual professionalism and work ethic is, quite often, a lot stronger. They are quite different to a number of the people we've recruited not from abroad, in the sense that they are very often a much more driven workforce." (Human resource manager)

UK immigration policies: implications for transnational social workers' mobility

Similar to social work reforms, there has been a dynamic process of immigration policy reforms in the UK. The UK has relied extensively, for many decades, on immigration to fill labour shortages, first during the 1960s and 1970s from Commonwealth states, formerly part of the British Empire (Redfoot and Houser, 2008). From the late 1970s, the UK gradually began to closely link migration policies to economic imperatives such as redressing workforce shortages. In 2004, 10 countries joined the European Union (EU): eight of them required further development to meet full joining requirements, these are referred to as the A8 accession countries.[1] The UK was one of a minority of EU states that permitted free labour flows from the A8 in 2004 prior to the agreed date of 2010. In 2008, the UK introduced a points-based system, based mainly on the skills of individual migrants, with specific quotas for various sectors and an occupation shortage list (which is reviewed yearly) reflecting national demand. This has reduced the ability of employers to recruit migrants from outside the EU (Dobson and Salt, 2009). In 2010, in his general election campaign, David Cameron promised to cut net immigration to the tens of thousands, and with no control over levels of immigration from the EU, the only alternative was to cut skilled migration from outside of Europe through an 'immigration cap' on non-EU migrants. Following this, some local councils, as presented in Figure 8.1, have initiated recruitment campaigns for TSWs from Romania, which is a member of the EU, since 2015; however, the impact of these campaigns was not captured in the period covered by the data obtained from the HCPC. During this period, children's social work was removed from the UK Border Agency occupation shortage list, but was shortly reintroduced to the list, while social work with adults never made it to the list. This meant that employers were still able to apply for Tier 2 visas to enable the recruitment of non-EU children and family TSWs; however, with an overall cap on numbers of non-EU migrants, the process was extremely onerous. In 2016, the UK voted to leave the EU ('Brexit'); the strategy for such an exit is not yet clear, but it is likely to have various implications on the ability of EU and non-EU TSWs to join the UK social work sector.

Figure 8.2 presents the number of overseas social workers registering to work in England from 2003 to 2015. The trend in the level of new TSW recruits reflects most of the UK's immigration policy developments during this period of time. It should be noted that the analysis used two data sources that present different levels of detail and coverage. Up until 2011, all social workers with non-UK qualifications were required to request registration to work in England through the GSCC; this responsibility was transferred to the HCPC after 2012. Thus, the year 2012 showed a 'loss' of data during the transfer; this figure has been imputed to smooth the curve presented in Figure 8.2. The other point to notice is the significant difference in the numbers of TSWs registered to work in England prior to, and after, 2012. This, in the main, is likely to reflect the changes in the UK's immigration system during this period but might also reflect some variations in the different data-recording processes employed by the GSCC and HCPC.

Figure 8.2 shows that the number of non-UK-qualified TSWs increased sharply from 2003 to 2009 when the UK allowed free mobility for the A8 countries and, at the same time, overseas recruitment campaigns continued to recruit TSWs from countries such as Australia, Canada and the US. The data also reflect the introduction of the immigration cap for non-EU migrants in 2010, when the number of newly registered TSWs in England declined sharply from 1,185 in 2009 to 413 in 2011.

Figure 8.2: Number of overseas-qualified social workers registered by the General Social Care Council and Health and Care Professions Council to work in England from 2003 to 2015

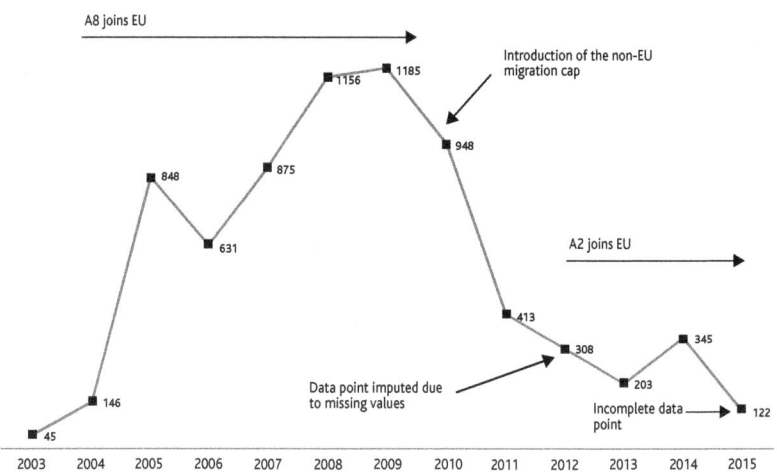

Note: Author's own calculations using data supplied by the GSCC and HCPC.

Data obtained from the GSCC for the period 2003–11 allowed further interrogation of source countries for TSWs in England, while the HCPC data were provided in an aggregated format with no detailed breakdown of country of qualification. Table 8.1 presents trends in the number of TSWs obtaining qualifications from different source countries from 2003 to 2011. The analysis clearly shows the changing profile of TSWs during this period, with more TSWs from Europe registering to work in England over those years; however, there was a peak during 2008–09 when active overseas social workers' recruitment campaigns were adopted by a number of local authorities.

Table 8.1: Number of overseas-qualified social workers registered to work in England by year of registration from 2003 to 2011 by country of training

Country and region of social worker qualifications	Year of registration in England									2003–11
	2003	2004	2005	2006	2007	2008	2009	2010	2011	
Traditionally sending countries (non-EEA[c])	*(28)*	*(77)*	*(587)*	*(422)*	*(526)*	*(741)*	*(725)*	*(557)*	*(224)*	*(3887)*
India	3	13	97	90	115	194	190	147	57	906
South Africa	8	28	235	112	97	127	108	72	34	821
Australia	3	1	64	62	112	162	144	119	51	718
US	6	18	62	66	99	125	161	124	40	701
Canada	2	2	21	45	37	43	57	41	19	267
Zimbabwe	3	10	75	23	34	41	30	21	7	244
New Zealand	3	5	33	24	32	49	35	33	16	230
EEA countries (excluding A8 and A2)	*(4)*	*(26)*	*(100)*	*(84)*	*(151)*	*(150)*	*(219)*	*(166)*	*(82)*	*(982)*
Germany	0	12	42	35	57	58	75	38	23	340
Ireland	2	3	6	8	15	6	33	29	10	112
Spain	1	2	6	13	19	21	25	11	11	109
Portugal	0	1	1	1	14	21	20	26	9	93
Netherlands	1	2	14	7	14	13	4	12	3	70
Sweden	0	3	8	3	7	5	19	14	7	66
Other[a]	0	3	23	17	25	26	43	36	19	192
A8 countries	*(1)*	*(6)*	*(22)*	*(24)*	*(37)*	*(85)*	*(79)*	*(79)*	*(36)*	*(369)*
Poland	0	4	12	13	22	47	39	29	20	186
Hungary	1	0	5	4	5	13	16	12	10	66
Lithuania	0	2	1	0	5	12	5	14	2	41
Slovakia	0	0	1	3	2	4	10	7	3	30
Other[b]	0	0	3	4	3	9	9	17	1	26
A2 countries	*(2)*	*(8)*	*(37)*	*(35)*	*(68)*	*(71)*	*(72)*	*(65)*	*(36)*	*394*
Romania	2	6	33	34	61	59	65	61	34	355
Bulgaria	0	2	4	1	7	12	7	4	2	39
Africa[d]	*(3)*	*(7)*	*(52)*	*(39)*	*(48)*	*(69)*	*(52)*	*(41)*	*(15)*	*(326)*
Ghana	0	4	15	20	16	29	18	12	2	116
Nigeria	1	1	14	8	13	21	14	16	5	93
Uganda	2	1	6	5	5	11	9	5	3	47
Other[b]	0	1	17	6	14	8	11	8	5	70
Asia	*(1)*	*(6)*	*(21)*	*(9)*	*(20)*	*(18)*	*(12)*	*(14)*	*(10)*	*(111)*
Philippines	0	4	15	5	13	10	1	5	3	56

Country and region of social worker qualifications	Year of registration in England									2003–11
	2003	2004	2005	2006	2007	2008	2009	2010	2011	
Other[b]	1	2	6	4	7	8	11	9	7	38
The Caribbean	2	2	8	9	10	7	6	10	3	57
Eastern and Central Europe (non-EEA)	1	12	6	1	6	8	5	6	1	45
South America	3	1	8	4	4	2	8	8	3	41
The Middle East	0	1	7	4	5	5	7	2	3	34
All countries	45	146	848	631	875	1156	1185	948	413	6246

Notes: Author's own calculations using GSCC registration data records. Sum of each group of countries is indicated between brackets (n). [a] Less than 50 social workers over 2003–11 from each other country in that region; [b] Less than 20 social workers from each other country in that region. [c] EEA (European Economic Area) refers to EU member states plus Iceland, Norway and Switzerland. [d] Excluding South Africa and Zimbabwe.

Transnational social workers navigating their way into British social work practice

For some TSWs, having social work qualifications was an enabling factor for migration and mobility. This was particularly the case for European social workers or those recruited directly from Commonwealth countries by British local authorities. Interview participants highlighted their ability to utilise their qualifications as an important facilitator factor, particularly when they were faced with recruitment challenges in their own countries:

> "It was really just the option of being able to choose a job here. I graduated in Germany and started looking around there. At this point in time, there were very few people employed and employers really had to choose between, say, 250 application forms for each job. I knew UK needed social workers so I came here." (Female, Germany)

Negotiating entry to employment was not the main hurdle; those arriving from outside the EU have to secure a 'work permit' with an attachment to certain employment for a period of four years. Due to such visa requirements, they experience considerable restrictions in relation to further labour mobility within the UK (though, in theory, they can change employment if the new employer is also able to offer them anther work permit): "Immigration status gave me limited work opportunities, as other Local Authorities and agencies do not offer work permit" (female, the Philippines).

While obtaining access to the UK job market was one step in the process, the next most important step was to get one's qualifications recognised in the UK. For EU TSWs, this process was governed by the European Directive (Hussein, 2011), but for others, these were decided on a case-by-case basis. Many social workers from the US, Canada and other nationalities faced constraints in skills and qualifications recognition, which resulted in many cases of deskilling and the acceptance of 'less-qualified' job roles. Moreover, the variability in the content, depth and emphasis of social work training had further implications on practice, as well as on the way in which qualifications were counted as relevant experience for career progression purposes:

> "The qualifications that I received in the US are not understood, and are not recognised in the same way that they are in the US, as they do not translate easily to UK higher education attainments." (Male, USA)

> "I think the [training] emphasis is just different, simply because, in Holland, we don't have social services. It's a completely different system. It just means that the education is different because it's tailored to the country that you are in…. So I don't really think they [the GSCC] had come across the degree very often." (Female, the Netherlands)

After acquiring entry to social work practice through a process of obtaining the right of entry and work in the UK, and overcoming the various hurdles of qualifications recognition processes, TSWs continued to face a set of challenges during their practice. These include: understanding social work legal and cultural systems; communicating effectively with colleagues, managers and service users; and adjusting to a new life with limited social networks. Many TSWs, even those who were recruited directly from their home countries, felt that there was little done to address these needs and regarded induction as a lost opportunity:

> "When I joined social work practice in the UK, there should have been a 'transition course' for those of us from abroad [could be linked to the Post Qualifying (PQ) framework]. I was given a full caseload in a busy child protection team, and had never heard of the Children's Act 1989! This lack

of training made my practice seem more inconsistent, and made the culture shock more severe." (Female, US)

"We felt like we got a lot of support when we were in the States [at the recruitment stage] but then when we got here [the UK], that [support] sort of tapered off ... I think it's important for the employer to sort of touch base with the individuals. I mean, you know, they put in all of this effort in terms of getting us here and then we got here, you know, sort of left to your own devices." (Male, US)

Social work is regarded as a culturally sensitive and 'nation-specific' profession (Kornbeck, 2004). In this research, 'cultural context' was defined to include the diversity of the host nation and its norms, as well as both home and host country social work practice cultures. Challenges associated with the diverse cultural context covered a wide spectrum, ranging from understanding and relating to different groups of service users, to fitting into the UK social work culture and the wider status of social workers within society. Data analysis indicated that TSWs from both the EU and other countries have experienced challenges in relation to cultural difference in some way or another. However, there were some differences between the two groups. Proportionally, more EU TSWs indicated that 'communicating with staff and service users' was most challenging when compared to non-European Economic Area (EEA) TSWs. On the other hand, more non-EEA TSWs indicated that 'colleagues and employers don't understand my culture'. Some participants felt that a greater level of cultural understanding would enhance both their professional and personal experience of working in the sector. Providing 'insider' knowledge of different cultures would enhance integration within the team and reduce potential social isolation and associated health risks. However, some were sceptical of how different cultures are actually valued by the British social work sector:

"I personally feel that the UK has very little space for outside social workers. After immigration, the professionals should have been attached with the relevant departments to gain experience for a reasonable period before practicing independently and to make use of his/her full potential. I had been trying my best to work voluntarily in the social care field but in vain. Maximum I could get was befriending with Asian service users." (Male, Pakistan)

The analysis of the online survey with TSWs indicated that relatively more TSWs from outside Europe had 'no difficulties at all' in relation to language requirements. However, working in a non-native language imposes its own barriers to communication flows and network building. Language interpretation is affected by communication style and cultural perceptions of different terms. This may occur between TSWs and users, as well as within teams, and sometimes between TSWs from different countries:

> "I have had an experience of working quite closely with an Italian social worker and I always think she's angry with me. I always feel like I've done something wrong. I've learned that it is actually her way of expressing herself. But it does sound, quite often she sounds very angry when she isn't, I realise that. There are some times you can sound more abrupt and your accent can make you sound more abrupt." (Female, Sweden)

Social work practice requires understanding situation-specific language styles for effective service delivery. Flow of communications was not necessarily guaranteed if TSWs arrived from English-speaking countries. Some of the latter group also acknowledged that communications were not always straightforward, particularly within the context of social work and associated 'jargon': "Even though we speak the same language – [there are] different value base[s] and references in different countries, which may make communications difficult" (female, New Zealand).

The stories of TSWs in the UK highlighted the serious implications of a complex journey to social work practice that can easily translate into stress spilling over to their personal lives, where they, in the majority, do not enjoy a large social network in the UK: "I had never been to the UK and didn't know anyone when I moved here. It was literally trial by fire" (female, Canada, with Dutch passport); "Some staff, relatives of service users and surprisingly some professionals do not accept working with people of colour" (male, Zimbabwe).

Conclusion

TSWs continue to be part of a growing global professional body utilising their skills to enable cross-border mobility. This is occurring within a context of a profession that is not easily internationally transferable, despite continued efforts by academics, educators and regulatory bodies for a comprehensive international social work identity. Drivers for skilled migrants are triggered by demand in host countries where it has proved difficult to recruit personnel with certain skills, and social work in the UK is no different. The UK social work sector continues to face considerable challenges in attracting highly skilled staff, particularly to work with children and families. A dynamic process of reforms has been occurring in the UK over the past decade in relation to social work education, policies and regulation. These played a part in facilitating or hindering mobility for some TSWs. Similar to other professionals' global mobility, the host country's immigration policies and legislation are key facilitating or hindering factors. The past decade has witnessed considerable changes and developments in UK immigration policy, restricting some and allowing other groups of migrants, including TSWs. These are still evolving with new dynamics in place, chief among them the recent decision (in June 2016) of Britain to exit the EU, with unclear implications for TSWs from within and outside of Europe.

A cornerstone in the debate around TSWs' mobility is concerned with the transferability and development of skills and training from a national to an international context. The very nature of social work in assisting the vulnerable in society entails a culturally sensitive and 'nation-specific' practice. The complexity in constructing social work training that is transferable to national and international contexts has been addressed by several writers and scholars, and these are directly reflected in the findings presented here. For TSWs, their individual ability to translate their training to a new context is influenced by their original qualification content and structure, their own analytical ability, and the different supports they receive from outside agencies. Induction in the host country that addresses commonalities and knowledge gaps is thought to be crucial in such dynamics; however, the findings from this study indicated limited usage of tailored, or even general, induction opportunities for TSWs. These, combined with linguistic and cultural challenges, place TSWs in a vulnerable situation, especially if they have limited support networks inside and outside of the workplace. The empirical findings presented here highlight the need for employers to take active responsibility in this process, acknowledging their role in facilitating this process through tailored induction and building work-based support networks.

Acknowledgement and disclaimer
The studies on which analysis in this chapter was drawn were funded by the Department of Health, through the Policy Research Programme

(DH/035/0095) core funding to the Social Care Workforce Research Unit (SCWRU), and a previous research grant (NIHR-CCF 056/0013) and Skills for Care and Development (PC125-10). The studies received ethical permission from the National Social Care Research Ethics Committee and King's College London's research ethics committee. I am grateful to colleagues participating in parts of these studies and to interview and survey participants. The views presented here are those of the author alone and do not necessarily represent those of the funders.

Note

[1] The A8 countries are a group of eight of the 10 countries that joined the EU during its 2004 enlargement. They are commonly grouped together separately from the other two states that joined in 2004, Cyprus and Malta, because of their relatively lower per capita income levels in comparison to the EU average. These are: Czech Republic, Estonia, Hungary, Latvia, Lithuania, Poland, Slovakia and Slovenia.

References

Bartley, A., Beddoe, L., Fouché, C. and Harington, P. (2012) 'Transnational social workers: making the profession a transnational space', *International Journal of Population Research*, doi:10.1155/2012/527510.

Dobson, J. and Salt, J. (2009) 'Point the way? Managing UK immigration in difficult times', *People and Place*, 17(2): 16–29.

Hussein, S. (2011) *Social work qualifications and regulation in European economic countries*, London: General Social Care Council and Social Care Workforce Research Unit.

Hussein, S. (2014) 'Hierarchical challenges to transnational social workers' mobility: the United Kingdom as a destination within an expanding European Union', *British Journal of Social Work*, 44(suppl 1): i174–92.

Hussein, S., Stevens, M., Manthorpe, J. and Moriarty, J. (2011) 'Change and continuity: a quantitative investigation of trends and characteristics of international social workers in England', *British Journal of Social Work*, 41(6): 1140–57.

Hussein, S., Stevens, S. and Manthorpe, J. (2013) 'Migrants' motivations to work in the care sector: experiences from England within the context of EU enlargement', *European Journal of Ageing*, 10(2): 101–9.

Hussein, S., Manthorpe, J., Ridley, J., Austerberry, H., Ferrelly, N., Larkins, C., Bilson, A. and Stanley, N. (2014) 'Independent children's social work practice pilots: evaluating practitioners' job control and burnout', *Research on Social Work Practice*, 24(2): 224–34.

Kornbeck, J. (2004) 'Linguistic affinity and achieved geographic mobility: evidence from the recognition of non-national social work qualifications in Ireland and the UK', *European Journal of Social Work*, 7(2): 143–65.

Orme, J., McIntyre, G., Lister, P.G., Cavanagh, K., Crisp, B., Hussein S., Manthorpe, J., Moriarty, J., Sharpe, E. and Stevens, M. (2009) 'What (a) difference a degree makes: the evaluation of the new social work degree in England', *British Journal of Social Work*, 39(1): 161–78.

Pullen Sansfaçon, A., Brown, M. and Graham, J.R. (2012) 'International migration of professional social workers: towards a theoretical framework for understanding professional adaptation processes', *Social Development Issues*, 34(2): 1–20.

Redfoot, D.L. and Houser, A.N. (2008) 'The international migration of nurses in long-term care', *Journal of Aging and Social Policy*, 20(2): 259–75.

Tandeka, T.M. (2011) 'Making Britain home: Zimbabwean social workers' experiences of migrating to and working in a British city', doctoral thesis, Durham University, UK.

Walsh, T., Wilson, G. and O'Connor, E. (2010) 'Local European and global: an exploration of migrations of social workers into Ireland', *British Journal of Social Work*, 40(6): 1978–95.

NINE

Transnational social workers and the Australian labour market

Gai Harrison

Introduction

Skilled migrants are actively recruited to fill perceived skills shortages in Australia and migrants now constitute the primary source of the country's net labour force growth (Birrell and Healy, 2014). Many overseas-trained social workers come to Australia with the expectation that they will be able to readily gain positions that match their qualifications and experience, although it is difficult to gain an accurate picture of their presence in the human services workforce (Papadopoulos, 2016). Some arrive under the skilled migration programme while others come to Australia via working holiday visas or family reunion programmes. An unknown number arrive as refugees. A concomitant trend is the growing number of international students who complete social work programmes in Australia, with the hope of gaining employment in Australia after finishing their studies (Harrison and Felton, 2013).

In 2013/14, the Australian government granted 136 permanent, independent migrant visas to overseas-trained social workers while a further 81 came to Australia on temporary employer-sponsored visas (Department of Education and Training, 2015). While not a large number, it is noteworthy that the number of social workers coming to Australia on permanent, independent migrant visas more than doubled from the previous year (57), while there was a reduction in employer-sponsored social workers (110). However, little is known about how these overseas-trained social workers are faring in the labour market.

Temporary workers currently comprise the majority of skilled migrants in Australia (Hawthorne, 2015). Due to their temporary status, Hawthorne (2015) contends that a large number of these workers are choosing to forgo full qualification recognition in Australia and instead seek employment within a restricted scope of practice. This suggests that official figures on the number of visas issued to overseas-qualified social workers might not reflect their real numbers in Australia. Social work is not a registered profession in Australia and a growing number of social workers are employed in the non-government community services sector, where job titles are commonly not profession-specific (Harrison and Healy, 2016). Accurately predicting the number of overseas-trained social workers in Australia is made more difficult by a lack of published data on their migration routes (Papadopoulos, 2016).

Despite this lack of hard data on their numbers, a small group of writers have drawn attention to the challenges faced by overseas-qualified social workers who move to Australia, as well as their potential contribution to the social work workforce (Zubrzycki et al, 2008; Harrison, 2013; Papadopoulos, 2016). Notably, more attention has been focused on the challenges, which include negotiating the application process for recognition of their qualifications, finding employment, adapting to a new work context, coping with the experience of cultural dislocation, dealing with discrimination and learning new policies, laws and service provision models. These challenges have similarly been identified by writers who have explored the experiences of transnational social workers practising in the UK, Canada and New Zealand (Welbourne et al, 2007; Bartley et al, 2012; Hussein, 2014; Brown et al, 2015). However, less attention has been focused on the broader, structural factors that mediate these social workers' experiences, such as a volatile job market, changeable migration policies and employers' screening and recruitment practices. Accordingly, the purpose of this chapter is to explore the potential impact of these structural factors on the experiences of social workers who migrate to Australia.

A shortage of social workers in Australia?

Many social workers come to Australia operating on the assumption that their skills will be in demand. Social work is currently listed on the Australian government's Skilled Occupation List (SOL), which identifies those occupations seen as 'meeting the medium to long-term skill needs of the Australian economy' (Department of Education and Training, 2015). The SOL website lists over 180 occupations, but it stresses that the list 'is not intended to be a list of occupations experiencing current shortages' (Department of Education and Training, 2015). The SOL is relevant for those social workers who apply to come to Australia as independent skilled migrants because they must nominate an occupation from the list in their application. They are assessed via a points system, which awards points based on criteria such as skill set, education, age, work experience and English-language proficiency.

The Australian government's Job Outlook website describes employment prospects for social workers as being 'very strong' until 2020 (Australian Government, 2016). In a submission made to the SOL for 2015/16, the Australian Association of Social Workers (AASW) drew on information from this website to present the case that there was a 'shortage of qualified social work professionals to meet workforce demand' (Daly, 2014, p 3). However, the government's Job Outlook website conflates the classification of 'social worker' with 'associated occupations with varying tasks' (Australian Government, 2016), which suggests that this is not a reliable indicator of job prospects for qualified social workers in Australia. This conflation of occupations is evidenced by the listings of job vacancies for social workers on the Job Outlook website, which include positions for carers, disability support workers, youth workers and childcare educators. In fact, very few of the positions listed refer to the job title of 'social worker'.

Some commentators are critical of the data that the Australian government uses to predict workforce demand, pointing out that in several professions identified as having strong growth prospects, there is actually an oversupply of professionals (Birrell and Healy, 2014, p 3). Sloan (2014, paras 15–16) has described the process by which occupations come to be listed on the SOL as 'shambolic', suggesting that it is far from a neutral endeavour:

> There are bureaucratic machinations, competing pieces of advice and self-serving, but unhelpful, input from the relevant professional associations.
>
> These associations are often more intent on spruiking a rosy outlook than providing accurate, short-term assessments of the state of supply and demand for their occupational group. There is also the potential conflict of interest of some office bearers whose links with higher education mean their first priority is to maximise the number of overseas students. Having the relevant occupation included on the SOL is one such means.

Social work is similarly listed on the Consolidated Sponsored Occupation List (CSOL), which includes over 500 occupations ranging from accountant to pig farmer (Department of Immigration and Border Protection, 2017). Social work's inclusion on this list allows social workers who are nominated by an employer to come to Australia on a temporary work visa. However, as indicated earlier in this chapter, the number of social workers coming to Australia via the sponsored route has declined in recent years, while the number moving to Australia as independent skilled migrants has increased.

Some migration agents actively encourage overseas-trained social workers to apply to come to Australia via the independent skilled migrant route, as exemplified by the following blog by an immigration agent:

> Down Under is rather keen to give a red-carpet welcome to skilled Social Workers and motivate them to stay and do a job in the country. Given this, in case your line-of-work is that of a Social Worker – as duly described in the Australian and New Zealand Standard Classification of Occupations (ANZSCO) 272511 – then your talents are presently in demand in Oz.
>
> Social Workers ... who dream of living and working in the Land of Kangaroos – would be happy to know that they may take the qualified assistance of professional Australia [sic] Immigration consultants and make the most of services to successfully live you [sic] dream in reality. (Abhinav, 2015)

The blog gives the impression that obtaining a social work position in Australia is a relatively straightforward process and that jobs for social workers are plentiful. Whether this is the case is debatable. As the previous discussion has identified, it is difficult to obtain an accurate picture of social work vacancies in Australia and part of this confusion lies in the conflation of social work with other, related, occupations. In 2012, the Australian Institute of Health and Welfare reported that on a national level, there was 'no shortage' of social workers in the community services sector, which employs approximately 40% of the social work workforce (AIHW, 2013). Although the community services industry is considered to be an employment sector with strong growth prospects, this industry covers a range of occupations, including psychology, social work, counselling and early childhood educators.

While social workers make up a substantial proportion of the allied health workforce in Australia, competition for these positions is usually keen in metropolitan areas and unfilled vacancies are more likely to be in rural and regional areas. Both federal and state governments have introduced schemes to attract skilled migrants to regional and rural Australia, which experiences more pronounced skills shortages. However, a review of the Australian health workforce concluded that

The formal and informal recognition of overseas-qualified social workers

There are currently no legal requirements for registration for social workers in Australia. However, if overseas-qualified social workers plan to apply for positions that require eligibility for membership of the AASW, they need to have their qualifications assessed by the association. Similarly, the AASW is the designated assessment authority for overseas-qualified social workers planning to migrate to Australia via the skilled migration programme. In 2013, 352 social workers applied to the AASW for an overseas qualifications assessment, which represents an increase of 10% on the previous year. The bulk of these applicants were from the UK, New Zealand, Ireland, India, the US, South Africa and Canada (Daly, 2014). There has been a parallel rise in overseas-trained social workers seeking an assessment for eligibility for the AASW.

The impact of language testing on the recognition of qualifications has received little attention in the literature. Yet, English-language assessment has been identified as 'the most powerful determinant in Australia of migrants' recognition and employment outcomes', with employers expressing a preference for workers from English-speaking countries (Hawthorne, 2015, p 181). Hawthorne (2015) claims that language testing has a greater impact than clinical examinations on the formal recognition of qualifications. Many Australian professional bodies require applicants to meet a specified English-language standard for registration purposes. For example, the Australian Health Practitioners Regulation has set a common English standard for the health professions. The English-language standard required for social work is similar to that of most health professions. For the purposes of an AASW qualifications assessment, if applicants have not completed three years of tertiary study in an English-speaking country, they need to complete an International English Language Testing System (IELTS) test and achieve a score of '7' in reading, writing, listening and speaking. It is not known how many applicants achieve the required test scores or, alternatively, do not apply for a qualifications assessment because of low test scores. However, research conducted by Scull (2016) on a range of professionals seeking registration in Australia indicated that a failure to achieve the required language test scores prevented many applicants from proceeding any further with the assessment process.

From 1998 to 2013, 3,400 applicants applied to the AASW to have their qualifications assessed, with the majority of these applicants (81%) deemed eligible for the AASW and 11% directed to undertake additional study in order to meet eligibility requirements (Papadopoulos, 2016). Overseas-trained social workers whose qualifications are not recognised in Australia and who are not in a position to upgrade their training may find that their work opportunities are limited. As Wagner and Childs (2006, p 50) wryly comment, 'social workers become hospital cleaners' when their qualifications are not recognised. This type of underemployment can result in 'skills atrophy', which, in turn, further hinders chances of professional employment (Wagner and Childs, 2006, p 51). Skills underutilisation is similarly an issue for many former international students who have completed studies in Australia (Gribble, 2014). However, overseas-trained social workers and students planning to move to Australia are not necessarily made aware of these employment outcomes.

While the formal recognition of qualifications is important, it does not guarantee a job. Several researchers have argued that 'informal recognition' in the labour market is an equally important factor, which is equated with gaining employment that is commensurate with their qualifications and experience (Chapman and Iredale, 1993; Wagner and Childs, 2006; Scull, 2016). Chapman and Iredale (1993, p 360) conceptualise informal recognition as 'informal acceptance by an employer or employing body of a person's qualifications and/or skills'. As Colic-Peisker (2011, p 639) points out, it is employers who ultimately judge the value of a person's credentials and work experience.

Minimal research has been conducted on informal recognition processes, such as how skilled migrants are screened by employment agencies and employers. Research suggests that this type of recognition is more challenging for overseas-trained workers whose language skills are viewed in a deficit light or whose cultural background is deemed to be dissimilar to that of the employer (Colic-Peisker, 2011). Notably, migrants from non-English-speaking countries now form the majority of skilled migrants in Australia (Birrell and Healy, 2008). A growing body of research has highlighted how professional workers from these countries have less success in securing employment commensurate with their qualifications and experience than those from English-speaking countries (Wagner and Childs, 2006; Birrell and Healy, 2008; Colic-Peisker, 2011; Scull, 2016). Remennick (2013, p 156) contends that professions vary in terms of their level of cultural dependency, or 'the extent to which a professional practice is embedded in the language, mentality and cultural codes of a specific society'. In contrast to technical professions such as engineering, which have a low level of cultural dependency and translate readily to other contexts, professions such as social work tend to be more embedded in the local cultural and linguistic milieu (Remennick, 2013). Arguably, this, in turn, makes it more difficult for social workers to transfer their skills and knowledge to new settings if they come from a markedly different cultural and linguistic background. Evidence also indicates that Australian employers place a high value on local work experience (Joint Standing Committee on Migration, 2012), which most overseas-qualified social workers do not have when they first arrive in the country.

A significant risk for overseas-qualified workers who do not gain informal recognition is skills underutilisation coupled with downward occupational mobility (Ho and Alcorso, 2004; Wagner and Childs, 2006; Ressia et al, 2017; Scull, 2016). The following social worker's documented experience of failing to find employment as a social worker in Australia demonstrates how this process occurs:

> David Kuel is a Sudanese Humanitarian entrant currently living [in] Tasmania. Upon his arrival to Australia in 1999, Mr Kuel decided to complement his experience as a social worker by undertaking study at an Australian university. During this time Mr Kuel worked as a university mentor for five years, a community volunteer, founded a multicultural youth group, and was awarded Young Citizen of the Year in 2004. Having successfully completed two degrees and a college certificate, Mr Kuel thought that his qualifications and experience in community volunteering would greatly enhance his employment opportunities in Tasmania. However, Mr Kuel has found it particularly difficult to get a job relevant to his qualifications and experience in Tasmania. Mr Kuel's ability to speak three different languages and engage with local migrant communities has had little effect on his employment outcomes. (Kuel, 2012, p 15, cited in Joint Standing Committee on Migration, 2012, p 192)

Despite having two degrees, extensive experience as a community volunteer and a command of three languages, David Kuel still experienced a poor employment outcome, which he believed was due to institutionalised racism (Joint Standing Committee on Migration, 2012). Although there have been concerted attempts to address workplace discrimination in Australia, Anglo-Australians and migrants from European countries still maintain a dominant place in the workplace, particularly in higher-status positions (Colic-Peisker, 2011). Anti-discriminatory legislation may offer individuals legal remedies to address particular acts of discrimination, but such laws do not challenge covert employer attitudes that devalue difference and thwart migrant workers' efforts to gain employment.

Over the past two decades, many workplaces have endorsed diversity policies that affirm the value of difference for the organisation and promote inclusion (Ahmed, 2012). 'Diversity management' has become a catchphrase in the contemporary workplace, with managers identifying both the social and economic benefits attached to having a diverse workforce (Noon, 2007). Conceivably, the skills and attributes of overseas-qualified social workers who come to Australia would be seen as an asset for those organisations that promote the benefits of diversity. However, critics of diversity policies claim that rather than creating a level playing field for workers, they have propagated the view of workers' differences as commodities that can be drawn on selectively to promote organisational goals (Noon, 2007; Ahmed, 2012; Harrison, 2013). As a result, existing power relations remain unchallenged in the workplace, while equity agendas are sidelined and structural barriers in the labour market are not addressed.

Some social workers from culturally and linguistically diverse backgrounds have been able to use their ethnic credentials to gain employment in ethno-specific or migrant services. Nonetheless, the danger associated with ethnic matching in employment is that workers may then be confined to these roles rather than having access to the broader labour market (Harrison, 2013). Moreover, it may mean that these workers are not able to secure employment that is concomitant with their qualifications and previous work experience.

Conclusion

There are several areas of research that merit further attention in relation to the employment of migrant social workers in Australia. Employers' perspectives and practices on recruiting overseas-qualified social workers have not been subject to any in-depth inquiry. Yet, their screening and selection practices can have significant ramifications for social workers who have made an investment in migrating to a new country with the expectation that they will find employment that matches their skill set and work experience. These activities are often conducted behind closed doors, but they play a crucial role in the informal recognition of overseas-qualified social workers. While many Australian employers place a high value on local work experience and favour applicants who have a similar cultural background to their own (Colic-Peisker, 2011), how these preferences shape the employment outcomes of migrant social workers is not known. In the UK, Hussein et al (2010) argue that the role of intermediaries such as employers has largely been ignored in the literature on international recruitment in social work. This is similarly the case in Australia. Employers have the ultimate power to offer or deny workers jobs (Hawthorne and To, 2014), and, on this basis, their practices warrant greater scrutiny in relation to how they use this power.

A further gap in the research is how international social work students who pursue the study–migration pathway fare in the Australian job market. More recently, the Australian government has sought to streamline qualification recognition by targeting international graduates as on-shore skilled migrants to meet workforce demand. However, as highlighted earlier in this chapter, many of these international graduates have struggled to find work in their respective professions. Work-based learning is viewed as critical to enhancing international graduates' employability, and universities are now being urged to do more to improve these graduates' employment outcomes (Gribble, 2014). In the case of social work, it is noteworthy that some agencies have expressed a reluctance to take international students on field placements (Harrison and Felton, 2013). These agencies have identified students' cultural and linguistic differences as being potentially problematic in the workplace, or have assumed that they will return to their home country after graduation and hence represent a poor investment for the organisation (Harrison and Felton, 2013). Possibly, these attitudes are indicative of broader discriminatory practices operating in the welfare sector that warrant further investigation.

Finally, there is a need to investigate the different pathways that overseas-qualified social workers use to come to Australia, as well as the numbers coming via these pathways. These data will provide a more accurate overview of their presence in Australia and assist with workforce planning. In addition, there is a need for more rigorous analysis of the job market that these social workers will encounter once they arrive in the country. Prospective migrants need to be provided with accurate information on workforce demand so that they can make an informed decision about relocating to another country. This is crucial to ensuring that the investment they make in their relocation is worthwhile and leads to a positive employment outcome.

References

Abhinav (2015) 'Attention social workers 272511, get Australia immigration services!', 17 March. Available at: http://blog.abhinav.com/2015/03/attention-social-workers-272511-get-australia-immigration-services

Ahmed, S. (2012) *On being included: Racism and diversity in institutional life*, Durham: Duke University Press.

Australian Government (2016) 'Job outlook – social workers'. Available at: http://joboutlook.gov.au/occupation.aspx?code=2725

AIHW (Australian Institute of Health and Welfare) (2013) *Australia's welfare 2013*, Australia's Welfare Series No. 11, Cat. no. AUS 174, Canberra: AIHW. Available at: http://www.aihw.gov.au/WorkArea/DownloadAsset.aspx?id=60129544075

AIHW (2015) *Australia's welfare 2015*, Australia's Welfare Series No. 12, Cat. no. AUS 189, Canberra: AIHW. Available at: http://www.aihw.gov.au/WorkArea/DownloadAsset.aspx?id=60129555153

Bartley, A., Beddoe, L., Fouché, C. and Harington, P. (2012) 'Transnational social workers: making the profession a transnational professional space', *International Journal of Population Research*, Article ID 527510.

Birrell, B. and Healy, E. (2008) 'How are skilled migrants doing?', *People and Place: Centre for Population and Urban Research*, 16(1): S1–S20.

Birrell, B. and Healy, E. (2012) *Immigration overshoot*, CPUR Research Report, November, Melbourne: Centre for Population and Urban Research.

Birrell, B. and Healy, E. (2014) *Immigration and unemployment in 2014*, CPUR Research Report, Melbourne: Centre for Population and Urban Research.

Brown, M., Pullen Sansfaçon, A., Éthier, S. and Fulton, A. (2015) 'A complicated welcome: social workers navigate policy, organizational contexts, and socio-cultural dynamics following migration to Canada', *International Journal of Social Science Studies*, 3(1): 58–68.

Chapman, B. and Iredale, R. (1993) 'Immigrant qualifications: recognition and relative wage outcomes', *The International Migration Review*, 27(2): 359–87.

Colic-Peisker, V. (2011) '"Ethnics" and "Anglos" in the labour force: advancing Australia fair?', *Journal of Intercultural Studies*, 32(6): 637–54.

Crawford, F. (2012) 'Learning cautious pragmatism from American social work education. Commentary on lessons from American social work education: caution ahead (Karger, 2012)', *Australian Social Work*, 65(3): 326–29.

Daly, K. (2014) 'Submission to the Skilled Occupation List (SOL) 2015/16', Department of Industry, Australian Government. Available at: http://industry.gov.au/Office-of-the-Chief-Economist/SkilledOccupationList/Documents/2015Submissions/AASW.pdf

Department of Education and Training (2015) '2015–16 SOL occupation summary sheets – social workers', Australian Government. Available at: https://docs.education.gov.au/node/38781

Department of Employment (2016a) 'The skilled labour market: a pictorial overview of trends and shortages 2015–16', Australian Government. Available at: http://www.employment.gov.au/

Department of Employment (2016b) 'Australian jobs 2016', Australian Government. Available at: https://cica.org.au/wp-content/uploads/Australian-Jobs-2016.pdf

Department of Immigration and Border Protection (2017) 'Consolidated Sponsored Occupations List (CSOL)'. Available at: www.border.gov.au/Trav/Work/Work/Skills-assessment-and-assessing-authorities/skilled-occupations-lists/combined-stsol-mltssl

Gribble, C. (2014) 'Employment, work placements and work integrated learning of international students in Australia', Research Digest 2, International Education Association Australia. Available at: http://www.ieaa.org.au/documents/item/257

Harrison, G. (2013) '"Oh, you've got such a strong accent": language identity intersecting with professional identity in the human services in Australia', International Migration, 51(5): 192–204.

Harrison, G. and Felton, K. (2013) Final report. Fair go in the field: Inclusive field education for international students in the social sciences, SD12-225, Sydney: Office for Learning and Teaching.

Harrison, G. and Healy, K. (2016) 'Forging an identity as a newly qualified worker in the non-government community services sector', Australian Social Work, 69(1): 80–91.

Hawthorne, L. (2015) 'The impact of skilled migration on foreign qualification recognition reform in Australia', Canadian Public Policy, 41(Supplement): S173–87.

Hawthorne, L. and To, A. (2014) 'Australian employer response to the study-migration pathway: the quantitative evidence 2007–2011', International Migration, 52(3): 99–115.

Ho, C. and Alcorso, C. (2004) 'Migrants and employment: challenging the success story', Journal of Sociology, 40(3): 237–59.

Hussein, S. (2014) 'Hierarchical challenges to transnational social workers' mobility: the United Kingdom as a destination within an expanding European Union', British Journal of Social Work, 44(1): i174–92.

Hussein, S., Manthorpe, J. and Stevens, M. (2010) 'People in places: a qualitative exploration of recruitment agencies' perspectives on the employment of international social workers', *British Journal of Social Work*, 40(3): 1000–16.

Joint Standing Committee on Migration (2012) 'Inquiry into migration and multiculturalism in Australia', Commonwealth of Australia, Canberra. Available at: http://www.aph.gov.au/Parliamentary_Business/Committees/House_of_Representatives_committees?url=mig/multiculturalism/report.htm

Karger, H. (2012) 'Lessons from American social work education: caution ahead', *Australian Social Work*, 65(3): 311–25.

Mason, J. (2013) 'Review of Australian government health workforce programs'. Available at: https://www.health.gov.au/internet/main/publishing.nsf/Content/D26858F4B68834EACA257BF0001A8DDC/$File/Review%20of%20Health%20Workforce%20programs.pdf

Noon, M. (2007) 'The fatal flaws of diversity and the business case for ethnic minorities', *Work, Employment & Society*, 21(4): 773–84.

Papadopoulos, A. (2016) 'Migrating qualifications: the ethics of recognition', *British Journal of Social Work*, Advance Access, published 3 May, doi:10.1093/bjsw/bcw038.

Remennick, L. (2013) 'Professional identities in transit: factors shaping immigrant labour market success', *International Migration*, 51(1): 152–68.

Ressia, S., Strachan, G. and Bailey, J. (2017) 'Going up or going down? Occupational mobility of skilled migrants in Australia', *Asia Pacific Journal of Human Resources*, 55: 64–85, doi:10.1111/1744-7941.12121

Robertson, S. (2013) *Transnational student migrants and the state: The education–migration nexus*, Basingstoke: Palgrave Macmillan.

Scull, S. (2016) 'Overseas-qualified professionals: the search for professional re-entry and its perceived impact on settlement', PhD, The University of Queensland, Brisbane.

Sloan, J. (2014) 'Migrants no threat to jobs', *The Weekend Australian*, 26 August, p 12.

Wagner, R. and Childs, M. (2006) 'Exclusionary narratives as barriers to the recognition of qualifications, skills and experience – a case of skilled migrants in Australia', *Studies in Continuing Education*, 28(1): 49–62.

Welbourne, P., Harrison, G. and Ford, D. (2007) 'Social work in the UK and the global labour market: recruitment, practice and ethical considerations', *International Social Work*, 50(1): 27–40.

Zubrzycki, J., Thomson, L. and Trevithick, P. (2008) 'International recruitment in child protection: the experiences of workers in the Australian Capital Territory', *Communities, Families and Children Australia*, 3(2): 30–8.

TEN

Pōwhiri: a safe space of cultural encounter to assist transnational social workers in the profession in Aotearoa New Zealand

Wheturangi Walsh-Tapiata, Helen Simmons, Litea Meo-Sewabu and Antoinette Umugwaneza

Introduction

Navigating the borders of a new country and a new area of work can be bewildering for the transnational social worker. This chapter introduces a cultural framework called 'pōwhiri', which challenges the reader to consider the experience of its process and metaphorical application to practice. It is our declared position that pōwhiri is a gift to practice from Aotearoa New Zealand for transnational social workers, for New Zealand-trained social workers and for those that we work with. In this chapter, we provide a context for our view and explain the role of host and the rationale for cultural encounter as crucial to our position. Pōwhiri is then introduced.

Relationships between parties are core to good social work practice. The social worker needs to understand their own values, principles and worldview, as well as those of the people they are working alongside. In Aotearoa New Zealand, understanding the Māori world and their history is a critical contribution to good social work practice. Māori, as the indigenous people of Aotearoa New Zealand, share a similar history of dispossession and injustice with other colonised indigenous peoples, and the history of their struggles over 175 years has been well canvassed elsewhere (Walker, 2004; Kawharu, 1989; Orange, 1989; see also Baines, this volume). As a colonised indigenous population, Māori have also been resilient in surviving their colonial history, with its considerable historical and current impacts. They have also maintained their constitutional status as a partner to the Crown through the Treaty of Waitangi (signed in 1840), and with its reassertion via the Treaty of

Waitangi Act 1975, some means of justice, redress and greater influence in the political, social and economic life of the country has started to occur (Eketone and Walker, 2013). The relationship between Māori and the Crown, or tangata whenua (hosts – people of the land) and manuhiri (visitors – people who have come from other places), is sometimes referred to as 'biculturalism'.

Social work is one of those professions (at least peripherally) that has shown a commitment to the Treaty of Waitangi and biculturalism. In particular, this has been the case since 1986 when *Puao-te-Ata-tu* (*Daybreak*) (Ministerial Advisory Committee on a Māori Perspective for the Department of Social Welfare, 1986) was published. The report identified widespread institutional racism across all areas of the department, including social work. Since that time, the profession has embedded a commitment to the Treaty and to biculturalism as core components of ethical social work practice (ANZASW, 2008). This commitment, while tenuous, is apparent in relationships, policies and practices that require regular review.

Moreover, Māori social workers and the expansion of culturally specific services have also strengthened a cultural positioning based on Māori worldviews. While there is still considerable development required in this area, as a contribution towards effective practice, this continues the evolution of a positive bicultural relationship. Critical to this relationship is an understanding and acceptance of the roles and responsibilities of tangata whenua (the host) and the role of manuhiri (the visitor).

The role of host in relation to this context expands to include all of those who already live in Aotearoa New Zealand. 'Host' means tangata whenua, colleagues, institutions, employers, the profession, the regulatory body and those we work with. Being host is a collective responsibility. Equally important, however, is that the transnational social worker recognises the importance of understanding the specific context of good practice in Aotearoa New Zealand and is committed to reconsidering their previous knowledge and practice on this basis.

Research suggests that the transferability of social work practice skills is less straightforward in a foreign context (White, 2006; Crisp, 2009; Simpson, 2009) – even though social workers in many countries are trained in anti-racist, anti-oppressive, cross-cultural contexts. Professional education is culturally specific and therefore transferring practice from one cultural context to another and developing a clear understanding of how culture and practice are intertwined are important considerations when making sense of a culture different to our own (Munford and Sanders, 2010). This is particularly so if the transnational social worker's culture and training has not taught them an appreciation of the particular cultural and historical context of their new country. When we consider the situation for transnational social workers who choose to come to Aotearoa New Zealand, it is therefore important that we offer them the opportunity to develop bicultural frameworks and practices that support the profession and the practice of social work in this land. Campinha-Bacote's (2011) research suggests that 'up close and personal' transformation through continuous 'cultural encounters' is pivotal in the process of becoming culturally competent as it develops one's awareness, knowledge, skill and desire to keep up with ongoing 'encountering'. Walker (2012) believes that the more practitioners are exposed to, and develop strong relationships with, the cultural and ethnic 'other', the more competent they are likely to become.

Māori agree with Campinha-Bacote (2011) that competency needs to be up close and personal and involves ongoing cultural encounters. Walsh-Tapiata and Webster (2004, p 18) suggest that a person's learning is a journey, where they start by being an ākonga (student), before progressing to being pia (learner) and then onwards to being tauira (apprentice), before attaining the status of pūkenga (graduate). This reflects the focus that cultural competency needs to be ongoing. It is not the sort of learning whereby one can be deemed competent after a single encounter or experience.

Penetito (2010) believes that bicultural frameworks provide Aotearoa New Zealand with an authentic social construct that, when used, can be acceptable to both Māori and non-Māori. Pōwhiri is one such framework that is used in establishing, developing and maintaining complex systems of ongoing human relationships (Thomas and Davis, 2005, p 202). It looks at a dual responsibility between the hosts and others, with each being equally responsible for the process.

Two of this chapter's contributing authors, Meo-Sewabu and Umugwaneza, both moved to Aotearoa New Zealand and have experienced pōwhiri. They believe that this has helped them to gain an understanding and appreciation of indigenous Māori, as well as providing them with a cultural process not dissimilar to their own cultural encounters, therefore making them feel more at home living in this country.

Meo-Sewabu participated in a pōwhiri to acknowledge the relationship between Fijians at a university and the local Māori tribe where the university was located. Included in the pōwhiri, the Fijian community were able to incorporate their cultural encounter of 'sevusevu' by sharing yagona, a traditional drink used in almost every

Fijian cultural protocol to bind and bring two groups together. The Fijians were able to pay their respects to their hosts (who had looked after them over several decades), to acknowledge their respective ancestors and to apologise for not acknowledging Māori as the traditional people of this land. The formalised process of pōwhiri was required in order to establish an ongoing relationship between the two parties (Simmons et al, 2013, p 73).

Umugwaneza came to New Zealand as a refugee, from Rwanda. In her early days, she had multiple social workers assisting her and her family. While she acknowledged that she would not have survived without the support of these social workers, she felt that her family were also irritated, frustrated and even annoyed by all the home visits and their suggestions, which were, at times, totally different from her cultural practices. Later Umugwaneza had the chance to visit a marae where a pōwhiri took place. She understood the importance of feeling welcomed and felt as though her identity and her values were acknowledged and respected. She felt that the pōwhiri at point of entry into the country could have helped her to feel welcome. A similar process in relation to working with social workers would have helped to develop a connection whereby she would have felt safe to talk openly about her issues, share her culture and be empowered in her role as host in her own home: 'In my culture, it takes time to trust people and I believe the pōwhiri could have helped me to create a safe space to share, have an equal respect, and build positive and genuine relationships' (Simmons et al, 2013, p 74).

These narratives offer examples of how pōwhiri could help the transnational social worker settle and feel at home in this new land and in their new area of work. Pōwhiri is guided by Māori knowing, thinking, understanding and wisdom, and highlights the potential for an indigenous worldview to offer contributions of consequence to good social work practice. A bicultural framework requires Treaty partners to share, learn and thereafter have an ongoing relationship with each other. This leads to a space of caring, protecting and safeguarding people and relationships.

Pōwhiri allows a critical relationship of encounter to occur. Māori believe that it is important to greet their manuhiri tūārangi (visitors from afar) when they come into the country and/or arrive into a specific tribal area. This helps to establish the nature of their mutual relationship. This practice is called pōwhiri and generally happens on the marae (traditional meeting place). Today, pōwhiri are also performed in a range of different settings, but there is no other like the marae. The marae is the traditional home and centre for the families, sub-tribes and tribes of that place. It provides everyone with a true understanding and appreciation of the connection between Māori, their land, their ancestors, their stories and their spiritual connections. In order to truly understand this cultural encounter, it needs to occur at the marae. A marae cannot simply be replaced by an office or a hall as it provides a unique environment in which two parties come together and are enabled to clearly understand their roles and their ongoing relationship with each other. It establishes a set of rules or ethical behaviours between parties, providing a cultural context of encounter between the two groups (Mead, 2003).

There is, however, some ambivalence from Māori about 'performing their cultural traditions to serve non-Māori purposes' (Stewart et al, 2015) simply to tick a box, and so a warning comes with the practice of pōwhiri. It is important to not trivialise or compromise the pōwhiri as an understanding of the Māori world, and key cultural concepts can be lost in translation and the integrity of the process diminished.

At the marae, Māori organise, participate and share their culture with other Māori and non-Māori. In this context, they are central to the organisation, they are in charge and take their roles seriously as hosts, educators, challengers and peacemakers (Edwards and Ellmers, 2010, cited in Stewart et al, 2015, p 97). It is important for those coming to the marae to know that despite the strangeness and challenges of what they might experience, they will be cared for. Pōwhiri is more than a physical process; it is one where there is a sharing of tradition through the use of language and culture, and where the history of the people becomes evident, including the resilience and right of 'Māori to exist' and to reassert their tino rangatiratanga. This is the last bastion of Māori culture and should not be denied. Every physical and metaphysical aspect of the marae has meaning: the house itself, the carvings and the photos represent an ancestor; and every person at the marae has a role that is interconnected with others. The pōwhiri and the marae where it occurs is more than an enjoyable cultural experience of authentic indigenous culture: rather, it shows respect and affirms the place of Māori people in society (Stewart et al, 2015). Pōwhiri disrupts dominant discourses and can therefore provide a critical moment in encouraging the participants to understand the context of what they are participating in (Stewart et al, 2015, p 92). While pōwhiri might confront newcomers as foreign at first, there is also a trust in the relationship that will ensure that all ultimately benefit from this process as each comes to know and understand each other in the context of living and working in Aotearoa New Zealand.

It is important, therefore, that the transnational social worker understands the theoretical and analytical underpinning complexities of pōwhiri as a representation of the Māori world. Table 10.1 outlines some fundamental principles about pōwhiri that people need to understand and recognise as representing essential elements of te āo Māori.

The pōwhiri process

Table 10.1: Elements of pōwhiri

Principles	Explanation
Tapu and noa	The pōwhiri is a formal event that moves from being tapu (sacred) to where human relationships are balanced and people can then meet more informally, or noa.
Ihi	Two groups coming together produce a range of emotions that contribute to the ihi (the sense) of the occasion. It is a connection with the spiritual world and where the two parties check each other out, and ihi changes as the relationship gradually changes as the pōwhiri progresses (Mead, 2003).
Manaakitanga	Sometimes identified as hospitality towards manuhiri (visitors), this is a critical part of the ritual of encounter and a reflection of the hosting by the marae. This is an expression of enhancing people's mana or dignity and reflects values such as generosity, fairness, respect and consideration (Mead, 2003).
Kaitiakitanga	Being a good kaitiaki (steward) is important for the hosts and occurs by ensuring that the manuhiri are cared for, nurtured, protected and sheltered.
Wairuatanga	A spiritual dimension lives in all present at the pōwhiri. Wairuatanga acknowledges the extensive web of relationships between the past, the present and the future, no matter where participants come from. This is present in many ways during the powhiri at the marae.
Kua ea!	'It is done!' (Mead, 2003). This state occurs when all the obligations, roles and responsibilities of the pōwhiri have been completed by both sides.

Pōwhiri is a complex set of practices that the hosts and visitors engage in, constituting a series of rituals of encounter leading to the parties' ability to then socialise in a more informal manner. Each of the following components of the pōwhiri plays a role in enabling a transformation of the encounter to occur (Mead, 2003).

Preparation

Both parties need to prepare themselves for the pōwhiri or embarking on to the marae. Each person needs to be aware of their role, the connections that they have to the marae and to the group, and the purpose or reason for participating in the pōwhiri.

> For transnational social workers this could occur soon after they arrive into the country, and/or when they start their employment in a particular organisation.

Wero

This is a challenge given to important hosts or on important occasions. The wero ascertains whether the visitors are friends or foes. A male is sent out onto the marae atea to lay down a little carved wooden dart or leaf for the visitors. If the visitors come in peace then they will slowly pick this dart up and then the home people will allow them to continue embarking onto the marae (Mead, 2003; Stewart et al, 2015).

> For transnational social workers, their initial challenge will be in choosing to come and live in Aotearoa New Zealand and then further challenges will be around their practice as social workers.

Karanga

Instantly, the atmosphere changes as karanga (calls) alternately ring out from women on both sides of the pōwhiri groups as they embark onto the marae. The karanga calls to the ancestors as well as those who are present. The karanga facilitates a state of released emotion that symbolises the spiritual and emotional bonds between the hosts and their visitors. The women's voices are the first heard on the marae and their role is pivotal as they have the power to negate the tapu (Walker, 2004).

> Whether refugees or immigrants, transnational social workers initially arrive in Aotearoa New Zealand as visitors. In the context of pōwhiri there is a moment

of discovery as each party acknowledges who they are, their past and their connections. They also need to acknowledge each other as Treaty partners. It is therefore important that, as good hosts, we organise, initiate and support such events as these can link to, and inform, the subsequent practice in Aotearoa New Zealand of transnational social workers.

Whakaeke

Generally, the women will be at the front and the men at the back (although there are tribal variations) as they embark onto the marae. The group needs to be conscious of their surroundings: the environment, the people involved in the pōwhiri and their respective roles. The wero and karanga are integral parts of the whakaeke.

Both parties have now committed to a relationship or encounter. This is the point where both groups are embarking on a new adventure. The journey might occur with some caution as the parties need to be aware of all the external senses, but new arrivals become aware of the place, the people and the roles and rituals in this new place just as astutely as those who are of this place and who are watching them.

For transnational social workers, this could be a phase when they are orienting themselves into the country and into their specific area of social work.

Tangi ki nga mate

While embarking onto the marae, the visitors will stop in front of the wharenui (ancestral meeting house) to acknowledge those who have passed on. It is a mutual merging of wairua (spirituality) by connecting to those from the past.

For transnational social workers, this is about remembering the people they have left behind, as well as the trauma and crises that they may have come from. This is a moment to acknowledge all of this 'spiritually'. It is a very emotive time but the shared understanding also enables some collective healing to occur.

As the transnational social worker becomes aware of the present situation that they are in, they also remember the past that they have come from. All of this makes up who they are as a social worker.

Whaikorero

Now that the visitors are on the marae grounds, they are seated (inside or out of the traditional meeting house) and the formal speech-making or whaikorero occurs. This Māori oratory from both sides includes greetings to those who have passed on as well as the living, and a focus on the purpose of the pōwhiri: 'Eloquences and expert oratory skills enhance traditional patterns with metaphor, recitation or genealogy, proverbs and tribal sayings, jokes and timing, and the connecting of past and present' (Stewart et al, 2015, p 96). The Māori language is the preferred medium of communication in this formal part of the ceremony as the marae is seen as the last bastion and sanctuary of the Māori language, and while it is acceptable to have translators sitting alongside the visitors, it is acknowledged that there is often something that is lost in the translation.

It is important for the transnational social worker to acknowledge the experiences, the knowledge, values and skills, that they bring with them, but it is just as important for them to recognise the new and different aspects of this environment. This will be a learning journey, one that they need to be open to if they are to be competent in their work with Māori.

Waiata

Each whaikorero is followed by a waiata (song). There are various versions of waiata that are generally recited to compliment, acknowledge or embellish the speaker and their speech.

For the transnational social worker, the waiata supports that they are in a new place. It is an acknowledgement of who they are, where they have come from and where they are now.

Hohou te rongo

At the end of the formal speech-making, a sign is given by the hosts and the two groups merge by literally sharing two breaths. This occurs by way of the hongi (a pressing of noses). The hongi is a symbolic merging of the two groups. The distance is closed, the groups merge and the group become one.

> The process of pōwhiri allows transnational social workers to consider appropriate cultural rituals of encounter within their work and how this might be included as a part of their work.

Hakari

The formal part of the pōwhiri finishes when a hakari (feast or sharing of kai) occurs. This is a noa agent and is a time when the hosts show their manaakitanga (hospitality) and kaitiakitanga (stewardship) to their guests. The sharing of food is a key cultural marker that enables formality and informality to merge (Mead, 2003; Stewart et al, 2015).

> This is a moment of celebration for the transnational social worker as they consciously recognise their practice and how it needs to change in order to work more effectively with Maori, including what they bring to the relationship.

Within the hui (gathering) at the marae, there are two other practices that cement the relationship established through the pōwhiri process.

Mihimihi

This generally occurs inside the wharenui, which is also known as the Whare of Rongo (the house of peace). This is a process whereby everyone introduces themselves, acknowledges where they come from and includes their connections to their mountain, river, land, tribe and family.

> For transnational social workers, this provides them all with an opportunity to talk about the place that they have come from, their connections to their places and the journey that brought them to Aotearoa New Zealand. These narratives strengthen the connection of the group with others.

Poroporoaki

When the hui or gathering is finished, the visitors will get up to acknowledge the hosts, both those in the kitchen who have fed them and those who have facilitated the hui. Acknowledging the hosts gives thanks for the way in which the guests have been looked after, in their space, with their cultural practices.

For the transnational social worker, this might offer an opportunity to consider how they conclude their meetings given that the end is just as important as the beginning from a Māori perspective.

Pōwhiri in practice

The pōwhiri framework can therefore be used in welcoming and orienting transnational social workers into Aotearoa New Zealand and into the practice of social work. Simmons et al (2013, pp 74–5) have developed a guide for transnational social workers to consider in applying the pōwhiri framework to their social work practice. The framework has application in both macro (ie institutional) and micro (ie interpersonal) contexts (see Table 10.2).

It cannot be assumed that because one is a qualified social worker in another country, one necessarily knows how to practise social work competently in Aotearoa New Zealand. Orientation (which includes the competency and registration of these workers) could use a pōwhiri process to contextualise their position, their role and their relationship within Aotearoa New Zealand and with the indigenous people of this country. This could form a part of their pathway to competency and thus enhance a relationship with Māori under a Treaty relationship. Using a pōwhiri framework should therefore become a necessary component for all transnational social workers who are seeking social work registration. This should include a pōwhiri as well as a deconstruction and analysis of it as part of their practice here.

Cultural competency is an ongoing journey of cultural encounters that can create meaningful reciprocal relationships to build a desire of *wanting* to, rather than *having* to, become competent ethical practitioners. Pōwhiri is both a process and a tool that provides an ethical framework for the competent engagement of transnational social workers in Aotearoa New Zealand. It is grounded in a Māori worldview and honours the need for practice based on Te Tiriti ō

Waitangi (ANZASW, 2008). The two narratives shared illustrate how identity and one's own culture can be affirmed through the pōwhiri process while welcoming, connecting and ultimately developing trust in order to build a genuine working relationship with a social worker. For transnational social workers, pōwhiri enables who they are and what they bring to be ethically grounded in their new context. Welcoming is not just a matter of providing transnational social workers with training and opportunities to meet the local challenges of working in Aotearoa New Zealand, but also about acknowledging the histories and skills that they bring and providing them with opportunities to contribute. Developing a process based on reciprocity enhances a sense of mutual respect (Kjellberg and French, 2011).

Explicit and implicit in the pōwhiri is the role of the kaitiaki (steward), which is formed in the relational encounter between two groups. As practitioners, managers, educators, professional bodies and the Social Workers Registration Board (SWRB), we all share in the reciprocal responsibility of ensuring that our manuhiri (visitors) have ample opportunity to seek out cultural encounters on the path to ethically ground their practice.

Table 10.2: Elements of pōwhiri in practice

Phases of pōwhiri	Macro	Micro
Preparation	Finding out about the culture and the context that you are walking into.	Finding out about the culture of the family you will be visiting. What protocols may be required? What processes may need to occur in order to build trust? Should refreshments or koha be taken? Is a translator needed in order to understand the client and family?
Wero	Gauging what needs to be done. With different cultures, we may need to consider how we relate to the Treaty and the historical context of Aotearoa New Zealand. We will also need to understand the journeys that have enabled other cultures to be in Aotearoa New Zealand.	How are cultural values respected and harnessed? How can you ensure that a safe space is created with the client? How does a wider understanding of the cultural context of the client help you understand your relationship with the client?

Karanga	Understanding the role of your culture in relation to the Treaty and how to address this. Understanding relationships and the role of the host alongside the role of visitor or guest.	Understanding that all stereotypical ideas about a culture need to be put aside. Be prepared to have your own worldview ruptured so that you can encounter the client's worldview.
Whakaeke	Being aware of what is expected mentally, physically and spiritually when entering the place of encounter.	Commit to a genuine relationship for a real encounter to take place. Acknowledging those present in a manner that is respectful in order to avoid any misunderstanding. Being aware of the environment where the encounter will occur and what is respectful, ranging from manners and clothing to what to take with you, which ensures that the encounter occurs in a safe space.
Tangi ki ngā mate	Understanding that, from various cultural perspectives, spirituality is pivotal to their well-being. Ensuring, therefore, that spaces are provided within the workplace in which spirituality can be acknowledged if needed, including ways in which those that have passed are acknowledged.	When working with the client, this may involve having to say a prayer or share some words of wisdom. Being open to spiritual understandings. An understanding of silence may also be needed.
Whaikorero	Ensuring that policies are conducive to creating an environment in which the past, present and future are acknowledged.	Acknowledging the purpose of the visit and attempting to form a genuine relationship with the client and family.
Waiata	How can the organisations ensure that Māori values are embellished and embraced? What other ways of effective communication can occur?	Clients may wish to serve you food, sing or perform a practice from their culture to honour you. This should be welcomed and not judged.
Hohou te rongo	Accepting different cultures, their differences and their possible similarities.	Reflecting the essence of genuinely trying to help the client – that you are there to work alongside them rather than tell them what to do.
Hakari	Agencies must allow spaces in which cultural encounters can occur, gifts can be exchanged and reciprocity can be acknowledged.	This is when sharing takes place and clients are able to gauge who you are and how you express yourself, and ensure that you are not judgemental in this process.

Mihimihi	Acknowledging that, as a responsible service in Aotearoa New Zealand, you are accepting the role of kaitiaki to induct transnational social workers to practise competently in Aotearoa New Zealand. As transnational social workers, accepting that you come with knowledge and skills but also have the ability to learn from this place about this space.	Ensuring that introductions take place where you allow the client to discuss their culture and who they are. This may allow you to take your professional hat off and be personable. This is an important stage as not achieving this makes it difficult to work with the client.
Poroporoaki	Ensuring that the cultural processes are reciprocated. Ensuring that the ending is as important as everything else from a cultural perspective.	Once trust is built and the client can sense genuineness in your approach, you will be able to address the issues and ensure self-determination is achieved.

References

ANZASW (Aotearoa New Zealand Association of Social Workers) (2008) *Code of ethics*, Christchurch, NZ: ANZASW.

Campinha-Bacote, J. (2011) 'Coming to know cultural competence: an evolutionary process', *International Journal for Human Caring*, 15(3): 42–8.

Crisp, B.R. (2009) 'Is there a role for foreigners as social work educators?', *Social Work Education: The International Journal*, 28(6): 668–77.

Eketone, A. and Walker, S. (2013) 'Kaupapa Māori social work research', in M. Gray, J. Coates, M. Yellowbird and T. Hetherington (eds) *Decolonising social work*, Surrey: Ashgate Publishing Ltd, pp 259–70.

Kawharu, I.H. (ed) (1989) *Waitangi: Māori and Pākehā perspectives of the Treaty of Waitangi*, Auckland: Oxford University Press.

Kjellberg, G. and French, R. (2011) 'A new pedagogical approach for integrating social work students and service users', *Social Work Education*, 30(8): 948–63.

Mead, S.M. (2003) *Tikanga Māori: Living by Māori values*, Wellington: Huia Publishers.

Ministerial Advisory Committee on a Māori Perspective for the Department of Social Welfare (1986) *Pūao-te-Ātatū = Daybreak: The report of the Ministerial Advisory Committee on a Māori Perspective for the Department of Social Welfare*, Wellington, NZ: New Zealand Department of Social Welfare.

Munford, R. and Sanders, J. (2010) 'Embracing the diversity of practice: indigenous knowledge and mainstream social work practice', *Journal of Social Work Practice: Psychotherapeutic Approaches in Health, Welfare and Community*, 25(1): 63–77.

Orange, C. (1989) *The Treaty of Waitangi*, Wellington, NZ: Bridget Williams Books.

Penetito, W. (2010) *What's Māori about Māori education?* Wellington, NZ: Victoria University Press.

Simmons, H.., Walsh-Tapiata, W, Meo-Sewabu, L. and Umugwaneza, A. (2013) '"Cultural encounters": a framework of ethical practice for transnational social workers in Aotearoa', in J. Duke, M. Hendrickson and L. Beddoe (eds) *Conference proceedings: Protecting the public – Enhancing the profession. E tiaki ana te Hapori-E manaaki ana I ngā mahi*, Wellington, NZ: Social Workers Registration Board, pp 66–78.

Simpson, G. (2009) 'Global and local issues in the training of overseas social workers', *Social Work Education: The International Journal*, 28(6): 655–67.

Stewart, G., Karaitiana, K. and Mika, C. (2015) 'Infinitely welcome: education pōwhiri and ethnic performativity', *Mai Journal*, 4(2): 91–103.

Thomas, C. and Davis, S. (2005) 'Bicultural strengths-based supervision', in M. Nash, R. Munford and K. O'Donoghue (eds) *Social work theories in action*, London: Jessica Kingsley Publishers, pp 189–204.

Walker, R. (2004) *Ka whawhai tonu matou: Struggle without end* (rev edn), Auckland: Penguin.

Walker, S. (2012) 'The teaching of Māori social work practice and theory to a predominantly Pākeha audience', *Aotearoa New Zealand Social Work*, 24(3/4): 65–74.

Walsh-Tapiata, W. and Webster, J. (2004) 'Do you have a supervision plan?', *Te Komako III, Social Work Review*, 16(2): 15–19.

White, R. (2006) 'Opportunities and challenges for social workers crossing borders', *International Social Work*, 49(5): 629–40.

ELEVEN

Consistency and change: internationally educated social workers compare interpretations and approaches in Canada and their countries of origin

Annie Pullen Sansfaçon, Marion Brown and Stephanie Éthier

Introduction

This chapter discusses findings obtained from interviews with 19 foreign-educated social workers who took part in a larger qualitative study aimed at understanding professional adaptation to social work practice in Canada. One of the research questions, explored in the context of the larger-scale project, was to investigate how social work experience and education in one country affects perspectives on social work practice in Canada – specifically, the assessment of client issues, social work intervention processes and interactions within the work environment. Following an iterative process whereby data were collected and then analysed in order to inform subsequent phases of data collection, we developed vignettes drawn from clinical cases. During this stage of data collection, we asked the participants to draw upon their knowledge, skills and values, and to reflect on their interpretations of each case's needs relative to the material and discursive conditions of their practice context, both in their country of origin and in Canada. This chapter analyses these data with a focus on knowledge transfer to internationally educated social workers who now work in Canada.

Transferability of social work

The profession of social work exists in a state of tension at the crux of several compelling forces: the familiar adage that practice is context-specific, referring to the need to understand the lived conditions of the people with whom we work, geopolitically and socioculturally; the substantive area of practice; and the notion of basic human needs that transcend time and space.

The capacity for social workers to transfer knowledge from one context to another is an important aspect of negotiating this tension, and is known to be an important aspect of professional adaptation overall (Remennick, 2003). Capacity to transfer knowledge may be facilitated by the fact that social work has access to 'Global standards' for practice (IFSW, 2012) and 'Global standards for social work education and training' (IASSW, 2004), which, for countries like Canada, might ensure a certain consistency in education and practice with other countries that adhere to these same principles through their professional associations and regulatory bodies. That said, not all countries adhere to these principles, and when they do so, they might have different standards of accreditation for social work practice and education. With regard to education, differences between countries at the level of standards or programme curricula are highly possible. For example, Spolander et al (2011) examined differences and similarities in social work curricula, regulation and ethical requirements in Canada, England and South Africa, and found that while the programmes examined are all members of the International Federation of Social Workers (IFSW), many differences exist between the three countries (Spolander et al, 2011). Social work practice is also subject to local variations in laws and social policy. Crisp (2009) suggests that the lack of knowledge about laws and the organisation of social services might prevent social workers from practising effectively in new contexts. Languages, as well as professional jargon, can also pose a specific barrier to social work practice abroad (Pullen Sansfaçon and Gérard-Tétreault, 2015). Remennick (2003) asserts that successful knowledge transfer may be closely linked to the similarities of standards between the countries of education and the host countries where social work will be practised. In other words, the more similar the standards are from one country to another, the more knowledge transfer should be possible.

Methodology

The data discussed here were generated from interviews carried out in the third wave (2012–16) of data collection of a pan-Canadian qualitative study (Pullen Sansfaçon et al, 2012). The 19 participants in this wave had immigrated to Canada after 2002 from Colombia (1), France (5), Lebanon (2), the US (3), Finland (1), the UK (3), the Czech Republic (1), Pakistan (1), Brazil (1) and India (1). At the time of interview, the participants were practising social work in the cities of Montreal, Calgary, Halifax and Charlottetown. Letters and targeted emails were sent to members of professional associations in the three provinces involved, and we successfully used the snowball method starting from these first contacts. Interviews were conducted in English or French based on the participants' preferences.

Individual in-depth interviews included semi-open questions and the discussion of clinical vignettes. This method allowed participants to reflect concretely on their experiences and compare sites of practice (Finch, 1987), while avoiding socially desirable responses (Hughes and Huby, 2002). According to Barter and Renold (2000), vignettes can be used to achieve three objectives: to put participants in action situations; to clarify judgements; and to be used as an inviting means to explore sensitive topics. The use of vignettes also offers the opportunity to explore the values and ethical dimensions of social work (Wilks, 2004).

Participants were asked to read the vignettes one at a time and to respond to questions about interventions in their country of origin compared to those made in the Canadian context; they were asked to reflect upon their values, their knowledge and the skills that underpin their thoughts on interventions. Congruent with grounded theory, axial and selective coding procedures were used to code the interviews and analyse the data. We analysed the participants' narratives to identify which aspects of their practice in Canada were similar to, and different from, what they experienced in their country of origin. Specifically, we aimed to explore issues related to values, theoretical models, skills, available resources, needs analysis, interventions and possible perspectives on the cases presented in order to identify what remained the same and what changed in their practice across contexts.

Presentation of data

Vignette 1

Maria is a social worker who works with the Hosta family. The Hosta family lives in public housing in an urban area. Both parents grew up as members of the working poor but managed to complete a high-school education. The family consists of a mother, father and three children under the age of five, including a new-born baby. The mother is not working due to the recent childbirth. The father is also currently unemployed. He was fired from his last job due to difficulties concentrating at work; he also has a back injury that limits the type of work he is able to look for. The oldest child, a four year old, is presenting with behavioural challenges, including tantrums, resisting the parents' instructions and hitting the younger children violently.

A common theme emerging in this vignette, wherever the participant emigrated from, was the goal to help the Hosta family. However, looking more closely at the responses, we noticed that participants from the Global North provided marginally differently responses from participants from the Global South with regard to the assessment of the situation, as well as the direction for intervention. Overall, participants from Europe and North America explained that they would act similarly both in their own country and in Canada. Participants from the Global North seem, overall, to apply similar intervention principles whether in Canada or in the country where they were educated: "I don't think I would approach them any different here than in the US, in terms of like ... to me, helping a family, I'm needing to know about that system or what other system they're attached to" (US-3). Participants from the Global North would focus on keeping the children safe, meeting the psychosocial needs of the family and connecting them with resources available to get appropriate support:

> "In the culture of England – but I guess I haven't mentioned it because it's so similar to Canada – you would want to support the family and keep them together so long as it is safe and no one's at risk of harm." (UK-2)

> "The values and the principles would be keeping the children safe, but also, as we've talked about before, empowering the family to help themselves." (Finland)

Participants from the Global North felt that their practice was similar both in their country of origin and in Canada. One notable exception emerged, however. Participants from France said that while they would want to protect the children in both places, the type of intervention they could provide was different: "I would say that what is different is at the level of funding, since the Canadian model is not only built around troubleshooting. The model is more about finding long-term solutions" (France-5).

Participants from the Global South, on the other hand, felt that their overall practice would be more different in Canada because of the availability of resources. Participants from South America, the Middle East and the Indian subcontinent, when reflecting on their practice in their countries of origin, paid more attention to meeting the basic needs of the family by increasing their income than to focusing on child protection. In comparison, when they discussed how they would intervene in Canada, they say that they would, instead, focus more on meeting the family's psychosocial needs because resources are more available to do so. Many noted that if they had access to the same resources in Canada as in their country of origin, their intervention would be similar: "I would have wanted to do the same in Colombia for a family like this one, but I did not have any resources to do so" (Colombia).

Many participants highlighted that their home country's government social safety net affects the intervention. For example, participants from Colombia, Brazil and Lebanon explained that the local government there would most likely not offer any financial assistance or social housing for the Hosta family:

> "Living in public housing in an urban area, we don't have this there.... If they don't have money, they go to favelas and they live in poverty there but there is no, nothing like group homes or public housing or community housing." (Brazil)

Facing a lack of institutional resources in their home countries, several participants mentioned that they would not hesitate to seek support through their personal networks to help this family.

The specific cultural and policy contexts therefore influence, in this case, the way in which social workers analyse the family's needs, and the possibilities of interventions to meet those needs. The analysis of this particular vignette, with regard to the ways in which people from different countries looking at the same case would handle assessment and intervention, shows that the approach is largely influenced by the context, which determines whether or not it is possible to fully meet service users' needs. Furthermore, while we found some differences in the ways in which assessment and intervention were considered between participants from the Global North and the Global South, both groups are nevertheless influenced by the context, and more specifically by the availability of resources and the social work mandate.

Vignette 2[1]

Jo is a 16-year-old assigned male inquiring about support to begin a medical transition towards affirming her identity as a woman. Jo was living as a boy until she reached puberty and then felt that she could no longer deny her true identity.

At the age of 14, she tried to speak to her mother about this but her father became aware of the situation and disowned Jo. Jo was instructed by her father to leave the community. Since then, Jo has been living on the streets, engaging in prostitution. She is trying to save enough money for medical treatments to undertake reassignment surgery. Jo has also had several episodes of self-harming and frequent suicidal thoughts. Now living as a girl on a full-time basis, Jo comes to see a social worker for a drop-in appointment at a youth counselling centre to get support and counselling.

The analysis of this vignette highlights that while participants asserted that professional values of respect and openness would be transferable, the lack of social acceptability and the resources available to work with transgender people in their countries of origin mediated their thoughts about how and whether they could intervene. Also, most participants explained that the values of social work would enable them to see the person as a whole, without judging them, but their own limited knowledge about possible interventions and restricted resources hampered their ability to elaborate further about interventions either in Canada or in their countries of origin.

All participants, whether from the Global North or the Global South, discussed the importance of universal social work values, abundantly citing the values of self-determination and respect. Despite some discomfort at first, all participants seemed to perceive the situation of Jo through the lens of social work's universal foundations – Jo is a human being and needs help:

> "Social workers have to have a very, very strong value base for [working with Jo] because this is where social work has to deeply move from the worker's personal self to their professional self." (India)

> "I could feel confronted by the situation of someone who changes sex because of my values, but I can still give them support because the most important thing for me is that a person who has needs can have support, whatever their choices." (Colombia)

> "Being open-minded, I think, in a situation like this one, is an obligation to respect, to respect the person and their identity." (France-5)

Social work values were therefore foundational to their assessment of the situation, and most participants said that they would welcome Jo with openness and compassion, whether in their home country or in Canada. However, although participants were open to Jo's situation, several of them shared their reservations and agreed that this would not necessarily be the same for all social workers in their country of origin:

> "As a social worker, you cannot just be openly accepting of everything, you can still have your opinions and views. So you would really have to find a social worker who is a good match to work with Jo because, especially in older generations, you might find very small-minded people towards this kind of, this kind of issue, or this kind of situation." (Finland)

Besides social work values, which were identified as transferable, if not essential in this case, cultural and social context were said to inevitably impact on the type of intervention that could have been carried out with Jo. While participants refer to Canada as a fairly liberal context within which to intervene with regard to issues facing lesbian, gay, bisexual and trans (LGBT) people, several openly spoke about the difficulties that Jo could meet in seeking help in their country of origin. Jo's reality – that is, being transgender – remains taboo in many societies:

> "I know that the concept of sex change would hurt immensely French social values. It is the only thing. And I would not want to be in this person's shoes because … I would say that society is really in conflict with a situation such as Jo's." (France-5)

> "So people are still living kind of in the shade, they don't come out with this, they don't talk about it, so there's lots of hidden issues." (Czech Republic)

Given the variations in the level of social acceptability of trans issues in their countries of origin, it is not surprising that participants suggested different types of interventions for working with Jo. Participants from countries where Jo could be ostracised or oppressed largely suggested individual interventions respecting confidentiality. However, when they assessed the same situation with a Canadian lens, participants explored the possibility of combining various types of interventions – for example, family counselling and participation in a support group.

Some wondered about the extent to which social workers are the most appropriate people to work with transgender people.

Vignette 3

Alia is seeking counselling to help her cope with her living situation at her home. Her living situation has become increasingly difficult due to marital conflict with her husband. She and her husband have been married for two years and they have a one-year-old baby boy. She is feeling anxious, depressed and scared because every day her husband criticises her, yells at her and makes negative comments. She wants her husband to stop treating her this way but she is afraid to confront him about it directly. In the past couple of weeks, her husband has also been getting physically forceful with her and she is growing fearful of him. However, she is financially dependent on him and she has not worked in any job for the last two years since they got married.

The assessment of this vignette was similar for most participants, insofar as they all identified a case of spousal abuse, but they discussed many values and perspectives to support intervention. No common threads emerged from this vignette, whether participants were from the Global North or the Global South. They emphasised the need to provide Alia with a place where she can be safe, and all stressed the importance of establishing trust with Alia. The availability of resources, and the cultural and religious context in which the situation was taking place, strongly influenced the assessment and the direction of intervention.

Some participants raised the question of the service user's religion and cultural context. Many participants identified the sociocultural context as important in terms of influencing the direction of the intervention, sometimes making it difficult to intervene according to professional values: "We can intervene [in Colombia] but we will do it very slowly because we do not necessarily want to break the family. We won't encourage breaking the family even if she is a victim of conjugal violence" (Colombia).

Due to the different contexts, participants explained that they might have to intervene differently in Canada than in their countries of origin. For example, participants from Pakistan, India and Columbia explained how they would draw on the community or the extended family and friends to intervene, whereas in Canada, they would be able to find other resources to help this person.

The question of the service user's religion was noteworthy in this case in a way that was not present in the other two vignettes.[2] Participants highlighted the importance of respecting Alia's religious affiliation and asserted that this would need to be considered as a significant aspect of their assessment:

> "The problem in Lebanon would be, depending, in Lebanon, there's no civil marriage, so there's no civil law. So, for example, if a Muslim gets divorced, they would follow the law of the Sharia, and if a Christian gets divorced, they would follow the law of the Catholic or the Orthodox Church. The custody of the child is the problem because the woman has the right to keep the child 'til age nine; from age nine to 12, it depends on – not religion, but – like in Lebanon, there's 18 denominations, like for Christians, you have Catholic, Mennonite, Orthodox, Protestant, okay? And for Muslims you have Sunni, Shia … so you have 18, 18 laws." (Lebanon-2)

When exploring how they would have intervened in their countries of origin, participants discussed other values. Issues around oppression, gender inequalities and the centrality of family were clear in the analyses provided by several participants since these issues are intimately linked to the sociocultural, political and even legislative contexts that influence intervention in their countries of origin. Even when self-determination was identified as an important value for them, they explained that the contexts in their countries of origin often prevented them from intervening according to this value and were not conducive to interventions that would let them work in coherence with their professional values.

With so many values emerging during the discussion of this case, not surprisingly, we observed some differences between participants' approaches in this situation. For example, despite the context of spousal abuse and the imbalance of power between Alia and her husband identified by the participants, some of them suggested moving forward with a meeting between the two in order to facilitate reconciliation. This type of intervention was, however, generally not put forward by the majority of participants when discussing their work in a Canadian context, and most of them favoured Alia's self-determination as long as the child is not in danger. This orientation for intervention was more frequently discussed among the social workers from the Global North, with some exceptions, such as the participant from Brazil:

"I am not here to say what she has to do, I would just show her what the situation is and what resources are available to help her; the decision is hers. But I keep very clear that the boy is my worry. She's adult, she can run away, whereas the young boy cannot. I would show her that if something happens and the boy's life becomes endangered, I could easily contact the court and even have the boy taken away from the family." (Brazil)

"The child is in danger at home, so if the mother does not take any action, I would tell her that we are going to have to take some." (France-3)

Finally, all participants mentioned that the services available to Alia in Canada are at least equivalent to, and more often enhanced when compared to, those that would be available in their countries of origin, which facilitates intervention with women who are experiencing domestic abuse. Apart from a minority of participants favouring a reconciliation approach to this situation, most advocated measures aimed at getting the violence to end, usually by working towards the goal of Alia leaving the situation and ensuring the protection of the child.

Discussion

In discussing the vignettes, participants explored a range of possible interventions, which highlight variations in how to engage in complex social situations that are experienced individually. For example, while some participants placed the protection of the child as a priority in vignette 1, others focused on finding financial resources for the family. This finding is coherent with the research findings of Weiss (2005) and Hendriks et al (2008). Weiss (2005) found that students across countries analysed the same case study very differently depending on their academic foundations. Similarly, Hendriks et al (2008), in a cross-national comparative study of social work students in 10 countries, highlighted important differences with regard to the goals of social work interventions to address client poverty.

Digging into the data, however, we identified how the changing context from one country to another impacts not so much on the assessment of cases, but, rather, on the type and direction of intervention. Indeed, the comprehension and assessment of the case tended to remain the same when discussing the case in the participants' countries of origin or in Canada. However, depending on whether they were discussing practice in their countries of origin or in Canada, it was possible to see how the political, economic, cultural or religious context influenced the intervention. For example, resources and the level of cultural acceptability of a situation helped determine the choice of one type of intervention instead of another. The data obtained in this research allowed us to precisely observe the impact that the context of practice can have on intervention.

Not surprisingly, we have noted major differences related to available resources from one country to another, which also impacted on the capacity, willingness or tendency for social workers to draw on familial or community-based support networks. All participants also stressed the multitude of available resources in Canada for economically or socially vulnerable people. At the same time, there is a concern that Canada's social safety net and community cohesion are eroding compared to those of other countries.

While the various changing contexts required the participants to adapt their practice, the participants' values, on the other hand, seemed to provide the most guidance on how to intervene, and remained relatively stable across the practice in the two countries. When we analysed the responses obtained through the three vignettes presented to participants, it became clear that values play an important role in the intervention process as much in the country of origin as in Canada. In looking closely at the way in which values were discussed in relation to the three vignettes, it seems that they helped participants to adjust their practice to the new context, providing a framework to carry on social work practice locally or abroad. For example, the value of respect and self-determination helped participants make sense of things even in a situation about which most of them were unaware (vignette 2). It also helped them reflect on how service users should be treated even if the user's situation was not socially acceptable in one country or another (vignette 3). Thus, even when the standards of practice may bear a greater difference, for example, as in the case of immigration from the Global South to the Global North, professional values may help internationally educated social workers to adapt. Lastly, participants noted that some of their values had adapted to their new context, but we did not see any evidence of complete value changes as a result of such adaptation. Indeed, looking closely at the description of intervention that was carried out in the country of origin compared to the description of the intervention in Canada, we identified only a small number of participants who explained that they have further developed a value (eg "I have become open"). No evidence of significant or wholesale value changes came up in the context of our research, which would indicate that social work values are fairly stable even after a process of immigration.

Conclusion

The data from these 19 social workers shines a light on the long-standing reality in social work that there are both foundational, common principles and context-specific applications to our practice. The analyses presented here make clear that social workers approach their practice in ways that uphold both a commitment to consistency and a willingness to change. A key factor in this ongoing negotiation is the embodiment of core social work values and a commitment to congruence in one's personal and professional ways of being in the world. Ultimately, while contexts and their structural impediments and opportunities shifted, these practitioners stayed true to their values, which formed the bedrock of their confidence and ability to practise in the new Canadian setting.

Notes

[1] This vignette was abbreviated for the purposes of this book.
[2] Participants talked about the possible impact of religious values on their assessment of Jo's situation in vignette 2, but in vignette 3, the role of religion is important from the service user's perspective, not from the social worker's perspective.

References

Barter, C. and Renold, E. (2000) '"I want to tell you a story": exploring the application of vignettes in qualitative research with children and young people', *International Journal of Social Research Methodology*, 3: 307–23.

Crisp, B.R. (2009) 'Is there a role for foreigners as social work educators?', *Social Work Education: The International Journal*, 28(6): 668–77.

Finch, J. (1987) 'The vignette technique in survey research', *Sociology*, 21(1): 105–14.

Hendriks, P., Kloppenburg, R., Gevorgianien, V. and Jakutien, V. (2008) 'Cross-national social work case analysis: learning from international experience within an electronic environment', *European Journal of Social Work*, 11: 383–96.

Hughes, R. and Huby, M. (2002) 'The application of vignettes in social and nursing research', *Journal of Advanced Nursing*, 37(4): 382–86.

IASSW (International Association of Schools of Social Work) (2004) *Global standards for social work education and training.* Available at: http://cdn.ifsw.org/assets/ifsw_65044-3.pdf

IFSW (International Federation of Social Workers) (2012) *Global standards.* Available at: http://ifsw.org/policies/global-standards/

Pullen Sansfaçon, A. and Gérard-Tétreault, A. (2015) 'Langage et adaptation professionnelle de travailleuses sociales immigrantes au Québec' ['Language and professional adaptation of immigrant social workers in Quebec'], *Intervention*, 142: 5–15.

Pullen Sansfaçon, A., Brown, M. and Graham, J. (2012) 'International migration of professional social workers: towards a theoretical framework for understanding professional adaptation processes', *Social Development Issues*, 4(2): 7–50.

Remennick, L. (2003) 'Career continuity among immigrant professionals: Russian engineers in Israel', *Journal of Ethnic and Migration Studies*, 29(4): 701–21.

Spolander, G., Pullen Sansfaçon, A., Brown, M. and Engelbrecht, L. (2011) 'Social work education in Canada, England and South Africa: a critical examination of curriculums and programmes', *International Social Work*, 54(6): 817–32.

Weiss, I. (2005) 'Is there a global common core to social work? A cross-national comparative study of BSW graduate students', *Social Work*, 50: 101–10.

Wilks, T. (2004) 'The use of vignettes in qualitative research into social work values', *Qualitative Social Work*, 3(1): 78–87.

Part Four:
Policy challenges,
professional responses

As has been noted throughout this edition social work is a profession that frequently appears on national skills shortage lists in many Western countries. While this has increased global mobility, and enabled transnational social workers to gain employment, professional registration and often permanent residency in foreign jurisdictions, this phenomenon has created additional opportunities and challenges. The relative ease of relocation creates significant opportunities for transnational labour market mobility. However, in an era when social work has faced increasing professional regulation in many jurisdictions, social worker mobility also presents challenges. These challenges include relocating models of practice, adapting and developing professional competencies (especially cultural competencies), clarifying professional identity in a new environment and the translation of knowledge of law and policy from familiar fields to unfamiliar foreign jurisdictions. These challenges confront government policy-makers, social service employers, service users and user communities and the whole of the social work profession, as well as transnational social workers themselves. Part Three, 'Employer/stakeholder views', provided examples of how social work employers and/or other key stakeholders encountered social work as a transnational professional space. The main focus of the four chapters in this section is to provide country-specific examples of the challenges and opportunities that are presented by the employment of transnational social workers in particular contexts.

Whether social work is self-regulating or regulated by statute, the primary obligation of such systems is the protection of the public and the maintenance of standards, equivalent to local systems. These systems become significant drivers for standardisation of professional competence and knowledge. This is by no means a straightforward matter, as is demonstrated by the chapters in this section. Four chapters offer insights related to the implications for regulators, policymakers and professional bodies in Canada, Australia and the Republic of Ireland of social work as a transnational professional space.

In 'Readiness and regulation: perspectives of Canadian stakeholders' Marion Brown, Annie Pullen Sansfaçon and Kate Matheson draw on insights gained in 'knowledge exchange fora' in two Canadian cities that involved both domestic and transnational social workers, employers and representatives from the provincial regulatory bodies. They note the significance of policies and practices in the assessment and licensing of transnational social workers. Employers in particular weave knowledge and values in their consideration of transnational social workers and Brown et al note that 'the move into the belief systems of employers and employees proves murky indeed' (p 195), citing the example of conflicts between religious values and the secularism of professional codes and practices in Canada.

In two chapters addressing social work regulation in Australia the tensions and challenges are discovered and addressed from two different perspectives, each in dialogue with the other. In 'Will she be right, mate? Standards and diversity in Australian social work', Karen Healy broadly explores the regulation of the health and human service professions in Australia, and some of the implications for social workers seeking to relocate to Australia. Healy explores the dynamics of professional self-regulation, in the absence of statutory registration of social workers. She addresses the challenges of self-regulation in achieving both professional standards and diversity within the social work profession, and implications of the self-regulating environment for transnational social workers seeking to migrate and practise in Australia. Healy notes the potential for collaboration, both between health and social professions and, more significantly, between countries.

In 'Recognising transnational social workers in Australia', Angelika Papadopoulos explores the ethical principles that frame social work practice to critique the politics of credentialing transnational social workers in Australia. Drawing on Honneth's work Papadopoulos notes that the professional recognition of transnational social workers relates to such recognition as both respect for, and esteem of, their acquired cultural capital. In the current climate, she argues that the systems that have emerged for assessing and recognising the qualifications and experience of transnational social workers wishing to practise in Australia reflect narrow technocratic imperatives that are split away from social work values. Papadopoulos makes a strong case for respectful recognition processes which assess their capabilities fully rather than 'comparing their educational attainments with (shifting) standards used in Australia' (p 235). She also argues for better information and induction for transnational social workers to enable them to practise safely and competently in Australia.

In the final chapter of this edition, 'Social work mobility in Europe: a case study from Ireland', Trish Walsh, George Wilson and

Erna O'Connor present a European case study of social worker mobility over a period of change, which will likely intensify in the decade to come. Data from the Republic of Ireland over the period 2004–13 capturing the years leading up to, and in the aftermath of, the global financial crisis of 2008 is contrasted with the situation in Northern Ireland. In this discussion, Walsh et al illuminate the sensitivity of social worker mobility patterns to rapidly changing economic and political factors in the countries, the region and more broadly in Europe. The Brexit referendum vote in the UK adds a new set of uncertainties to the European setting. The many debates and questions swirling around migration, borders and people's freedom of movement that have emerged in the politics of Brexit and the refugee crisis mean that this chapter provides a closing to the book that affirms our view of social worker mobility as ever-changing.

TWELVE

Readiness and regulation: perspectives of Canadian stakeholders on the labour mobility of internationally educated social workers

Marion Brown, Annie Pullen Sansfaçon and Kate Matheson

Background

While the scholarly literature is sparse on data and analyses from social work employers in Canada, anecdotal accounts suggest that they are eager to hire social workers who come to the field of practice as seasoned professionals in both substantive content and contextual knowledge. They cite the fast pace of the work environment, the narrowing of service provision to only the most complex situations and dynamics, and the volume of the work as the driving forces behind needing new hires to 'hit the ground running' (Newberry-Koroluk, 2014). There is little time or energy for an accompanying adaptation process. These stories are not surprising given that, over the past 35 years, Canadian social work has been restructured to parallel the capitalist premises that good social welfare policy and programming is that which is productive and cost-efficient, with a focus on individualism and autonomy not only for service recipients, but also for employees. The joint ideologies of neoliberalism and economic rationalism prioritise productivity and deliverables, documentation, and external accountability. This is the context in which social work employers govern agency work, and into which internationally educated social workers enter when they arrive in Canada seeking to work in the field.

Similarly, there is little documentation on the experiences of regulators of the profession, those charged under legislation to enact the social work statutes in every province of Canada. As a self-regulating profession, the primary obligation is the protection of the public, which rationalises the driver for the uniformity of expectation and measurement of competence. In this chapter, we present data from both employers and regulators and seek to bring together their priorities and needs relative to the adaptation processes of internationally educated social workers.

Method

As part of a four-year federally funded study, Canadian researchers Pullen Sansfaçon et al engaged in qualitative interviews with 66 internationally educated social workers and held two Knowledge Exchange Fora (KEF), in Montreal and Halifax, respectively (Pullen Sansfaçon et al, 2012, 2014; Brown et al, 2015; Fulton et al, 2016). The KEF gathered social workers, both internationally and domestically educated, social work supervisors and employers, and representatives from the Quebec and Nova Scotia regulatory bodies. Data were collected via individual written reflections and focus group discussions. Focus group discussions were transcribed and analysed as components of the full data.

Twenty-nine participants attended the Montreal KEF and 23 participants attended in Halifax. Social workers, social work supervisors and employers represented government and non-governmental social welfare agencies, ranging in size from small, community-based, not-for-profit agencies with four employees to large governmental departments. This chapter presents data from these fora, where the findings of the four-year study were shared, and subsequently responded to, by KEF participants. The KEF were designed as a method for both disseminating data and analysis resulting from the individual interviews, and collecting data from employers, regulators and internationally educated social workers. Dialogue at the KEF began with the current Canadian social work practice context, and then prioritised the knowledge, values and skills transfer, cultural adaptations, and understanding of the Canadian social welfare system of the internationally educated social workers. These themes align with many of the concerns of migrant social workers themselves (Pullen Sansfaçon et al, 2014); however, the perspective is distinct, born as it is from distinct positioning relative to the issues.

The context: Canadian social welfare and social work today

The profession of social work is grounded in and committed to advocating for equitable social structures and responses to people and communities in need; these are the aspirations of the profession. However, in Canada, given the prevailing ideology of neoliberalism, the context of social service delivery has shifted over the past 35 years to prioritise economic rationalism, privatisation and the overall retrenchment of the welfare state. This contextual analysis is well documented in Canadian social work literature (Carniol, 2005; Baines, 2006; Smith, 2007; Mullaly, 2008; Wilson et al, 2011; Weinberg and Taylor, 2014), where social work scholars have been writing for years about the socio-political threats to the fundamental value base of the profession of social work. The political allegiance of Ronald Reagan in the US, Margaret Thatcher in Great Britain, Brian Mulroney in Canada, Malcolm Fraser in Australia and Roger Douglas in New Zealand solidified the principles and practices of economic rationalism, the essence of which is that good policy is that which meets economic priorities. It is upheld by commitment to capitalism's free market and the conviction that maximising individual economic freedom and minimising overt regulation should lead the way for all policy. Inequality is accepted as par for the course, government spending is considered a risk to economic health and government spending on social welfare is seen as a particular threat to productivity and profit.

This review of the socio-political context is required because social welfare is always the product of a particular time and place, underscored by the prevailing values and beliefs of the influential classes. In Canada, social welfare has shifted because these prevailing values and beliefs have shifted. Far different from the post-war expansion of government services and income supports, which saw the introduction of Medicare, unemployment insurance and the Canada Pension Plan, among other welfare policies, for 35 years, we have been living under a federal commitment to transnational corporations, capitalism, free trade and multilateral agreements. Concern for the welfare of people, equity and the accessibility and availability of resources conflict with global economic priorities, which consider all decisions in financial terms. Social welfare is seen as an impediment to sound economic policy.

This is the shifted sociocultural, political and economic context in Canada within which social work clients live, and in which social workers – those educated within Canada and beyond – do their work. Social work supervisors and employers who attended the KEF spoke about these changes to social service organisations over the course of their careers. The focus on efficiency has led to standardisation in orientation, which leaves little room for adjusted timelines to assist the internationally educated social worker, often a newcomer to Canada, in the adaptation process. In short, workers are expected to arrive already versed in culture and context, legislation and language:

> "I know it's tough on people from away who come to work at [the agency]. But I have no time to help them along, to help them figure it out. They have to figure it out, like all of us do. I know there's more to figure out for them, being new to Canada and all. But we need them to just get to work." (Social work employer)

Social work supervisors similarly report increased focus on accountability measures and the disappearance of clinical supervision. Studies corroborate that these lead to an increase in workloads and supervisory scrutiny (Aronson and Sammon, 2000). Part-time and contractual positions and reliance on volunteers have increased, contributing to heightened job insecurity and decreased salaries and benefits (Smith, 2007; Wilson et al, 2011). These changes have eroded relationships among staff members and knowledge transfer between veteran and newer social workers (Baines, 2006). Our data align with these findings:

> "There was a time when I would meet with the social workers in my unit and go over all their cases – what was happening, how they felt about it, what we thought the plan should be. Now it's only high risk cases we go over, and in the team. There's a risk assessment tool we use, so we don't talk about it in the same way either. Things are rated on scales more than talked about. And there's no time for talking about the regular cases." (Social work supervisor)

This tightening of focus, combined with increased complexity of need and often decreasing resources, emphasises productivity and the meeting of outcomes. Participants in the KEF noted a distinct shift in the language of the workplace as a result:

> "I remember about five or six years ago when we started using a logic model – I didn't know what it was. Someone had gone to some training and came back wanting us to

put all these things into a logic model. There were sections for deliverables and outcome measures. And I just thought, 'Am I in the right place? This is social work!'." (Social work supervisor)

This participant is calling attention not only to shifts in context, but also to how they connect to ideological shifts. Here, we can see the insidious infiltration of neoliberal priorities into the very foundations of a profession founded upon social justice, not surprising, perhaps, given that neoliberalism organises economic, political and social life in most Western societies. Given that its economic tenets are free markets, free trade and a non-interventionist state, governments that adopt its ideology scale back any institutions, programmes and services that function at the expense of market freedom (Wilson et al, 2011). For several decades, a top priority of Canada's federal government has been to decrease its deficit, a common concern under neoliberalism. Methods are both covert and overt: politicians commit rhetorically to quality-of-life improvements for their constituents while dismantling what remains of federal social welfare programmes. Provincial governments follow suit in their jurisdictions, ramping up efforts to get people off income assistance, cut disability benefits and cut back or eliminate special diet, transportation and employment-related benefits. Countrywide, the social safety net has shrunk, and distributions of wealth and resources have become polarised. An intersectional understanding of oppression reminds us that the colluding forces of white privilege, capitalism and patriarchy make these cuts more devastating for some than for others (Mananzala and Spade, 2008).

The internationally educated social workers engaged in our study, new to Canada in the past 10 years, do not have this historical comparison of the working conditions within the social welfare system, nor the understanding of the socio-political shifts. Indeed, most compared Canada favourably to their country of origin, in particular, noting the availability of resources and the broad terms of engagement for social workers. One social worker from Lebanon said:

"Well, this situation [of a trans youth seeking services] would not happen at home because it is illegal. People would help, but not out in the open. Here, it is so much better. The youth can come talk to social workers openly, and not get in trouble with the governments." (Internationally educated social worker)

Knowledge, values and skills transfer

The transfer of knowledge, values and skills across international borders is a central concern for employers and regulators of social work, who are eager to hire seasoned social workers who have expertise. Through three phases of data collection in our study, we queried the knowledge bases of internationally educated social workers: the theoretical foundations, the core social work values and the practice skills of the profession. With little variation, participants self-reported competence in knowing social work fundamentals and confidence in their applicability across contexts. Provincial regulatory body personnel who participated in our KEF did not disagree. However, regulatory bodies require applicants for licensing to have their internationally earned academic credentials assessed, an appraisal most often undertaken by the Canadian Association of Social Work (CASW). This process includes a review of degree requirements, including course syllabi and transcripts. If, in this review, there is a gap identified between the degree requirements of the country of origin and a Canadian social work degree, the provincial regulatory body identifies this as a concern regarding equivalence and may deny the social work licence:

> "Like, if we hear from CASW that the person doesn't have a social work policy course in their BSW [Bachelor of Social Work degree], then they don't have equivalent to a Canadian BSW, and they aren't eligible for a licence in [province] if they don't have equivalent to a Canadian BSW. That's the end of it. They may know everything about how to be good to people, be a good social worker with people, but their degree isn't recognised, so that's the end of it." (Provincial regulator)

Congruent with the interviews conducted with internationally educated social workers, employers and regulators at each KEF cited knowledge of local, provincial and federal laws as essential for competent practice. In Montreal, participants added "notions of national and provincial history", which may be particular to Quebec and its unique, contemporary and historical separatist movement. Further, practical knowledge related to technology and Robert's Rules of Order were cited by participants in Halifax as gaps in knowledge for migrant social workers.

Employers and regulators in both Montreal and Halifax expressed positive perspectives on the foundational social work knowledge and skills of migrant social workers. However, a significant gap was identified in migrants' "knowledge of secularist approaches in the government context". One supervisor said:

> "Sometimes, I find that newcomers who come from a country that is really religious can't accept that we can't bring that stuff to work. I can't talk with clients about God and praying. Or I can't talk about clients as 'all God's children'. I can talk about compassion and empathy, but not because we're all God's children. We can't talk like that. We have to be neutral." (Social work supervisor)

The weaving of knowledge and values is clear here, and the move into the belief systems of employers and employees proves murky indeed. The CASW's (2005) 'Code of ethics' forms the basis for the values and ethics of the profession in Canada, and it inherently supports a secularist approach to practice. Supervisors and employers expect allegiance with the code and attest that they, indeed, find this to be the case with internationally educated social workers. Internationally educated social workers themselves cited no challenge to the transferability of these values and ethical standards across national borders. Our research evidences that the broad aspirations of the social work profession to uphold the dignity and worth of all persons, to act with integrity and competence, to hold client information confidential, and to pursue causes of social justice (CASW, 2005) do, indeed, form the foundation for social work across international contexts. At the Halifax KEF, a collection of internationally educated social workers, employers and regulators shared a joint statement that "It's a matter of knowing the laws and ethics and how to respect confidentiality".

As we know, however, there are nuances to values and ethics, and a range of interpretations thereof. In Montreal, participants discussed varied opinions on how much personal information a practitioner should disclose and how much physical contact is appropriate. In Halifax, a social worker raised the concern that the provincial regulatory body was itself not aligned with the value of the pursuit of social justice in its treatment of internationally educated social workers: "The things they put us through – it's just not right. The cost, the waiting for answers, the runaround. And this is an organisation of social workers?" (internationally educated social worker).

Cultural adaptations

In Halifax, employers and regulators highlighted the benefits of diverse cultural adaptations and the lived experience of migrant social workers, noting that they bring unique perspectives precisely as a result of their lived experiences. One employer noted: "Internationally educated social workers bring their own practice experiences and unique worldviews to practice in Canada. Their lived experiences and diversity in culture could be seen as allowing them to work from a more culturally experienced lens" (social work employer).

Stakeholders in Montreal added that the personal attributes of internationally educated social workers reflect those they want to hire into their workplaces. Attributes such as "flexibility, perseverance, resourcefulness, self-confidence, courage to give one's opinions, initiative, optimism, the capacity to adapt, curiosity [and] patience" were thought to be not only required, but often found, in social workers new to Canada.

These data are a point of divergence from the experiences of some internationally educated social workers themselves, who reported feeling undervalued through their experiences of bureaucracy with credential recognition and licensing, and discrimination in job seeking (Brown et al, 2015). One participant at the Halifax KEF shared her view that employers lack understanding of cultural differences, which may manifest in professional practice; for example, she felt pressure to adapt to the Canadian norm of smiling as an expression of friendliness:

> "It is different if you come from Ukraine, you don't just smile at everyone. Some cultures don't smile and believe smiling is a sign of stupidity. You can do something that is normal in your culture and seen as really mean from a Canadian." (Internationally educated social worker)

Unique to Montreal's experience of social work migration is an agreement of labour mobility and credential recognition between Quebec and France. Due to shared culture and history, and this legislated agreement, there is an assumption of ease in transition between these two countries. Most internationally educated social workers did, indeed, find this to be the case; however, one talked about the difficulty adjusting his documentation style and learning the nuanced language of psychosocial reports in his new practice environment.

At both the Montreal and Halifax KEF, adapting to and integrating cultural practices was cited as critical for newcomer social workers. In Montreal, employers and stakeholders expressed the importance of migrant social workers understanding that indigenous people and people of African descent are members of unique groups with important histories that must be known. In Halifax, participants suggested that more education in local cultures be made available to newcomers. However, this was not a significant theme among internationally educated social workers themselves. Only a few spoke of needing to build awareness and understanding regarding populations and histories new to them; all others continued to cite the foundational values and ethics of the profession as assisting in adaptations to particular client groups. One social worker from the US explicitly named his comfort in working with Hispanic populations and 'American Indians', but that he was aware in moving to Canada that he needed to pay particular attention to the history of First Nations peoples in Canada. Migrant social workers themselves come from a range of countries, each with their own historical and contemporary experiences of colonialism. As Canada takes reconciliation action to change relationships, processes and systems between settlers and indigenous people (Truth and Reconciliation Commission of Canada, 2015), migrant social workers who have experience with colonialism and post-colonial dynamics can bring wisdom to the cultural adaptations under way.

Understanding of the Canadian social welfare system

The final substantive area of focus for employers and regulators in considering the readiness of internationally educated social workers was the need for understanding of the Canadian social welfare system. As with knowing the jurisdictional laws for the relevant field of practice, being oriented to federal policies of health care and justice, as well as provincial systems of education and child welfare, is considered critical. One supervisor said:

> "There are these things that you just have to know about, like how health care works in Canada and the child welfare laws of the province. Lots of us know it because of growing up here, or we learn it early on. All social workers have to know about those things. We always talk about context – well, this is like the political and legislative context, or parts of it anyway." (Social work supervisor)

Internationally educated social workers similarly named this factor as critical to their successful adaptation. Aligned with the previous quote, social workers know that context is important, both in understanding clients' lives and in understanding the role and scope of social work practice. Social workers from the Global North, notably, the US and the UK, experienced the fewest barriers in coming to understand the socio-political context.

Where there is a need to become oriented to the Canadian social welfare system, a representative from the regulatory body in Nova Scotia called on the School of Social Work at Dalhousie University to play a role:

> "The person might have taken a policy course, which is required to be equivalent to the Canadian degree, but that doesn't mean they know the Canadian policies. I think the School of Social Work should offer courses to newcomer social workers to help bridge. That's what [a particular school of social work] does." (Social work regulator)

Discussion

Readiness for practice comprises a nexus of factors among the internationally educated social worker, the site of social work practice and the regulation of the profession. Our research has clearly evidenced that adaptation is not solely a personally rooted and individually held phenomenon (Pullen Sansfaçon et al, 2014; Brown et al, 2015; Fulton et al, 2016). While complicated, the interaction of the efforts and intentions of employers, supervisors, colleagues and regulators, as well as the social workers themselves, is a necessary site of facilitation because each position rests upon the others in the ultimate aim of expanding the possibilities of social workers finding their place in Canadian social work practice. Indeed, one discussion group at the Halifax KEF squared the onus of social worker adaptation on the receiving province and local context rather than on the migrating practitioner, saying: "Very often we train immigrants to adapt to Canada. Perhaps we should change Canadians to adapt to immigrants". Another participant suggested that cultural competency education begin in public schools so that children unlearn the xenophobia for which, sadly, Nova Scotia is known. This shift in perspective and responsibility suggests a consciousness of removing barriers.

This example illustrates the need for the concepts of readiness and adaptation to broaden and include examination of the sociocultural and ideological context. This brings our analysis around again to neoliberalism, for the neoliberal tenets of self-sufficiency, personal responsibility, competition and merit underscore not only Canadian immigration policy (Shapaizman, 2010; Root et al, 2014), but also the nature and process of foreign credentials and experience assessment: equivalence with Canadian experience and Canadian education is the benchmark and neoliberal meritocracy upholds the illusion that this standard is equally available to all. Those who succeed do so because they deserve to, and those who do not succeed are personally responsible for their failing. This meritocracy masks the racism and xenophobia that are woven into the Canadian societal fabric, and the stories of internationally educated social workers substantiate that speculation about who is 'like us' and who is 'not like us' is always in operation. A participant from Nigeria sensed that employers viewed him with suspicion because of his foreign credentials; a social worker from Israel said, "I know it's very sad that I'm saying that, but ... I was lucky that I'm Caucasian. It's very sad for me to tell this. I know that that's a factor in the ability to get a job". These accounts connect migration, racism and neoliberalism. They are not surprising given that operations of the market – both labour markets and trade markets – are always underpinned by operations of material and discursive power. In the Canadian context, the white coloniser, wrapped in a cloak of neoliberalism, drives the machinery of who belongs.

Neoliberal federal and provincial social welfare policies have discontinued or reduced social spending, leading agencies to scale back resources and cut programmes, which increases the psychological and emotional toll on the practitioner (Baines, 2006; Smith, 2007; Wilson et al, 2011). Practitioners facing concurrent challenges like immigration, the assessment of foreign credentials and securing a licence are further pressured by demands at work and at home, creating a disconnect between what is required of migrating social workers in order to obtain employment and what is realistic. Bauder (2003, p 702) finds that 'rigorous certification systems favour individuals with Canadian education, training and experience, and disadvantage immigrants' across professions. Creese and Wiebe (2012) assert that this discrepancy is a strategic method of exclusion on the part of employers and professional associations, and assert that employers and professional associations are implicated in the deskilling and marginalisation of professionals who migrate to Canada. The authors cite Grace-Edward Galabuzi (2006) in naming this systemic marginalisation as 'economic apartheid' (Creese and Wiebe, 2012, p 58). This systemic discrimination is echoed by internationally educated social workers in our study (see

Brown et al, 2015). However, in contrast, Fouché et al (2014) found that migrant social workers in New Zealand are perceived positively by employers given the diversity of experience, knowledge and skills that they bring to their new professional context.

Internationally educated social workers in our study were clear that their adaptation to Canadian social work would be facilitated if there was a coordinated system wherein employers, regulators and educators in social work understand each other's roles and work together to streamline information and processes that build towards employment. In Halifax, such a consortium was, indeed, established – the International Social Workers Stakeholder Group – organised with administrative support from the Immigrant Settlement Association of Nova Scotia (see: www.isans.ca). The group has representation from the Dalhousie University School of Social Work, the Nova Scotia College of Social Workers and several large employers, government included, with guest membership from the CASW and Citizenship and Immigration Canada. The group is currently developing a proposal to the Dalhousie University School of Social Work for a 'bridging programme' to educate in the areas assessed by the CASW as lacking in the migrant social worker's degree from the country of origin. The group's genesis and momentum grew from the KEF held in Halifax. A different platform (but a similar initiative) is the website developed as a result of the Pullen Sansfaçon et al study during 2012–15 (available at: www.socialworkmigration.ca). The website serves as a portal for internationally educated social workers, employers, regulators and educators to learn about the other positions relative to the issues and to communicate with one another in an effort to ease adaptation to social work in Canada.

It is clear that internationally educated social workers, employers and regulators are bound together in this matrix of credentialing, licensing and employment. Along with all practising social workers, educators, researchers and scholars, service users, and the specifics of contexts of practice, all are engaged in constructing and refining definitions and expressions of social work practice (Beddoe et al, 2012). As social workers continue to work amid the constraints of neoliberal ideology and policy, we need to actively build collaboration among the stakeholders to not only remove barriers to licensing and employment, but strive to achieve the aspirations of the profession as set out by the CASW (2005) and the Canadian Association for Social Work Education, grounded in the 'Global standards for social work practice' developed jointly by the International Federation of Social

Workers (2012, 2014a, 2014b) and the International Association of Schools of Social Work.

Conclusion

This chapter presented data from employers, supervisors and regulators of social work, along with internationally educated social workers, which was generated through KEF held in Montreal, Quebec, and Halifax, Nova Scotia, at the end of a four-year study exploring the adaptation processes of migrant social workers. There are many shared priorities among these stakeholders. At the same time, there is a call for increased collaboration among stakeholders to facilitate the adaptation of internationally educated social workers and assist their integration into the profession. Partnership generated among employers and regulators, internationally educated social workers and other practitioners, educators, researchers, and service users can resist the material and discursive manifestations of neoliberalism. Together, we can reach for the social justice aspirations of the profession, not only in direct client and community practice, but in its workforce as well.

References

Aronson, J. and Sammon, S. (2000) 'Practice amid social service cuts and restructuring: working with the contradictions of small victories', *Canadian Social Work Review*, 17(2): 167–87.

Baines, D. (2006) 'Social work and neo-liberalism: if you could change one thing', *Social Work*, 59(1): 20–34.

Bauder, H. (2003) '"Brain abuse", or the devaluation of immigrant labour in Canada', *Antipode*, 35(4): 699–717.

Beddoe, L., Fouché, C., Bartley, A. and Harington, P. (2012) 'Migrant social workers' experience in New Zealand: education and supervision issues', *Social Work Education*, 31(8): 1012–31.

Brown, M., Pullen Sansfaçon, A., *Éthier*, S. and Fulton, A. (2015) 'A complicated welcome: social workers navigate policy, organizational contexts and socio-cultural dynamics following migration to Canada', *International Journal of Social Science Studies*, 3(1): 58–68.

Carniol, B. (2005) *Case critical: The dilemma of social work in Canada*, Toronto: Between the Lines.

CASW (Canadian Association of Social Workers) (2005) 'Code of ethics'. Available at: https://casw-acts.ca/sites/casw-acts.ca/files/documents/casw_code_of_ethics.pdf

Creese, G. and Wiebe, B. (2012) '"Survival employment": gender and deskilling among African immigrants in Canada', *International Migration*, 50(5): 56–76.

Fouché, C., Beddoe, L., Bartley, A. and Brenton, N. (2014) 'Strengths and struggles: overseas qualified social workers' experiences in Aotearoa New Zealand', *Australian Social Work*, 67(4): 551–66.

Fulton, A.E., Pullen Sansfaçon, A., Brown, M., Éthier, S. and Graham, J. (2016) 'Migrant social workers, foreign credential recognition and securing employment in Canada', *Canadian Social Work Review*, 33(1): 65–86.

International Federation of Social Workers (2012) 'Global standards'. Available at: http://ifsw.org/policies/global-standards/

International Federation of Social Workers (2014a) 'Global definition of social work'. Available at: http://ifsw.org/policies/definition-of-social-work/

International Federation of Social Workers (2014b) 'Global agenda for social work and social development: first report – promoting social and economic equalities', *International Social Work*, 57(S4): 3–16.

Mananzala, R. and Spade, D. (2008) 'The nonprofit industrial complex and trans resistance', *Sexuality Research & Social Policy*, 5(1): 53–71.

Mullaly, R. (2008) *The new structural social work*, Toronto: Oxford.

Newberry-Koroluk, A.M. (2014) 'Hitting the ground running: neo-conservatism and first-year Canadian social workers', *Critical Social Work*, 15(1): 42–54.

Pullen Sansfaçon, A., Brown, M. and Graham, J.R. (2012) 'International migration of professional social workers: toward a theoretical framework for understanding professional adaptation processes', *Social Development Issues*, 34(2): 37–50.

Pullen Sansfaçon, A., Brown, M., Graham, J. and Michaud, A. (2014) 'Adaptation and acculturation: experiences of internationally educated social workers', *Journal of International Migration and Integration*, 15(2): 317–30.

Root, J., Gates-Gesse, E., Shields, J. and Bauder, H. (2014) 'Discounting immigrant families: neoliberalism and the framing of Canadian immigration policy change', RCIS Working Paper No. 2014/7, Ryerson Centre for Immigration and Settlement.

Shapaizman, I. (2010) *The influence of neo-liberal ideas and political conflict on the privatization process of immigrant policy: A comparison of Israel, Canada and the Netherlands*, Maryland, MD: Centre for International Policy Exchanges.

Smith, K. (2007) 'Social work, restructuring and resistance: "Best practices" gone under-ground', in D. Baines (ed) *Doing anti-oppressive practice: Building transformative, politicized social work*, Halifax: Fernwood Books.

Truth and Reconciliation Commission of Canada (2015) 'Final report', Winnipeg, Manitoba. Available at: http://www.trc.ca/websites/trcinstitution/index.php?p=11

Weinberg, M. and Taylor, S. (2014) '"Rogue" social workers: the problem with rules for ethical behaviour', *Critical Social Work*, 15: 1.

Wilson, M.G., Calhoun, A. and Whitmore, E. (2011) 'Contesting the neoliberal agenda: lessons from Canadian activists', *Canadian Social Work Review*, 28(1): 25–46.

THIRTEEN

Will she be right, mate?
Standards and diversity in Australian
social work

Karen Healy

Australia's National Regulation and Accreditation Scheme

Health and human service professions work with people who experience a range of life challenges. In Australia, as in other wealthy countries, governments provide a framework for the regulation of the health and human services professions. Considerable variation exists internationally as to how governments regulate these professions and which professions are subject to government regulation. As we will discuss in this section, in Australia, a national regulation scheme exists for some health and human service professions; however, social work is not included within this scheme.

In Australia, a National Registration and Accreditation Scheme (NRAS) was introduced by the commonwealth government in 2010. The NRAS is administered by the Australian Health Practitioners Regulation Agency (AHPRA), which is a government body. At the time the NRAS was established, national registration was confined to those health professions that were already regulated or partially regulated by state or territory governments (Commonwealth Department of Health, 2016). The NRAS was intended to replace the patchwork of state- and territory-based registration schemes, which were costly and cumbersome to administer.

Ten professions were included in the NRAS when it commenced in 2010. The 10 professions are: chiropractors; dental practitioners (including dentists, dental hygienists, dental prosthetists and dental therapists); medical practitioners; nurses and midwives; optometrists; osteopaths; pharmacists; physiotherapists; podiatrists; and psychologists. In 2012, a review of NRAS led to the inclusion in the scheme of four further health professions (AHPA, 2012). These professions are: Aboriginal and Torres Strait Islander health practitioners; Chinese medicine practitioners (including acupuncturists, Chinese herbal medicine practitioners and Chinese herbal dispensers); medical radiation practitioners (including diagnostic radiographers, radiation therapists and nuclear medicine technologists); and occupational therapists. In 2015, the Council of Australian Governments Health Council (COAG Health Council, 2015) announced that paramedics will be included in the NRAS, although the time frame for this remains unclear.

The NRAS provides a legal and policy infrastructure for regulating professional competence of the health and human service professions under its jurisdiction. Each of the 14 professions included in the NRAS has its own regulatory board that oversees and monitors professional education and standards. The monitoring role includes requiring registered practitioners to have completed specified qualifications and engage in ongoing professional development in order to maintain currency of practice, as well as requirements for additional support and education for practitioners re-entering practice after a period of absence. The regulatory boards also manage concerns about individual practitioners. These boards have the power to sanction (including removal of the right to practise) individual practitioners who are found to have breached professional standards as specified by the NRAS. Furthermore, severe financial penalties apply to individuals or services who falsely claim to hold registered qualifications.

Many health and human service professionals, such as social workers, audiologists, speech pathologists and dieticians, are not included in the NRAS and, as such, are largely unregulated by the government. Remarkably, social workers were not included despite being the largest allied health profession in Australia (AASW, 2011, p 9). The exclusion of social workers from national registration is not well known to the public. A survey conducted in 2010 on a representative sample of Australians found that more than 90% of people believed that counselling professionals, including social workers, can be struck off or prohibited from practising if they are found guilty of serious misconduct (AASW, 2011, p 11). This public confidence in safeguards to address misconduct is not well founded in the unregulated context in which social workers and many other allied health professionals practise.

Entry to the NRAS is determined by Australian health ministers, which includes the ministers of health of each state and territory and the commonwealth minister of health. The Australian Health Ministers' Advisory Council (AHMAC) indicates that public safety can be achieved without the further extension of the NRAS (AHMAC, 2014; COAG Health Council, 2015). In 2013, the AHMAC introduced a national code of conduct (NCC) as a strategy for protecting the public from misconduct by unregistered health-care practitioners, including social workers (AHMAC, 2014). The NCC involves a form of negative licensing through which members of currently unregulated health professions such as social workers can be subject to disciplinary action through various state and territory complaints tribunals. The NCC for unregistered health practitioners strengthens government authorities' power to investigate alleged breaches of conduct by health-care practitioners and to issue prohibition orders against those found to have engaged in serious misconduct. While the NCC does go some way to addressing professional misconduct, it does not provide a framework for educational preparation, professional workplace support and the monitoring of professionals that could assist in preventing malpractice and misconduct (AASW, 2013). The NCC is not yet in place in all states and territories of Australia and so the patchwork of even this weaker form of regulation is not yet available to users of the services of self-regulating health professions. Furthermore, the NCC will only apply to workers in health occupations, so, for example, concerns about social workers working in child protection or community services will not be addressed by the code.

While the profession of social work continues to be excluded from the NRAS, there is some recent political pressure for health ministers to reconsider the government regulation of the social work profession. Following the tragic death of Chloe Valentine (who was a child known to child protection authorities), the South Australian coroner called for the regulation of social workers either through inclusion in the NRAS or through the establishment of a state-level regulation scheme (Johns, 2015). In 2015, the COAG Health Council issued a communiqué which stated that:

> Ministers discussed a South Australian proposal to include social workers in the NRAS following two coronial inquests in SA which recommended such national registration. This issue has been referred to the Australian Health Ministers' Advisory Council for further work and advice back to Ministers at a future meeting. (COAG Health Council, 2015)

This is the second time since 2012 that health ministers have reconsidered the case for the inclusion of social work in the NRAS. Previously, a national review of NRAS did not support the case for its further extension to any currently unregistered health professions

(Snowball, 2014). At the time of writing, no further information on health ministers' deliberations on whether they will reconsider the inclusion of social work in the NRAS was available.

Self-regulating professions: implications for standards and diversity

For the time being, social work in Australia remains a self-regulated profession. This section will define professional self-regulation and its implications for maintaining standards and promoting diversity within the profession.

The term 'self-regulated' means that the profession takes it upon itself to be a 'reliable guarantor for the competence and conduct of its members' (Dixon-Woods et al, 2011, p 1452). In Australia, professional standards for social workers are regulated through the Australian Association of Social Workers (AASW), a membership-based voluntary organisation comprising professional social workers and students studying for AASW-accredited social work degrees. The AASW's regulatory functions include setting and monitoring standards of ethical behaviour for its members through its code of ethics. In the case of serious misconduct, sanctions can include the removal of eligibility for membership, which can affect the individual's employment status and eligibility for service-fee rebates through the Commonwealth Medicare Scheme.

The AASW also establishes education standards and practice standards. The Australian Social Work Education and Accreditation Standards (ASWEAS) provide the guidelines through which the AASW establishes and monitors universities and colleges providing social work education in Australia. Social work programmes must maintain compliance with the education standards in order for graduates to be eligible for AASW membership. While, under Australian competition policy, employers cannot insist that employees are members of the AASW, they can require that social work staff are eligible for AASW membership. In a context of self-regulation, eligibility for AASW membership has become the primary standard for employers and consumers to identify whether a social worker has either a recognised Australian social work qualification or an international social work qualification approved by the AASW.

The ASWEAS are structured around nine graduate attributes. These attributes are consistent with the 'Global standards for the education and training of the social work profession' (Sewpaul and Jones, 2004). To meet the attributes, Australian social work education programmes need to support students to develop: a professional identity as a social worker; understanding of social work ethics and of principles pertaining to social justice and human rights; knowledge of human behaviour and of society; and a sound base in practice methods with individuals, groups and families. While social work programmes internationally specify the importance of social workers' appreciation of cultural difference, the Australian standards emphasise the importance of students' awareness of culturally competent practice with Aboriginal and Torres Strait Islander people. The ASWEAS standards require that students develop an appreciation of the impact of European colonisation on Aboriginal and Torres Strait Islander people and an understanding of culturally competent practice in face of this history and its ongoing negative influence on the life opportunities and experiences of Aboriginal and Torres Strait Islander people. In addition to the emphasis on culturally competent practice with Aboriginal and Torres Strait Islander people, social work education programmes must also provide core curricula in mental health practice, child well-being and protection, and intercultural practice.

The AASW does have some additional capacity to authorise and monitor professional practice in the field of mental health social work. Through the AASW, members with relevant professional experience in mental health social work can apply to be accredited mental health social workers. The AASW approval of a social worker to practise as such enables the practitioner to be eligible for various fee-for-service rebates through the Commonwealth Medicare rebate scheme. The commonwealth has authorised the AASW to accredit appropriately qualified mental health social workers and obliges the AASW to ensure that the practitioner retains currency of practice. Employers and consumers can use eligibility for AASW accreditation to assess whether the social worker has completed a programme of social work education approved by the AASW.

Whereas the NRAS scheme requires all registered practitioners to maintain currency of practice, self-regulating professions are more limited in their capacity to set and monitor professional standards for practitioners after they have met the basic entry requirements for their profession. Nonetheless, the AASW has established strategies to encourage members to maintain currency of practice. These strategies include:

• The introduction of an accredited social worker status to provide public recognition of workers who maintain currency of practice. Only AASW members who can demonstrate ongoing engagement in continuing professional development to at least 30 hours of such activity annually are eligible for accredited social worker status.

• The implementation of a credentialing system to recognise social workers' expertise and engagement in ongoing learning in specific fields of practice. The AASW credential system will recognise practitioners in a range of fields, including in child protection, family violence, health services, school social work and social work in disability services. This credential system is intended to encourage practitioners to develop expertise and to provide employers and service users with indicators of service provider capacity.

Assessing international social work qualifications

Australia has a high migration inflow relative to its population (Czaika and Haas, 2014). Australian government migration policy places a high priority on attracting 'skilled' migrants 'in order to meet Australia's labour needs' (Phillips and Spinks, 2012, p 1). Almost 70% of Australia's migrant intake are skilled migrants (Phillips and Spinks, 2012), and social work is currently on the skills shortage list.

The Australian government has delegated authority to the AASW to assess social work qualifications for internationally qualified social workers seeking to migrate to Australia. The AASW uses the ASWEAS to assess whether an international social work qualification is commensurate with Australian social work education standards. To be regarded as equivalent to the AASW standard, the qualification must be in social work and be regarded as the professional social work qualification of the country of the international applicant. In addition, the learning outcomes must be similar and there must be equivalent levels of field education included in the programme. Applicants must also demonstrate high standards of English proficiency.

The AASW encourages social workers who have qualified in other countries to develop an understanding of the history and continuing impact of European colonisation on Indigenous Australians. The AASW has developed a learning resource that outlines this history and its continuing impact, which also includes reference to a range of resources for further professional development. However, beyond this introduction, neither the Australian government nor the AASW requires internationally qualified social workers to undertake further professional learning activities relevant to adaption to Australian history or culture, or of the ongoing legacy of European colonisation. Social workers migrating to the country can engage in continuing learning opportunities but they are not required to do so. This limited preparation for cultural transition has been noted in many other national contexts (Fouché et al, 2016).

Self-regulation: standards and diversity

Self-regulation has some advantages in relation to professional standards and responsiveness to diverse service user needs. The main advantage of self-regulation is that the profession retains autonomy over defining its scope of practice. In the context of self-regulation, membership of the AASW through its elected board defines the scope of social work practice and the educational, ethical and practice standards for the profession. These standards are regularly reviewed with the membership and by invitation to stakeholder groups, including employers, educational bodies and consumers. By contrast, the NRAS requires each of the professional boards to include people who are independent of the profession and also to include service users. Thus, government regulation of the social work profession would necessarily require the involvement of people other than social workers in defining the profession's scope of practice.

International experience also indicates that the involvement of a government regulatory authority can dilute the critical focus and values orientation on which our profession prides itself and shift the focus of regulation to the demonstration and monitoring of practitioners' technical capacities (Kirwin and Melaugh, 2015). International evidence also suggests that government regulation changes the way in which concerns and complaints about individual practitioners are managed (Kirwin and Melaugh, 2015). Under a government regulatory scheme, complaints about professional practice are formalised, and in the Australian context, findings of misconduct against individual practitioners are published in detail on the NRAS site. By contrast, as a self-regulatory body, the AASW seeks as far as possible to support practitioners to address concerns about misconduct through a confidential process of professional review and, where appropriate, through reconciliation with the person who has complained about the conduct. The names of practitioners who are currently ineligible for AASW membership are published on the association's website but details of misconduct remain confidential. The AASW is committed to preserving the privacy of the complainant and the practitioner, and to support, as far as possible, the practitioner's capacity to address practice failings and misconduct. If the social work profession becomes regulated through NRAS, the AASW will lose its authority to manage complaints or to determine the process through which complaints are managed.

Self-regulation also, potentially, offers the profession scope to determine its own boundaries and thus, potentially, to support diversity within the profession. Any form of regulation requires the regulatory authority to articulate a range of professional standards, including: educational standards for entrants to the profession; annual continuing professional development requirements; and professional conduct standards. Some commentators express concern that government regulation will lead to the exclusion of competent practitioners who lack the qualifications or experience required to meet registration requirements (McDonald, 2006; Van Heugten, 2011). In particular, concerns exist about how government regulation could recognise and support the diverse qualification base that exists among the Australian community service workforce (Chenoweth and McAuliffe, 2011). Yet, this argument about the exclusionary character of government regulation also applies to self-regulation, where the professional association assumes responsibility for determining who is eligible for membership of the professional association and for the various credentials developed within the AASW.

In summary, the advantages of self-regulation are that it offers opportunities for members of a profession to determine their identity and to monitor the practice of those members who agree to participate in a self-regulatory body. The second advantage that self-regulation offers is greater scope for diversity within a profession; however, in practice, both government and self-regulation require educational criteria and compliance with practice standards that, in effect, operate to exclude those who do not comply with these requirements.

Problems of self-regulation: standards and diversity

Having considered the advantages of self-regulation for supporting professional standards and diversity, we turn now to the challenges. The first challenge is that self-regulating professions have very little authority to compel members of the profession or employing agencies to recognise the standards set by the professional regulation body. The AASW, as a self-regulating body for social work in Australia, has jurisdiction only over its members and over those institutions that wish to offer 'AASW-accredited' educational programmes. The government regulation authority that oversees the NRAS has a range of legally enforceable sanctions for misconduct by individual practitioners or their employers, such as in relation to false or misleading claims about qualifications held by a practitioner. In contrast, the options available to the AASW for managing concerns about individuals or educational institutions are more constrained. The most significant penalty that the AASW can apply to an individual member is to withdraw their eligibility for membership, and, similarly, the AASW can withdraw accreditation for educational programmes that fail to meet the national educational standards outlined by the AASW.

Beyond some limited authority over members and educational institutions, the AASW's capacity to assert professional standards in the broader community is limited. The AASW has no power to protect the title 'social worker', with the consequence that the AASW has little right of reply to public reporting of scandals involving unqualified personnel in social work roles. The AASW has no authority to compel employers to confine social-work-designated positions to social workers who have graduated from AASW-accredited programmes, nor to require individuals or employers to ensure that graduates show evidence of recent and current practice. Furthermore, the COAG has refused even to support the AASW (and other self-regulating health professions) to operate a 'voluntary register' of professionals so as to support the public recognition of workers who choose to participate in self-regulation through their professional association, as recommended by the independent reviewer of the NRAS (Snowball, 2014, p 6).

In the case of Australian social work, the capacity of the professional body to effectively regulate the profession is further weakened by the relatively low uptake of membership by social work practitioners and students. In recent years, there has been a significant increase in AASW membership, with the membership numbers close to doubling between 2011 and 2016 to reach 10,000 members. Even with this large growth, the proportion of practising social workers who are members of the AASW is, at best, 50% of those eligible for membership. This contrasts markedly with other self-regulating professions in Australia. For example, the workforce data on dieticians indicate that more than 90% of qualified dieticians in Australia are members of their professional association (Health Workforce Australia, 2014; Dieticians Association of Australia, 2015). One reason for this is that many members of these professions maintain a private practice and, in Australia, governments authorise the professional associations to assess and monitor eligibility for Medicare rebates for fee-for-service work. Among dieticians and speech therapists, then, there exists a financial incentive for graduates to maintain membership of their professional body and, as such, to submit to the standards required of their professional association.

A further challenge associated with self-regulation relates to the ambivalence and, in some cases, the hostility of employers to workforce professionalisation in the community services sector.

For example, in 2007, the Queensland child protection authority announced a workforce policy focused on 'diversifying' the child protection workforce. The Department of Child Safety workforce consultation document asserted that the knowledge and skills base held by professional social workers and human services professionals was no longer relevant to front-line child protection work. The position of the Department of Child Safety (2007, p 7) was that:

> Historically, these degrees [in social work and behavioural sciences] were well aligned with the underpinning knowledge required to work in the child protection sector. In all cases they contain material relevant to child and family issues which matched respective roles of CSOs [Child Safety Officers]. This role has now changed. The change is [sic] not merely been in the form of repositioning the department to a solely statutory child protection focus, but in the specialization of roles and the sophistication of systems and processes essential to working in a high risk, statutory environment. This sophistication has occurred in the form of increased evidentiary requirements, familiarity with the pseudo legal discourse [sic], records management, forensic investigation, workload management and other specializations.

While the AASW made representations to the child safety authority advocating for the value of social work professionals in front-line practice, the capacity of the AASW to influence workforce policy was limited. Continuing escalation of high turnover rates of front-line workers following the introduction of this workforce diversification policy was ultimately reviewed in a commission of inquiry. Drawing on AASW evidence, the commissioner found that the workforce policy of the Department of Child Safety had contributed to workforce turnover and recommended that front-line staff be appropriately qualified in social work or related disciplines (Carmody, 2013).

The absence of government regulation in social work and many other allied health professions might also increase the vulnerability of service users in the context of consumer-directed care policies. In particular, the Australian government is currently introducing a National Disability Insurance Scheme (NDIS), which proposes to revolutionise the way in which disability services are organised and provided. A key characteristic of the NDIS is consumer choice over service providers and service types (Fawcett and Plath, 2014). Without government regulation of professional standards, consumers will have little guarantee that the professional providing services to them is appropriately qualified or has maintained currency of their practice. Furthermore, service users will have limited recourse regarding substandard services provided by practitioners who are not regulated by the NRAS and who have chosen not to be members of their professional organisations. This lack of consumer protection is a concern given research findings indicating that when support services are opened to private enterprise, as proposed in the NDIS, for-profit providers tend to be of poorer quality than not-for-profit and government services (Meagher, 2010, cited in Fawcett and Plath, 2014, p 755).

Another area of challenge to maintaining high professional standards by self-regulating professions relates to the inherent difficulties associated with the peer assessment of professional standards. Whereas government regulation involves the independent assessment of complaints of professional misconduct, self-regulating professions must maintain their own processes for managing such concerns. This reliance on peer review can compromise the monitoring of professional conduct and educational standards. In their analysis of the demise of the self-regulation of the British medical profession, Dixon-Woods et al (2011) point to the failures of the British General Medical Council in preventing or adequately addressing the medical scandals that resulted in the abuse, serious injury or death of patients. Indeed, the litany of failures by the General Medical Council led doctors to pass a motion of no confidence in their own council (BBC, 2000). Dixon-Woods et al (2011, p 1455) concluded that within the self-regulatory model, the 'system imperative to engage in monitoring and correction of deviant behaviour was in conflict with the social imperatives for collegial cooperation'. Similar institutional and professional failings have been exposed in a myriad of public inquiries into health and welfare institutions in Australia. Repeatedly, those before these inquiries have highlighted the tendency of powerful groups to serve their own interests rather than those of the most vulnerable with whom they are practising (Healy, 2015).

What, then, of diversity within the profession in the context of self-regulation? There is little evidence that self-regulation offers greater prospects than government regulation for achieving cultural or gender diversity in health and human service professions. Social work in Australia is characterised by strong female participation in the profession and with high participation of older workers. The ageing profile of the social work workforce is due, in part, to the older age at which workers enter this profession, which is, on average, much later than in other allied health and human service occupations (Healy and Lonne, 2010). In the para-professional workforce, people from culturally and linguistically diverse backgrounds and Indigenous people are represented at higher levels than in the general population, but this is not so for graduates at degree level (Meagher and Healy, 2005; AIFS, 2009). Workers from culturally and linguistically diverse backgrounds and from Indigenous communities are underrepresented in the social work professional workforce, compared to both their numbers in the population and among para-professionals in the workforce (Meagher and Healy, 2005; AIFS, 2009).

Furthermore, self-regulating professions might have fewer opportunities and requirements for consumer participation than do regulated professions. Currently, all boards operating under the NRAS are required to include members from outside the profession and people who are consumers of services. By contrast, insofar as self-regulating bodies require members of their boards and advisory committee to be members of their professional association, their capacity to include consumers and other people in decision-making roles is limited.

Social work standards: the importance of collaboration

In the absence of government regulation, the social work profession in Australia is almost entirely dependent on the professional association, the AASW, to establish and monitor professional standards. The authority of the AASW to enforce these standards is constrained because the AASW has low membership rates, relative to other allied health professions, and very little standing in law to enforce its standards among non-members and within the community. The AASW does not even have the legal entitlement to protect the title 'social worker'. The broader policy environment also contains challenges as funding bodies, employers and consumers may express ambivalence towards the need for professional standards, especially where this increases the costs of services. As has been outlined, the AASW has established a series of protocols for establishing and monitoring professional standards; however, these are largely dependent on a voluntary agreement between those who choose to be members of the AASW or for institutions that wish to avail themselves of AASW accreditation. In this challenging environment, the AASW has also recognised the value of collaboration with other organisations that share a commitment to professional standards in social work and related fields. We will discuss these collaborations here.

First, the AASW is collaborating with other self-regulating allied health and human service professions to develop a model of self-regulation that mirrors many of the features of the NRAS (see AHPA, 2012). The AASW is a founding member alongside other self-regulating professions, such as speech therapists and dieticians, of the National Alliance of Self-Regulating Health Professions (NASRHP). The AASW will have a seat on the board of NASRHP and the alliance will support the monitoring of professional standards, including fitness to practise and continuing profession educational standards, for members of self-regulating health professions. As a member of NASRHP, the AASW will continue to advocate for the government to provide legislative support for voluntary registers within self-regulating professions. Legislative support may increase public confidence and safety by obliging social workers on the voluntary register to participate in a system of professional self-regulation.

Second, in 2014, the AASW signed a memorandum of understanding (MOU) with the New Zealand Social Workers Registration Board (SWRB). The MOU applies only to social workers who have completed an AASW-accredited social work qualification, *or* social workers who have completed a recognised New Zealand social work qualification, are currently fully registered with the SWRB and are eligible to hold an Annual Practising Certificate. The MOU facilitates the expedited assessment of the qualifications of social workers from either country seeking accreditation in the other country. Through this partnership, the AASW and SWRB together commit to maintaining agreed standards of social work education and practice, and, as such, each partner consults the other in relation to any review of a proposed change of standard. The partnership recognises cultural differences between the two countries and, as such, both the AASW and SWRB require social workers seeking recognition to engage in preparation for culturally responsive and inclusive practice relevant to the country where they seek to practise. For example, as part of the accreditation process, the AASW provides social workers qualified in New Zealand with information about preparing for culturally responsive and inclusive social work practice in relation to Aboriginal and Torres Strait Islander communities in Australia.

Third, the AASW is striving to increase its accountability to those who use its services. An important lesson of the failure of the British General Medical Council as a self-regulating body is that it reminds us 'of the practical problem of confronting deviance, and [that] the tolerance and protection of the inept, are pervasive features of all organised groups' (Dixon-Woods et al, 2011, p 1458). This flaw of organised groups becomes magnified in the context of self-regulating professions when the profession loses sight of the interests of outsiders, particularly service users and those who care for them. The involvement of outsiders to the profession in determining standards and in monitoring conduct is recognised under national law for registered health professions and protects those standards from collusion or misuse within the profession. The AASW has begun to involve consumers in key consultations, such as in the review of the Australian Social Work Education and Accreditation Standards. Similarly, as the NASRHP develops, it will be important to include voices outside the social work profession, particularly those who use services and those who care for them, in assisting the NASRHP to improve standards. For public safety, it seems important that this is the case.

Conclusion

In the absence of government regulation, the AASW is the self-regulating body responsible for establishing and monitoring professional education, practice and ethical standards for social work in Australia. The AASW also has delegated government authority to assess the qualifications of social workers seeking to migrate to Australia. In this process, the AASW does encourage internationally qualified social workers to develop awareness of the Australian cultural context, particularly the ongoing legacy of European colonisation for Indigenous Australians. However, beyond a basic introduction to the Australian context, it becomes the responsibility of the social workers migrating to Australia and their employers to promote the person's cultural transition.

As a self-regulatory body, the AASW has limited capacity to challenge employer ambivalence towards a professionally qualified workforce, with the consequence that the position of professionally qualified workers in traditional areas of social work practice, such as child protection, has, at times, been eroded. Changes in the policy environment, particularly an increasing focus on consumer-directed care, have the potential to increase consumer choice but also consumer vulnerability in the absence of government regulation of professional standards and conduct. Collaboration with other organisations and individuals with a stake in high professional standards is vital to strengthening the Australian social work profession's capacity to establish and enforce these standards. To this end, the AASW is actively collaborating with partners in New Zealand and other self-regulating professions in Australia, and is seeking to strengthen consumer voices in establishing and maintaining professional standards. While the professional association continues to advocate for inclusion in the NRAS, it is also recognised that the collaborations across the Tasman, with other allied health professions and with consumers, are important in supporting high standards and responsiveness to diverse human needs.

References

AASW (Australian Association of Social Workers) (2011) *Protecting the health and wellbeing of Australians: Submission to health ministers on the national regulation of the profession of social work*, Canberra: AASW. Available at: http://www.aasw.asn.au/social-policy-advocacy/key-documents

AASW (2013) *Registration and title protection for AASW members: Directions paper for practice*, Melbourne: AASW. Available at: https://www.aasw.asn.au/social-policy-advocacy/latest-campaign-actions

AHMAC [Australian Health Ministers' Advisory Council] (2014) *A National Code of Conduct for Health Care Workers*, Canberra: Australian Government. Available at: www.coaghealthcouncil.gov.au/NationalCodeOfConductForHealthCareWorkers

AHPA (Allied Health Professions Australia) (2012) *Harnessing self-regulation to support safety and quality in healthcare delivery: A comprehensive model for regulating all health practitioners*, Melbourne: AHPA.

AIFS (Australian Institute of Family Studies) (2009) 'Workforce issues across the family relationship services sector: models, responses and strategies', AFRC Issues No 5. Available at: https://aifs.gov.au/cfca/publications/workforce-issues-across-family-relationship-services-sec/3-workforce-composition-and

BBC (British Broadcasting Corporation) (2000) 'GMC loses doctors' backing', 29 June. Available at: http://news.bbc.co.uk/2/hi/health/811421.stm

Carmody, T. (2013) *Taking responsibility: A roadmap for Queensland child protection*, Brisbane: Queensland Government. Available at: http://www.childprotectioninquiry.qld.gov.au/publications

Chenoweth, L. and McAuliffe, D. (2011) *The road to social work and human services practice*, South Melbourne: Cengage Learning.

COAG (Council of Australian Governments) Health Council (2015) 'Communique', 7 August, Independent Review of the National Registration and Accreditation Scheme for Health Professions. Available at: http://www.coaghealthcouncil.gov.au/Publications/Reports/ArtMID/514/ArticleID/68/The-Independent-Review-of-the-National-Registration-and-Accreditation-Scheme-for-health-professionals

Commonwealth Department of Health (2016) 'National Registration and Accreditation Scheme'. Available at: http://www.health.gov.au/internet/main/publishing.nsf/content/work-nras

Czaika, M. and Haas, H. (2014) 'The globalization of migration: has the world become more migratory?', *International Migration Review*, 48(2): 283–323.

Department of Child Safety (2007) *Review of the qualifications and training pathways: Department of Child Safety, Queensland, consultation paper*, Brisbane: Department of Child Safety.

Dieticians Association of Australia (2015) 'About DAA'. Available at: http://daa.asn.au/for-the-public/about-daa/

Dixon-Woods, M., Yeung, K. and Bosk, C. (2011) 'Why is UK medicine no longer a self-regulating profession? The role of scandals involving "bad apple" doctors', *Social Science and Medicine*, 73: 1452–9.

Fawcett, B. and Plath, D. (2014) 'A national disability insurance scheme: what social work has to offer', *British Journal of Social Work*, 44(3): 747–62.

Fouché, C., Beddoe, L., Bartley, A. and Parkes, E. (2016) 'Are we ready for them? Overseas-qualified social workers' professional cultural transition', *European Journal of Social Work*, 19(1): 106–19.

Health Workforce Australia (2014) *Australia's health workforce series – dietitians in focus*, Canberra: HWA. Available at: https://www.google.co.nz/url?sa=t&rct=j&q=&esrc=s&source=web&cd=1&cad=rja&uact=8&ved=0ahUKEwiPuOCS4IrWAhWCVbwKHSoRDt4QFgglMAA&url=http%3A%2F%2Fiaha.com.au%2Fwp-content%2Fuploads%2F2014%2F03%2FHWA_Australias-Health-Workforce-Series_Dietitians-in-focus_vF_LR.pdf&usg=AFQjCNHoWec76lGoSTFmdQIOPsjG0eW1yA

Healy, K. (2015) 'Becoming a trustworthy profession: doing better than doing good', *Australian Social Work*, 70(sup 1): 7–16, doi:10.1080/0312407X.2014.973550.

Healy, K. and Lonne, B. (2010) *The social work and human services workforce: A report from a national study of education, training and workforce needs*, Sydney: Australian Learning and Teaching Council, Strawberry Hills.

Johns, M. (2015) *Coronial inquest into the death of Chloe Lee Valentine*, Adelaide, South Australia: State Coroner.

Kirwan, G. and Melaugh, B. (2015) 'Taking care: criticality and reflexivity in the context of social work registration', *British Journal of Social Work*, 45(3): 1050–9.

McDonald, C. (2006) *Challenging social work: The institutional context of practice*, Basingstoke: Palgrave MacMillan.

Meagher, G. (2010) 'Is choice the enemy of equality?', keynote address at the Transforming Care Conference, Copenhagen, 21–23 June.

Meagher, G. and Healy, K. (2005) *Who cares? Volume 1: A profile of care workers in Australia's community services industries*, Sydney: ACOSS.

Phillips, J. and Spinks, H. (2012) *Skilled migration: Temporary and permanent flows to Australia*, Canberra: Parliament of Australia.

Sewpaul, V. and Jones, D. (2004) 'Global standards for the education and training of the social work profession', International Association of Schools of Social Work. Available at: https://www.iassw-aiets.org/global-standards-for-social-work-education-and-training/

Snowball, K. (2014) *Independent review of the National Registration and Accreditation Scheme for Health Professions*, Canberra: Council of Australian Governments Health Council. Available at: http://www.coaghealthcouncil.gov.au/Publications/Reports/ArtMID/514/ArticleID/68/The-Independent-Review-of-the-National-Registration-and-Accreditation-Scheme-for-health-professionals

Van Heugten, K. (2011) 'Registration and social work education: a golden opportunity or a Trojan horse?', *Journal of Social Work*, 11(2): 174–90.

FOURTEEN

Recognising transnational social workers in Australia

Angelika Papadopoulos

Introduction

> The migrant is the political figure of our time. (Nail, 2015,
> p 235)

This chapter explores the Australian approach to the recognition of transnational social workers migrating to Australia. Prior research into transnational social work has: questioned the portability of values, skills and knowledge across cultural contexts (McDonald et al, 2003; Walsh et al, 2010; Pullen-Sansfaçon et al, 2012); explored the experiences of migrant social workers' adaptation to destination country practices (Kornbeck, 2004; Hussein et al, 2010; Bartley et al, 2011; Beddoe et al, 2012; Sims, 2012; Harrison, 2013; Beddoe and Fouché, 2014; Hussein, 2014); and also noted the ethical implications of social workers migrating from countries that need their services (IFSW, 2012), and the obligations of destination countries to migrant social workers (McDonald et al, 2003; Walsh et al, 2010; Pullen-Sansfaçon et al, 2012; Fouché et al, 2016). As the opening quote from Nail suggests, these themes all touch on the political, and they inform the background to a critical analysis of current processes of professional recognition in Australia. Empirical research has recently begun to explore the complexity of recognition processes as a significant variable in the migration experiences of social workers in Canada (Fang, 2012; Brown et al, 2015) and New Zealand (Fouché et al, 2014a, 2014b). In the Australian case, there is a lack of scholarship and data illustrating the migration patterns of social workers, the absence of which relates to Australian social work's ambiguous professional status.

While the occupation of 'social worker' comprehends a broad range of practices across myriad contexts, one characteristic of social work that clearly transcends national boundaries is the espoused self-concept of the profession as ethical. This is expressed through codes and standards of practice to which practitioners are expected to adhere across fields of practice, framed both nationally and internationally. Comparing national codes of ethics of social work practice, Banks (2012, p 111) identified common orienting ethical principles across nations: 'respect for persons, respect for and promotion of the autonomy of service users, promotion of human welfare, social justice and professional integrity' – a commonality she attributes to the influence of the International Federation of Social Work (IFSW). Importantly, as illustrated by Fouché et al (2016) in their discussion of the concept of self-determination as it is variably understood in Aotearoa New Zealand, on analysis, ostensible commonalities can reveal considerable semantic variation.

The argument in this chapter is that recognition processes are a form of social work practice, and that professional associations responsible for assessments are therefore bound by the same ethical principles as are practitioners working with clients. Processes of recognition therefore have both professional and ethical significance. Further, what is recognised as social work in accordance with the assessment process illustrates the tension between the apparent universality of particular principles and standards, and their interpretation in specific local contexts.

Recognition as ethical practice

Theorists of recognition trace their lineage back to Hegel, who formulated intersubjective recognition as the core of modernity – meaning that the possibility and feeling of human freedom is contingent on, and grounded in, the recognition by others of us as free. Honneth's (1995, 2008, 2014) work asserted recognition as the precondition of respect for persons as rights-bearing beings. He further refined this conceptualisation, acknowledging a difference between intersubjective recognition without condition and more conditional forms of recognition that are mediated by social norms; within the latter, Honneth distinguished between recognition as *respect* and recognition as *esteem*. Professional recognition of transnational social workers relates to recognition as both respect for, and esteem of, their acquired cultural capital. Taylor (1994) argued that non-recognition imprisons a person in a deficient mode of being, and is an act of social injustice. The material consequences of non-recognition implicate recognition processes in questions of distributional and procedural justice.

Recognition processes also constitute the space of transnational social work. Credentials become a form of capital that can be exchanged for value (Bourdieu, 1986, 1987) in a field that is expanding as the international exchange of ideas and peoples increases. As noted elsewhere:

> The qualification 'social worker' signals certain capabilities that can be exchanged in the labour market, however, the value of this form of capital relies both on there being a field in which it is recognised as having value, and on processes of recognition that enable mobility within the field. Recognition of capabilities across national borders is a process which expands the field of possible transaction of the cultural capital acquired, from local contexts to international ones. Simultaneously, it constitutes the field of international social work through recognizing and enabling the conversion of capital acquired across national boundaries. (Papadopoulos, 2016, p 3)

Who is recognised and the procedures by which they are recognised are based on representations of social work practice that have both global dimensions and nationally specific inflections. There is a common set of core representations recognised internationally as social work. National inflections, on the other hand, give rise to specific obligations for receiving countries with respect to enabling the sociocultural adaptation of migrating social workers (Brown et al, 2015; Fouché et al, 2016). Analysis of recognition processes illuminates understandings of what it is to be a social worker, and what knowledge and skills are valued and therefore considered convertible. For social workers migrating to Australia, their main avenue is the skilled migration programme, which is discussed in the next section.

Australian skilled migration policy

The first policy challenge for transnational social workers is negotiating the skilled migration programme application process and satisfying preliminary requirements to be invited to apply to migrate to Australia. Through the Department of Immigration and Border Protection (DIBP), Australia utilises a highly selective points-based process for assessing prospective migrants' applications. An applicant must surpass a points threshold through a computerised expression-of-interest process before being invited to formally apply: the 'highest ranked clients by points score are invited to apply for the relevant visa' (DIBP, 2016). In the past decade, policy has increasingly given preference to skilled migration over family migration through the use of skilled occupation lists to signal occupations with workforce needs and providing prospective migrants in required occupational groups with bonus points in their skilled migration application. After the 2007–08 financial crisis, the skilled migration programme was further amended to shift from a 'supply-' to 'demand-side' approach, increasing the onus on applicants to demonstrate that they have skills that Australia needs (Phillips and Spinks, 2012).

The assessment process discriminates with respect to age, with bonus points given for being under 40 years old, and English-language proficiency (points for 'superior' English). An attitude of border protection imbues current policy and procedures for establishing eligibility to apply to migrate; while Australia relies on migration to maintain its workforce (Hawthorne, 2015), formal reviews have concluded that the procedures are complicated, difficult to negotiate and expensive, even prior to migrants' seeking recognition of their professional status (Joint Standing Committee on Migration, 2006; Commonwealth of Australia, 2013; ECCV, 2014).

Professional status is assessed by separate application to professional associations gazetted by the DIBP to perform this function, with a successful outcome translating into the bonus points accruing to professions, of which social work is one, appearing on skilled occupation lists. For social workers, this critical process of recognition is conducted by the Australian Association of Social Workers (AASW).

There are three main ways to migrate to Australia as a social worker. One is to attain professional recognition through application to the AASW for a skilled migration assessment as part of the skilled migration process. Another is to complete an accredited Australian degree as an international student, which creates access to professional association recognition and, in the first instance, temporary graduate visas. The third is to seek an employer-sponsored visa to reside and work in Australia subject to the employer warranting a need for skills that cannot be locally sourced. Social workers who are employer-sponsored are outside of the AASW's oversight except where the employer requires membership. They therefore have no warrant for their credentials beyond an employer's indication that they possess certain skills that are not available in Australia.

The Australian Association of Social Workers and professional recognition

The AASW is responsible for the accreditation of social work programmes in Australia. This means that graduates of accredited programmes are eligible for membership of the association. As the designated 'assessing authority', the AASW is also responsible for the professional recognition process establishing eligibility to apply for the skilled migration programme. The association's energies over the past five years have been directed towards building membership to 10,000 members (AASW, 2016), and furthering the recognition of social work as a profession within Australia. Unlike other countries to which social workers migrate (eg New Zealand, Canada and the Republic of Ireland), social work in Australia currently lacks formal legal status as a registered profession, which means that social workers in Australia do not currently hold a monopoly over the use of the title 'social worker'. To secure this monopoly, the AASW has sought registration with the health practitioners' National Registration and Accreditation Scheme in order to establish social work alongside psychology and other health professions as a registered profession under uniform health practitioner legislation enacted in each state of Australia (DOHA, 2012; AHPRA, 2016). The AASW (2012a) has argued that regulation of the profession is crucial to protect the interests of populations served by social workers. A lack of legal registration also creates challenges for the recognition process.

The AASW approach to skilled migration assessment is a comparative approach that treats formal credentials as signalling possession of the requisite capital. Overseas-qualified social workers apply for recognition by submitting certified copies of their qualifications, accompanied by transcripts of results and evidence of work experience. In 2014, the AASW reviewed procedures for the recognition of migrant social workers, distinguishing between applications for membership of the association and recognition of overseas qualifications for migration purposes, and changing the criteria by which applications are assessed.

Prior to 2014, documents were compared against an Australian four-year Bachelor of Social Work (BSW) degree, using five 'essential criteria' derived from the structure and content of the BSW (AASW, 2014a). A significant change in the 2014 procedure was the recognition of qualifying credentials such as diplomas that were previously excluded from consideration (AASW, 2014b).

Instead of the BSW as the reference for the comparison, applicants are required to demonstrate how their qualifications compare to nine learning outcomes required of Australian accredited social work programmes, as outlined in the revised *Australian social work education and accreditation standards* (ASWEAS) introduced in 2012 (AASW, 2012b, pp 10–13). A further requirement is evidence of completion of between 500 and 960 hours of field education in two separate placements covering two separate fields/methods of practice, 'at least one of which was in direct practice' (AASW, 2014b).

To provide confirmation that they have achieved comparable learning outcomes, the applicant is required to send a 'course information form' to be completed by the institution from which they received their qualification. With this requirement for institutional confirmation, the AASW has adopted a similar procedure to that used internationally (eg by the Health and Care Professions Council in the UK and the Council on Social Work Education in the US).

In 2009, the AASW announced that applicants whose first language (or language of instruction) is not English are also required to demonstrate English-language proficiency, understood as achieving an International English Language Testing System score of 7 in each component of the academic version of the test (AASW, 2014a). Exemption from this requirement arises through completion of either primary, secondary or at least three years of tertiary education (or three years of full-time employment) in Australia, Canada, New Zealand, the Republic of Ireland, the UK or the US.

Migration skills assessments can result in qualifications and experience being regarded as not comparable, as comparable (ie full recognition) or as partly recognised, which results in the recommendation to seek further study to bridge curriculum or field education 'deficits' (AASW, 2015). Appeals of decisions are reviewed internally. For applicants with three years of post-qualifying work experience overseas, or one year in Australia, the AASW also offers optional skilled employment assessments, which may further enhance the application's merits in the DIBP's skilled migration assessment; however, this assessment is contingent on the prior recognition of their qualifications (AASW, 2014a).

In summary, professional recognition is afforded by the same organisation that accredits Australian social work education programmes and also performs the role of quasi-regulator of practice for its membership ('*quasi*' given the current professional status of social work in Australia). Current practice generates a number of challenges for both migrating social workers and Australian social work.

Challenges for migrating social workers

The assessment process

The devolution by DIBP of the role of professional recognition to the AASW in 1999 presented an opportunity for the association to consider the recognition process in light of social work's commitment to ethical practice. An early advocate for this perspective suggested that the standards against which qualifications were compared encoded a 'Western mode of social work', which was challenged by globalisation and increasing mobility, and that the recognition process could be seen as an opportunity to recognise migrant social workers' experience and expertise as potential contributors to the evolution of Australian social work (Rodopoulos and Tong, 1999).

The current assessment process, however, requires that qualifications should principally conform to the understanding of social work expressed in the ASWEAS (AASW, 2012a). These standards are the object of regular revision (the current standards have been revised twice between 2012 and 2014, and further revision is slated for 2017) in order to reflect changing conceptions of required knowledge and skills for practice. They were designed for the accreditation of social work programmes, rather than the assessment of migrant social workers, whose experience may exceed the qualifying requirements but whose qualifications may not map easily against current standards incorporated in the ASWEAS. A social worker whose education and experience has primarily been community/social development or political practice, for example, will not necessarily be able to demonstrate proficiency in individual case management.

There is a further challenge emerging from the critique of settler grammars originating from First Nations scholarship in North America (Tuck and Yang, 2012; Calderon, 2014).[1] In Tuck and Yang's analysis, migrants and the processes through which they are invited to become part of 'settler colonies' are implicated in the ongoing project of settler colonialism. Calderon's work shows how educational standards can encode both the appropriation and simultaneous effacement of the existence and rights of First Peoples, and act as colonising forces. While the preamble to the ASWEAS incorporates the *Code of ethics* acknowledgement of Australia's First Peoples and commits educational programmes to enacting this acknowledgement, the learning outcomes expected of graduates are at once highly ambitious and limited in their scope:

Knowledge and understanding of Aboriginal and Torres Strait Islander cultures and ways of knowing and be able to apply these to practice [and] [a]n appreciation of the historical and contemporary interface between non-Indigenous and Indigenous cultures in Australia and the ability to apply that to practice. (AASW, 2012a, p 12)

For applicants whose credentials do not reflect the ASWEAS learning outcomes, experience is considered only insofar as it addresses educational 'deficits'. The assessment process is therefore not strictly a skills assessment, but rather a comparison of educational qualifications.

Opportunities for Australian social work

Migrant social workers bring with them not only their qualifications, but also their experience and cultural backgrounds. While analysis of AASW data shows that the majority (81%) of nearly 3,500 applications over 12 years (1998–2013) resulted in full recognition, what is also apparent from this analysis is that there was insufficient information retained about applicants to draw strong conclusions about the impact of recognition procedures beyond the apparent fact that 'applicants from (current or former) Commonwealth countries and countries in which English is the *lingua franca* dominate applications' (Papadopoulos, 2016, p 8). This apparent fact together with the expectations embedded in the graduate attributes against which migrant social workers are compared reinforce the view that Australia is supplementing its social work workforce from anglophone countries with similar curricula, rather than assessing by reference to applicants' capabilities or identified workforce development needs.

While recent procedural changes expanded the range of social work qualifications considered eligible for assessment, the current assessment process incorporates standards that were not designed for this purpose. The practice standards (AASW, 2013) by which the AASW articulates what is expected of current practitioners would arguably be a more appropriate reference point for skilled migration assessments; however, these standards were also formulated with the locally trained population in mind.

Recent years have seen growing recognition of transnational social work in the form of a commitment to internationalising social work, from the perspective of universities seeking recognition of the global currency of their degree offerings and in professional responses such as the development of the global standards (IFSW, 2012). Increasing international mobility requires that transnational social workers are recognised not as exceptions that need to meet the rule of the country to which they migrate, but, rather, as part of a broader kinopolitical (Nail, 2015) phenomenon consequent on globalisation.

The announcement of a mutual recognition agreement between the AASW and the New Zealand Social Workers Registration Board (SWRB) in 2014 signals an appreciation of the benefits of international exchange. Should Australian social work attain professional registration, the current agreement will be replaced by the Trans-Tasman Mutual Recognition Arrangement, which, under the *Trans-Tasman Mutual Recognition Act 1997*, provides for reciprocal recognition between Australia and New Zealand for registered occupations. Advice for applicants cautions that the two countries have different cultural competence requirements, accompanied by the reservation of the right to require further study to meet these requirements (SWRB, 2016). This caution is consistent with scholarly concern regarding the differences between both countries with respect to their engagement with First Peoples and progress on reconciliation (Beddoe and Fraser, 2012; Fouché et al, 2014a) and how educational preparation for practice sensitises students to local requirements (Razack, 2009; Bartley et al, 2012).

The following discussion considers alternative strategies that reconcile the need for standards that have international transferability with local particularities of the Australian social context. The *Global standards* (IFSW, 2012) conceptualises the core curricula in four domains: the domain of the social work profession; the domain of the social work professional; methods of social work practice; and the paradigm of the social work profession. If they are considered prerequisite for the assessment of a social worker's capabilities, qualifications could be assessed with reference to these four domains and how they are articulated in the social worker's home country (eg with reference to 'knowledge of social welfare policies (or lack thereof), services and laws' [IASSW, 2012, n.p.]). This approach would provide the basis for an assessment not only of how their education might, or might not, prepare them for the specific context of their destination country, but also of the characteristics of their origin country's approach to the provision of social welfare, thus facilitating the international exchange of ideas.

'England and America are two countries separated by a common language'

As this observation commonly attributed to George Bernard Shaw reminds us, shared language does not necessarily entail shared understandings or shared cultural capital. When considering the portability of migrant social workers' skills and knowledge, the Australian approach seems too ready to equate education and English-language proficiency with required cultural capital. Similarity between qualifications taken in different cultural contexts, however, does not guarantee their transferability. Studies in Canada, New Zealand and Australia further affirm the need for local interventions to support sociocultural adaptation (Fang, 2012; Harrison, 2013; Fouché et al, 2014a, 2014b, 2016).

The AASW's involvement in skilled migration assessments provides discretionary space for the association to expand the assessment to recognise the capabilities that migrant social workers bring. This would involve moving beyond the technocratic, paper-based comparative approach that it currently utilises. The national characteristics outlined in the following provide the basis for reconsidering the recognition process in light of Australia's history and current demographic composition.

Australia is multicultural and multilingual, with one quarter of Australians speaking a language other than English at home, and over 300 different language groups in addition to the many languages spoken by Aboriginal and Torres Strait Islander peoples (ABS, 2013). There is a need for social workers who have multilingual capabilities; however, only English-language proficiency is currently assessed. Recognition processes should also value social workers' proficiency in a range of community languages.

Australia continues to struggle with the legacies of its colonial history; this legacy, in the sphere of social welfare in particular (Zubrzycki et al, 2014), means that migrant social workers, beyond the demonstration of '[ability] to work with diversity and demonstrate respect for cultural difference' (AASW, 2012b, p 12), require a comprehensive orientation that historically contextualises Australian social work and the consequences of that history for the present. The 'ten core competence standards' used by the SWRB (2016) in New Zealand provides one example of the articulation of cultural responsiveness requirements to social workers whose country of qualification or origin may not face similar challenges. While Fouché et al (2016) suggest that there are varying views on its adequacy, the Australian version is currently limited to a brochure with hyperlinks (AASW, 2016).

Finally, the relationship between social work and the state in Australia has, over three decades, been transformed by the increasing conditionality of welfare provision and the ascension of workfare and risk management policy frameworks (McDonald et al, 2003, McDonald, 2006). Current practice approaches informing educational standards have been shaped as much by federal and state policy priorities as developments within the professional knowledge base. This has led to more emphasis on time-constrained, individualised, therapeutic practice, and less emphasis on community or social development and political practice (notwithstanding an enduring tradition that describes itself as progressive). Australian social work could be enlivened through the exchange of ideas with respect to practice modalities and responses to changing governance arrangements.

Conclusions

Critical appraisal of recognition processes is increasingly important in the context of the emergence of transnational social work and the increasing movement of peoples around the world. Processes treating the ethical implications of recognition and non-recognition as extraneous amount to professional gatekeeping without acknowledgement that recognition is a form of social work practice. This criticism can be made of assessment processes that take parts of a social worker's portfolio of qualifications and experience to reflect the whole.

The standards used in the Australian approach do not exhaust the scope of legitimate social work practice; they are an evolving dialogically constituted standard, subject to revision in light of developments in knowledge and in the situations with which social workers engage. To use them to arbitrate an assessment is to reify a socioculturally and temporally specific understanding of social work. This is equivalent to misrecognition of the context-specific drivers that have historically informed the development of social work in Australia, and to setting the Australian approach as the inherently superior standard. Such ethnocentrism is not written into the standards, but is an unintended consequence of their use in the assessment of overseas-qualified social workers. The current process therefore incorporates an a priori assumption that an applicant demonstrates their qualifications not as equivalent to, but as the same as, the Australian qualifying educational credential. The consequence for some applicants is that their skills and experience will not be recognised as legitimate social work. Consequently, migrant social workers whose qualifying training does not ostensibly conform to the model of social work practice on which the assessment process is based are excluded from recognition and inclusion in the professional association. This creates the risk of excluding contributions to internationalising Australian practice through transnational migration, to the detriment of the profession's continuing development.

Given social work's unregistered status in Australia, there is a related consequence for migrant social workers entering and practising in Australia through employer-sponsored migration pathways. This group of social workers, unrecognised by the professional association, sits outside of its processes of ethical accountability and review, and thus provides an avenue for the state or other agencies to promote practices that are divergent from the articulated values and ethics of the profession. Brown et al (2015) also proposed the use of the global standards as the preliminary basis of assessment of claims to recognition as a social worker. While contentious (see, eg, Gray and Fook, 2004; Yip, 2004), the global standards carry the advantage of being the product of a democratic and international process of development (Sewpaul, 2005; Sewpaul and Jones, 2005; IFSW, 2012). No generic standards can be expected to capture the situational specificity created by each destination country, its historical development and the development of social work within its national boundaries.

While receiving countries continue to use qualifications as human capital signals, there will be an enduring need to ensure that populations most vulnerable to poor social work practice – which, in Australia, must include Aboriginal and Torres Strait Islander peoples and migrant and refugee populations – are offered some kind of assurance that social work is committed to cultural responsiveness and safety, and that people who identify as social workers, whether transnational or local, have capabilities that reflect the specific needs of the country in which they practise.

Regardless of the specific standard used in recognition processes, there is an ethical responsibility for receiving countries to provide orientation to those characteristics of the country that could not be expected to be included in other countries' educational systems, for the benefit of both the migrant social worker and service users. This requires that a fully developed recognition process includes professional induction to orient transnational social workers to the unique history of the country and of social work in that country.

To approach professional recognition as an ethical responsibility, at a minimum, Australian social work is bound by values of respect for persons, a commitment to social justice and professional integrity (AASW, 2010). It follows from these values, first, that the recognition process show respect for applicants by assessing their capabilities and knowledge in addition to – or perhaps instead of – comparing their educational attainments with (shifting) standards used in Australia. Second, the commitment to social justice requires that the process provides access to sufficient information to practise safely and competently in Australia. Finally, professional integrity entails that appropriate orientation and induction to the history and current context of Australian social work are provided for migrant social workers on their arrival, and that recognition processes acknowledge that we have as much to learn from transnational social workers as they have to offer Australia.

Note

[1] I would like to acknowledge my colleague Dr Nikki Moodie for suggesting this thought path.

References

AASW (Australian Association of Social Workers) (2010) *Code of ethics*, Canberra: Australian Association of Social Workers.

AASW (2012a) *Registration and title protection for AASW members: Directions paper for 2013*, Canberra: Australian Association of Social Workers. Available at: http://www.aasw.asn.au/document/item/3826

AASW (2012b) *Australian social work education and accreditation standards*, Canberra: Australian Association of Social Workers. Available at: http://www.aasw.asn.au/document/item/3550

AASW (2013) *AASW English language requirements*, Canberra: Australian Association of Social Workers. Available at: http://www.aasw.asn.au/document/item/139

AASW (2014a) *Application for assessment of post qualifying social work experience (after having a positive migration skills assessment completed by the AASW)*, Canberra: Australian Association of Social Workers. Available at: https://www.aasw.asn.au/document/item/6481.

AASW (2014b) *MRA with New Zealand, Canberra: Australian Association of Social Workers*. Available at: www.aasw.asn.au/membership-information/mra-with-new-zealand/mra-membershipeligibility-assessment

AASW (2015) *Overseas social work qualifications assessment for migration*, Canberra: Australian Association of Social Workers. Available at: https://www.aasw.asn.au/document/item/5422

AASW (2016) *About AASW*, Canberra: Australian Association of Social Workers. Available at: https://www.aasw.asn.au/about-aasw/about-aasw

ABS (Australian Bureau of Statistics) (2013) 'The average Australian', Australian Bureau of Statistics 4102.0 Australian Social Trends, April. Available at: http://www.abs.gov.au/AUSSTATS/abs@.nsf/Lookup/4102.0Main+Features30April+2013

AHPRA (Australian Health Practitioner Regulation Agency) (2016) 'About AHPRA'. Available at: http://www.ahpra.gov.au/About-AHPRA/What-We-Do/Legislation.aspx

Banks, S. (2012) *Ethics and values in social work*, London: Palgrave Macmillan.

Bartley, A., Beddoe, L., Duke, J., Fouché, C., Harington, P. and Shah, R. (2011) 'Crossing borders: key features of migrant social workers in New Zealand', *Aotearoa New Zealand Social Work*, 23(3): 16–30.

Bartley, A., Beddoe, L., Fouché, C. and Harington, P. (2012) 'Transnational social workers: making the profession a transnational professional space', *International Journal of Population Research*, 1: 1–11.

Beddoe, L. and Fouché, C. (2014) '"Kiwis on the move": New Zealand social workers' experience of practising abroad', *British Journal of Social Work*, 44(suppl 1): i193–208.

Beddoe, L. and Fraser, H. (2012) 'Social work in Australasia', in K. Lyons, T. Hokenstad, M. Pawar, N. Huegler and N. Hall (eds) *The Sage handbook of international social work*, London: Sage Publications, pp 421–35.

Beddoe, L., Fouché, C., Bartley, A. and Harington, P. (2012) 'Migrant social workers' experience in New Zealand: education and supervision issues', *Social Work Education: The International Journal*, 31(8): 1012–31.

Bourdieu, P. (1986) 'The forms of capital', in J. Richardson (ed) *Handbook of theory and research for the sociology of education*, New York, NY: Greenwood, pp 241–58.

Bourdieu, P. (1987) 'What makes a social class? On the theoretical and practical existence of groups', *Berkeley Journal of Sociology*, 32: 1–17.

Brown, M., Pullen-Sansfaçon, A., Éthier, S. and Fulton, A. (2015) 'A complicated welcome: social workers navigate policy, organizational contexts and socio-cultural dynamics following migration to Canada', *International Journal of Social Science Studies*, 3(1): 58–68.

Calderon, D. (2014) 'Uncovering settler grammars in curriculum', *Educational Studies*, 50(4): 313–38.

Commonwealth of Australia (2013) *Joint Standing Committee on Migration inquiry into migration and multiculturalism in Australia*, The Parliament of the Commonwealth of Australia, Canberra: Australian Government Publishing Service. Available at: http://parlinfo.aph. gov.au/parlInfo/download/publications/tabledpapers/67834/ upload_pdf/committee_mig_multiculturalism_report_fullreport.pd f;fileType=application%2Fpdf#search=%22Overseas+qualifications +assessment%22

DIBP (Department of Immigration and Border Protection) (2016) *SkillSelect – 8 January 2016 round results*, Canberra: Department of Immigration and Border Protection. Available at: https://www. border.gov.au/Trav/Work/Skil/08-01-2016-round-results

DOHA (Department of Health and Ageing) (2012) *National registration and accreditation scheme for health practitioners*, Canberra: Commonwealth of Australia Department of Health and Ageing. Available at: http:// www.health.gov.au/internet/main/publishing.nsf/Content/work-nras

ECCV (Ethnic Communities Council of Victoria) (2014) *Qualified but not recognised*, Carlton: Ethnic Communities Council of Victoria. Available at: http://www.eccv.org.au/library/ECCV_Discussion_ Paper_-_Qualified_but_not_Recognised_2015_Final.pdf

Fang, C. (2012) 'Foreign credential assessment and social work in Canada'. Available at: http://sasw.in1touch.org/uploaded/web/ council/FQR-Report2012-Final.pdf

Fouché, C., Beddoe, L., Bartley, A. and Brenton, N. (2014a) 'Strengths and struggles: overseas qualified social workers' experiences in Aotearoa New Zealand', *Australian Social Work*, 67(4): 1–16, doi:1.1080/0312407x.2013.783604

Fouché, C., Beddoe, L., Bartley, A. and De Haan, I. (2014b) 'Enduring professional dislocation: migrant social workers' perceptions of their professional roles', *British Journal of Social Work*, 44(7): doi: 10.1093/ bjsw/bct054

Fouché, C., Beddoe, E., Bartley, A. and Parkes, E. (2016) 'Are we ready for them? Overseas-qualified social workers' professional cultural transition', *European Journal of Social Work*, 19(1): 106–19.

Gray, M. and Fook, J. (2004) 'The quest for a universal social work: some issues and implications', *Social Work Education: The International Journal*, 23(5): 625–44.

Harrison, G. (2013) '"Oh, you've got such a strong accent": language identity intersecting with professional identity in the human services in Australia', *International Migration*, 51: 192–204.

Hawthorne, L. (2015) 'The impact of skilled migration on foreign qualification recognition reform in Australia', *Canadian Public Policy*, 41(s1): 173–87.

Honneth, A. (1995) *The struggle for recognition: The moral grammar of social conflicts*, Cambridge, MA: The MIT Press.

Honneth, A. (2008) *Reification: A new look at an old idea*, New York, NY: Oxford University Press.

Honneth, A. (2014) *Freedom's right: The social foundations of democratic life*, Cambridge: Polity Press.

Hussein, S. (2014) 'Hierarchical challenges to transnational social workers' mobility: the United Kingdom as a destination within an expanding European Union', *British Journal of Social Work*, 44(suppl 1): i174–92.

Hussein, S., Manthorpe, J. and Stevens, M. (2010) 'People in places: a qualitative exploration of recruitment agencies' perspectives on the employment of international social workers in the UK', *British Journal of Social Work*, 40(3): 1000–16.

IFSW (International Federation of Social Work) (2012) '*Global standards for the education and training of the social work profession*'. Available at: http://ifsw.org/policies/global-standards/

Joint Standing Committee on Migration (2006) *Negotiating the maze: Review of arrangements for overseas skills recognition, upgrading and licensing*, The Parliament of the Commonwealth of Australia, Canberra: Australian Government Publishing Service.

Kornbeck, J. (2004) 'Linguistic affinity and achieved geographic mobility: evidence from the recognition of non-national social work qualifications in Ireland and the UK', *European Journal of Social Work*, 7(2): 143–65.

McDonald, C. (2006) *Challenging social work: The institutional context of practice*, London: Palgrave.

McDonald, C., Harris, J. and Wintersteen, R. (2003) 'Contingent on context? Social work and the state in Australia, Britain, and the USA', *British Journal of Social Work*, 33(2): 191–208.

Nail, T. (2015) *The figure of the migrant*, Stanford, CA: Stanford University Press.

Papadopoulos, A. (2016) 'Migrating qualifications', *British Journal of Social Work*, advance access, first published online 3 May, doi:10.1093/bjsw/bcw038.

Phillips, J. and Spinks, H. (2012) *Skilled migration: Temporary and permanent flows to Australia*, Canberra: Commonwealth of Australia. Available at: http://www.aph.gov.au/About_Parliament/Parliamentary_Departments/Parliamentary_Library/pubs/BN/2012-2013/SkilledMigration#_Toc342559467

Pullen-Sansfaçon, A., Spolander, G. and Engelbrecht, L. (2012) 'Migration of professional social workers: reflections on challenges and strategies for education', *Social Work Education: The International Journal*, 31(8): 1032–45.

Razack, N. (2009) 'Decolonizing the pedagogy and practice of international social work', *International Social Work*, 52: 9–21.

Rodopoulos, L. and Tong, Q. (1999) 'The recognition of overseas trained social workers for practice in Australia', conference proceedings, 'Promoting inclusion – Redressing exclusion: The social work challenge', joint conference of the Australian Association of Social Workers, International Federation of Social Workers, Asia and Pacific Association for Social Work Education, and Australian Association for Social Work and Welfare Education.

Sewpaul, V. (2005) 'Global standards: promise and pitfalls for re-inscribing social work into civil society', *International Journal of Social Welfare*, 14: 210–17.

Sewpaul, V. and Jones, D. (2005) 'Global standards for the education and training of the social work profession,' *International Journal of Social Welfare*, 14: 218–30.

Sims, D. (2012) 'Intercultural consolidation: exploring the experiences of internationally qualified social workers and the English post-qualifying framework', *European Journal of Social Work*, 15(2): 241–55.

SWRB (Social Workers Registration Board) (2016) 'Overseas qualified social workers', Social Workers Registration Board. Available at: http://www.swrb.govt.nz/new-applicants/overseas-qualified-social-workers

Taylor, C. (1994) 'The politics of recognition', in D.T. Goldberg (ed) *Multiculturalism: A critical reader*, Oxford: Blackwell, pp 25–73.

Tuck, E. and Yang, K.W. (2012) 'Decolonization is not a metaphor', *Decolonization: Indigeneity, Education and Society*, 1: 1–40.

Walsh, T., Wilson, G. and O'Connor, E. (2010) 'Local, European and global: an exploration of migration patterns of social workers into Ireland', *British Journal of Social Work*, 40(6): 1978–95.

Yip, K. (2004) 'A Chinese cultural critique of the global qualifying standards for social work education', *Social Work Education: The International Journal*, 23(5): 597–612.

Zubrzycki, J., Green, S., Jones, V., Stratton, K., Young, S. and Bessarab, D. (2014) *Getting it right: Creating partnerships for change. Integrating Aboriginal and Torres Strait Islander knowledges in social work education and practice. Teaching and learning framework*, Sydney: Australian Government Office for Learning and Teaching.

FIFTEEN

Social work mobility in Europe: a case study from Ireland

Trish Walsh, George Wilson and Erna O'Connor

A case study of social work mobility in Ireland

The phenomenon of transnational social worker mobility can be viewed against the background of the ambition to internationalise social work, dating from 1928 (International Conference of Social Work, Paris, 1928 – see the International Federation of Social Workers [IFSW] website, available at: http://ifsw.org/news/milestones-in-the-early-history-of-the-ifsw/). Such mobility occurs in a context of the increased global movements of people. Mobility has been shown to be a fluid process impacted by political and economic factors, as well as national and regional policies in a globalised world (Bartley et al, 2012; Williams and Graham, 2014). International mobility is not a universal right. In the case of the European Union (EU), one of the foundational principles and ambitions of the European project has been the free movement of workers between the member states as part of the concept of the Common Market. However, significant differences have always existed between mobility *within* the member states and from *outside*.

Pan-European contextual factors

Since the international war on terror following the 2001 '9/11' attacks on the US, a confluence of separate but intertwined global events have thrown established European migration policies into disarray. These events include the global financial crisis of 2007/08 and the subsequent Eurozone crisis, which saw the Republic of Ireland (ROI) and other indebted peripheral European states (Spain, Portugal, Greece and Cyprus) enter a 'bailout' programme provided by a 'troika' of international lenders comprising the European Commission (EC), the International Monetary Fund (IMF) and the European Central Bank (ECB). Financial assistance was accompanied by the imposition of stringent austerity measures in all cases. Ireland exited its bailout programme in 2013 but the legacy of austerity endures across health, social services and other sectors.

More critically, the Syrian and Iraqi wars and resultant humanitarian refugee crises have given rise to severe tensions between European partners on the issue of migration. The threat to the Schengen passport-free zone for Europeans and the tightening of European borders in the wake of the Daesh terrorist attacks in Belgium, France and Germany since November 2015 are also having a profound impact. In the UK, the 'leave' outcome of the 'Brexit' referendum vote in June 2016 illustrates how fraught the question of international mobility has become and is seen as not only a backlash against immigration to the UK, but also a manifestation of the alienation felt by many impoverished working-class communities that have suffered disproportionately through globalisation. The European project appears to have reached a turning point and member states are divided on the need for stronger or less stringent pan-European structures and controls. The Brexit vote has created considerable uncertainty about the continuation of the free movement of labour in Europe, although, at this point, the precise implications for social work mobility into and between both parts of the island of Ireland are unclear.

Methodology

The research reported in this chapter is based on an analysis of empirical data obtained from the social work regulatory bodies in the ROI and Northern Ireland (NI) in relation to the recognition of social work qualifications gained outside the respective jurisdiction, focusing on the years leading up to the 2004–07 global financial crisis and the aftermath of the crisis from 2008 to 2013. This constitutes phases one and two of an ongoing project on the experiences of migrant and ethnically diverse social workers (MEDSWS) based in Trinity College Dublin (TCD), funded by two grants from the university's Arts and Social Sciences Benefaction Fund. Ethical approval for the study was provided by the TCD School of Social Work and Social Policy Ethics Committee. Previous reports from this study have been published (Walsh et al, 2010) and presented at international social work conferences in the UK and Portugal. Further papers are planned on phase three – a national online survey conducted with 130 internationally qualified social workers across the island – and phase four – qualitative research including two small sets of interviews conducted with migrant social workers (Roche, 2015; Skuterud, 2016).

In Ireland, as social workers are employed across a range of sectors, and not necessarily in jobs entitled 'social worker', there are no robust national statistics available on the numbers in employment, nor on the proportion of these who obtained their qualifications outside the state. The situation is improving somewhat since the introduction of statutory registration in both parts of the island (NI in 2005 and ROI in 2011). However, in the ROI, if a professional social worker holds a job title other than the protected title of 'social worker', for example, 'caseworker' or 'probation officer', they may opt not to register and therefore are not counted in official statistics which indicate that 3,928 social workers had registered as of 31 December 2015 (CORU, 2016). Workers in the residential care sector are separately registered as social care workers in ROI, whereas in NI, they are registered as social workers in one generic category. NI has a considerably larger social work workforce, with 5,885 social workers registered in September 2016 (personal communication with Northern Ireland Social Care Council [NISCC], 2016). While statistics collected by national professional registration bodies are not definitive, they can nonetheless give a strong indication of patterns of mobility. It is not in any way assumed that, as a 'case', Ireland is typical or representative of other European countries; instead, it is viewed as unique (Yin, 1984) and probably atypical in its geographical position as a small island on the edge of what has been described as the 'jagged and ragged end of the Eurasian landmass' (Jacobs and Maier, 1998, p 13).

European social policy on worker mobility

The free movement of workers, a fundamental aim of the European project, has resulted in instruments (such as Directive 89/48/EEC Article 1, Directive 92/51/EEC and Directive 2005/36/EC) requiring member countries to implement policies on the mutual recognition of university degree courses and named professions, including social work. Under these directives, national recognition bodies (competent authorities) are required to provide mechanisms for social workers from other European countries to have their qualifications reviewed with the aim of enabling them to practise in that country. The 1997 Lisbon Recognition Convention requires a country to recognise other European qualifications unless it can demonstrate substantial differences between the two. In addition, the 1999 Bologna Declaration set out to create an ambitious universal European Higher Education Area by 2010. Central to this is the aim of introducing a common, third-level framework translatable through concepts of credit ratings and specified learning outcomes. Underlying these initiatives is a relatively unquestioned assumption that such universality is 'a good thing'. The European Association of Schools of Social Work (EASSW) suggests that the Bologna Declaration has had three beneficial effects on social work education: a stronger academic focus (in the move of more social work courses into universities and as an independent academic speciality); an increasing emphasis on generalist foundation training (eg as opposed to separate courses for probation officers and youth and community workers); and a strengthening focus on an international or European orientation, as required under Bologna guidelines (Labonte-Roset, 2007).

Notwithstanding the perception that at broad structural levels, social work courses across Europe may be converging, Johnson and Wolf (2009) question whether the Bologna vision will prove realisable in creating genuinely transferable qualifications. Their reservations centre on two concerns: that learning outcomes operate as minimum standards only; and translatability – whether standards are understood and interpreted in the same way across national borders. Language competence and financial resources are also identified as factors that can hinder or facilitate student and graduate mobility.

The Republic of Ireland: contextual factors

Having achieved independence from Britain in 1922, Ireland remained a largely agricultural society until the 1960s. The economic history of Ireland has been characterised by cycles of 'boom and bust' and corresponding cycles of immigration and emigration. In 1988, due to high unemployment, a slow growth rate, high inflation and taxation, and a heavy burden of debt, Ireland was deemed 'the poorest of the rich nations' by the *Economist* magazine (Cairncross, 1988). However, the period from the mid-1990s up to the global financial crisis brought sustained job creation and rising standards of living. Economic growth was built on factors such as an open economy, low corporate taxation, a social partnership model of industrial relations, investment in education and infrastructure, and the benefits of EU membership. Ireland joined the European Economic Community in 1973. It assumed the presidency of the EU in 2004 at a time of the largest single expansion to include 10 new member states predominantly from Eastern Europe. By then, Ireland had been dubbed the 'Celtic Tiger', with economic growth rates comparable to the East Asian economies. Rising employment and living standards brought a reversal of emigration patterns, which had been a feature of Irish life since the mid–1880s. Members of the Irish diaspora returned home and workers from the newest EU member states came to Ireland to seek employment. The population increased by almost 15% from 1996 to 2005. In 2002, when a question on nationality was included for the first time in the census in the ROI, 5.8% of the population had been born outside the country; this had risen to 12% in 2011 (CSO, 2008, 2016). In the latest 2016 census data, inward migration continues to be a strong feature and is contributing to a return in 2016 to net inward migration for the first time since the economic crash (see Figure 15.1).

Figure 15.1: Migration rates, Republic of Ireland, 2006–16

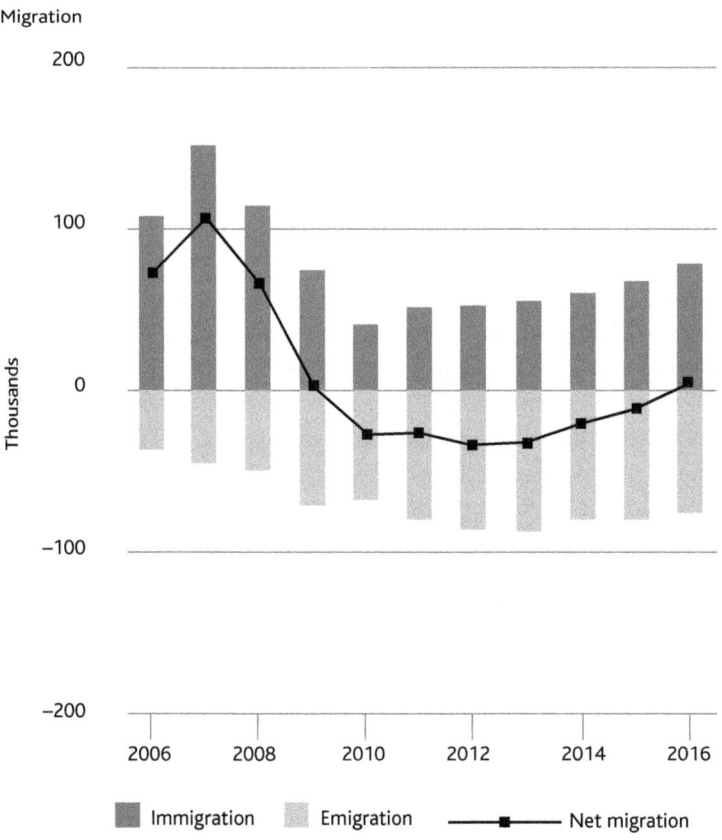

Source: CSO (2016).

Social work immigration into the Republic of Ireland

Social work developed in Ireland from a tradition of hospital almoners and is now an established discipline within health care, the criminal justice system and disability services, and a lead profession in the Child and Family Agency 'Tusla'. From 2000 onwards, a number of developments, including reorganisation of health and social services, increased responsibilities under new children's legislation and an expansion in posts in key sectors, led to specific shortages of qualified social workers in the ROI. While there was an increase in training places in the late 1990s (to a total of approximately 200 newly qualified practitioners annually), it was insufficient to meet demand. In 2001 and 2002, the largest sector of child and family services launched recruitment drives in Canada, South Africa and Australia (Moran, 2004).

This initiative had a significant impact on migration patterns. Figures of the annual inward migration of social workers increased from 96 in 2000, to 302 in 2002 and dropped to 99 in 2007. The numbers of internationally qualified social workers applying to have their qualifications recognised peaked across the years 2001–05, topping over 300 in 2002, before dropping below 100 (the 1999 level) in 2007 for the first time. Applicants from 42 countries applied for recognition of their qualifications between 1996 and 2007 (NSWQB, 2008; see also Table 15.1). The countries most represented were Great Britain (26), India (17), Australia (16) and the US (7) (NSWQB, 2008). Individually motivated mobility in the years 1996–99 suggests the strength of linguistic and cultural factors in attracting people to Ireland. No data exist on the onward mobility of workers who came to Ireland in response to these recruitment drives. Anecdotal evidence suggests that most did not remain in Ireland.

In the ROI, immigration remained high in 2008 (see Table 15.2), with a total of 116 international qualifications approved, decreased to 18 in 2009 and increased again to 103 in 2010. Applications fell again from 2011 to 2013, ranging from 27 to 33 annually in this period. Local movements from the UK and NI remained the predominant trend and account for the spike in numbers in 2010, with 73 people from the UK, including NI, joining the register in that year. The next highest numbers are from Australia and the US, at five each. In fact, Australia and the US are the most significant sending nations after the UK across the time frame 2008–13, with 25 each. India is next, at 17. Poland and Germany are the biggest EU sending nations, at 14 and 11, respectively. An embargo on public sector recruitment coupled with reputational damage to the Irish economy post-2008 is likely to account for this predominantly downward trend. The establishment of a new registration body, the Health and Social Care Professions Council (CORU), in 2011 saw the introduction of a more complex and expensive registration process, which may also impact on the numbers applying for and meeting registration requirements.

Table 15.1: Inward mobility of social workers to the Republic of Ireland, 1996–2007

Country	1996	1997	1998	1999	2000	2001	2002	2003	2004	2005	2006	2007	Total
Australia	7	7	8	6	14	34	55	19	15	12	13	16	206
Austria			1						1				2
Belgium	1		2				1		1				5
Brazil				1									1
Bulgaria								2	1			1	4
Canada	4		3		3	3	15	6	5	2	1	2	44
Columbia										1			1
Croatia							2	1					3
Czech Republic								1					1
Denmark				1		1	2		1	2			7
Finland		1					3					1	5
France						1					1	1	3
Germany	5		6	5	2	4	4	8	12	6	3	1	56
Greece	1									1			2
Hong Kong							1						1
Hungary										1			1
India	1					1	5	2	1	10	15	17	52
Israel									1				1
Italy								1		1			2
Lithuania										2		1	3
Malta								1			1		2
Mauritius												1	1
Netherlands	3				1		1	2					7
New Zealand			1			6	9	3	1	2	1	5	28
Nigeria								1	1	4	4	2	12
Northern Ireland	6	3	16	10	24	33	24	3	17	9	12	6	163

Country	1996	1997	1998	1999	2000	2001	2002	2003	2004	2005	2006	2007	Total
Pakistan									2				2
Philippines						1	1	3		2			7
Poland							1		3	1	2	2	9
Portugal						1						1	2
Romania						2		1	3	1	1	1	9
Slovakia									3	1	1	1	6
South Africa	1		1	1		3	58	15	4	5	3	5	96
Spain		3				1	1		2	3	1		11
Sweden	1		2	2		1	7	2	4		2	1	22
Tanzania							1						1
Thailand						1							1
Turkey								1					1
Uganda												1	1
UK	28	15	20	20	44	39	46	17	44	27	26	26	352
USA	18	7	8	8	8	15	56	13	27	18	13	7	198
Zimbabwe						2	9						11
Total	76	33	71	54	96	149	302	102	149	110	101	99	1,342

Source: National Social Work Qualifications Board (NSWQB) Annual Report 2007, in Walsh et al (2010).

Table 15.2: Social workers with international qualifications who registered in the Republic of Ireland, 2008–13

Country	2008	2009	2010	2011	2012	2013	Total
UK incl NI	57	24	73	27	12	15	208
Australia	15	3	5	0		0	23
India	11	0	4	2		0	17
USA	10	3	5	2	5	0	25
Nigeria	7	3	0	0		0	10
Poland	4	0	2	0	6	2	14
Germany	3	5	3	0	0	0	11
South Africa	2	2	2	0	0	0	6
Canada	2	0	0	0	0	0	2
New Zealand	0	2	0	0	0	0	2
Romania	0	0	3	0	0	0	3
Slovakia	0	0	0	0	3	0	3
Others	5	6	6	2	3	10	32
Total	116	48	103	33	29	27	356

Source: Based on figures supplied by the NSWQB and CORU.

Northern Ireland: contextual factors

While NI and the ROI have had different systems of welfare provision attached to their specific nation-state status since 1922, social work in these neighbouring jurisdictions share some common history and features (Kearney, 2005; Wilson et al, 2009). Although educational programmes have tended to follow different trajectories, similarities remain in relation to professional standards and requirements. Regulating authorities in both parts of the island have undertaken joint initiatives to encourage and facilitate cross-border social work mobility (NSWQB and CCETSW (NI), 1998). This section briefly explores the particular challenges affecting social work in NI and their likely impact on trends and opportunities for job mobility. The discussion also considers the opportunities for developing forms of social work in NI that transcend national borders and the future challenges that Brexit might present for social work migration.

One of the most distinctive and difficult challenges facing social work in NI is the legacy of the 'Troubles' and the continuing impact of civil and political conflict and violence on the population. Alongside high levels of unemployment and social deprivation, the legacy of the 'Troubles' is understood to be a key factor accounting for high levels of poor mental health in NI, which are greater than anywhere else in the UK or Ireland, for example, the prevalence of mental health problems in NI have been estimated to be 25% higher than in England (Wilson et al, 2015). During the 'Troubles', it has been argued, social workers in NI were able to develop a neutral and non-sectarian identity but this was at the cost of remaining aloof and rather disengaged from civil society (Traynor, 1998). Following the Belfast (Good Friday) Agreement in 1998, which marked the beginning of the current peace process, it was hoped that an end to violence would create greater occupational space for new forms of social work to emerge in NI that would allow practitioners to become more engaged with local communities and take a more proactive approach in promoting social justice within NI's divided society (Pinkerton and Campbell, 2002). However, more than a decade later, it is debatable to what extent new forms of social work have emerged in NI. Although violence has undoubtedly diminished, this period has also witnessed recurring bouts of political unrest that have threatened the peace process and created instability for NI's power-sharing governmental institutions. Arguably, social work, particularly within the statutory sector, remains largely wedded to the type of bureau professionalism and managerialism that are characteristic of social work in other parts of the UK (Wilson et al, 2009).

In spite of these continuing bouts of instability, there has been increased immigration to NI and significant growth in the numbers of non-UK/ROI nationals employed in both the private and public sectors. At the height of the economic boom in 2006, it was noted that just over 3% of people of working age in employment in NI were non-UK/non-Irish nationals, compared with 11% in the ROI (CSO, 2008). While the rate of immigration has been lower than in the ROI, it is clear that NI has also become more diverse ethnically and culturally. Of a total population of just over 1.8 million, recent census data indicate that about 4.5% of residents were born outside the UK or the ROI (Migration Observatory, 2014). The most common country of origin of non-UK nationals was Poland (19,658 residents), followed by Lithuania, India, the US and Germany (Migration Observatory, 2014). However, NI's legacy of inter-communal violence has had a significant adverse impact on new immigrants to the country over a prolonged period of time. A government-sponsored survey in 2007 found that racist attitudes to migrant workers in NI were among the strongest in Europe (DHSS&PS, 2007). Since then, there has been a steady rise in the number of racist incidents and racist 'hate' crime in NI. For example, while there were 750 racist incidents in 2012/13, this figure increased to 982 during 2013/14 (Nicem, 2014). The Annual Human Rights and Racial Equality survey in 2014 stated that racism in NI was beginning to supplant 'traditional' sectarianism as the main reason for employees being harassed, bullied or threatened in the region's workplaces (Nicem, 2014).

Social work immigration into Northern Ireland

After 1997, NI also experienced (although to a lesser extent than did the ROI) an increase in social work migration of non-UK/ROI nationals. Between 2004 and 2007, the data indicate that NI experienced a significant rise in the number of new social work registrations with NISCC by non-UK nationals from a range of 21 different countries (see Table 15.3). The total number (65) was lower in comparison to the migration of non-Irish nationals to the ROI during the same period and peaked in 2005 with 29 registrants (Walsh et al, 2010).

Statistics supplied by the NISCC (see Table 15.4) indicate that, in the years 2008–13, the number of new registrations of non-UK nationals in NI peaked at 25 in 2008, declining each year to a low of seven in 2011, with slight increases in 2012 and 2013.

Table 15.3: Social work mobility into Northern Ireland, 2004–07

	2004	2005	2006	2007	Totals
Irish		4	5	1	10
NI (qua ROI)		3		1	4
British	1	1			2
American	1	5	3		9
Australian		4	1	3	8
Botswanian			1		1
Bulgarian				1	1
Canadian		3			3
Dutch		2		1	3
Egyptian	1				1
Filipino			1		1
German		1		1	2
Ghanaian				1	1
Hungarian				1	1
Indian		3	5	3	11
Kenyan		1			1
New Zealander			1	1	2
Romanian		1			1
South African				1	1
Swedish				1	1
Swiss		1			1
Totals	3	29	17	16	65

Source: Adapted from Walsh et al (2010).

Discussion

From 2004 to 2007, at the peak of the 'Celtic Tiger' years, there was a pattern of sustained inward migration across the island of Ireland. Taking the cumulative figures for Ireland as a whole for 2004–07 (see Table 15.5), the highest numbers of incoming workers continued to come from former Commonwealth and/or English-speaking countries – Great Britain had the most (125), followed by the US (74), Australia (64), India (54) and NI to the ROI (44). The only non-English-speaking country to enter double digits is Germany (24). The next four in rank were: South Africa (18), Nigeria (11), Canada (13) and New Zealand (11).

Table 15.4: Social workers with international qualifications who registered in Northern Ireland, 2008–13

Country	2008	2009	2010	2011	2012	2013	Total
Ireland (ROI)	1	3	3	1	5	3	16
Australia	7	1	1				9
Zimbabwe	3						3
Brazil				1			1
Portugal				1		2	3
Lithuania	1	1				2	4
India	5	3	1				9
USA	2	3		1	1	1	8
Nigeria	1	1					2
Poland	1		2		2		5
Germany		2	1				3
South Africa	1	2		1			4
Canada	1					1	2
Romania			1				1
Ghana		1					1
Sweden	1						1
Italy	1						1
Switzerland		1					1
Slovakia				1			1
Total	25	16	10	7	8	9	75

Source: Based on figures from NISCC (2016, unpublished data provided by private communication).

While in a context of economic expansion, labour-force shortages and international recruitment drives, the period 2000–07 saw sustained growth in immigration, statistics from 2008–13 present a different picture, demonstrating how volatile social work inward migration patterns are. While NI figures grew from a low base of 54 in the four-year period 2004–07 (see Table 15.5) to 75 in the six-year period 2008–13 (see Table 15.6), cumulative figures for Ireland as a whole dropped from 481 to 431. ROI figures dropped from 427 to 356 over these time frames. Migration from ROI accounted for 21% of all immigration to NI from 2008 to 2013, while 58% of registrants with international qualifications in ROI in this period came from the UK, including NI. The US (33), Australia (32) and India (26) continued to account for the next highest numbers migrating to the island of Ireland as a whole. This shows a drop to about 50% of the

2004–07 figures of US (74), Australia (64) and India (54). Numbers from Nigeria increased minimally from 11 to 12. The cumulative figure from Germany reduced from 24 to 14 in the 2008–13 period. Small numbers of registrants came from other European countries, including three from Portugal and four each from the EU accession states, Slovakia, Romania and Lithuania. However, the figure for Poland more than doubled from eight to 19. This relatively high figure may be understood in the context of an established Polish diaspora in both jurisdictions (Migration Observatory, 2014; CSO, 2016). Marked decreases are evident in numbers from South Africa (which dropped from 18 to 10), Canada (from 13 to four) and New Zealand (from 11 to two).

Table 15.5: Mobility into the Republic of Ireland and Northern Ireland, 2004–07

Country	Into the ROI	Into NI	Total
Great Britain	123	2	125
USA	65	9	74
Australia	56	8	64
Northern Ireland	44	n/a	44
India	43	11	54
Germany	22	2	24
South Africa	17	1	18
Nigeria	11	0	11
Canada	10	3	13
New Zealand	9	2	11
Poland	8	0	8
Sweden	7	1	8
Slovakia	6	0	6
Romania	6	1	7
ROI	n/a	14	14
Totals	427	54	481

Source: Extracted from figures supplied by the NSWQB and NISCC (Walsh et al, 2010).

Table 15.6: Mobility into the Republic of Ireland and Northern Ireland, 2008–13

Country	Into ROI	Into NI	Total
Ireland (ROI)	n/a	16	16
UK (incl NI if applicable)	208	0	208
Australia	23	9	32
Zimbabwe	0	3	3
India	17	9	26
USA	25	8	33
Nigeria	10	2	12
Poland	14	5	19
Germany	11	3	14
South Africa	6	4	10
Canada	2	2	4
New Zealand	2	0	2
Romania	3	1	4
Portugal	0	3	3
Lithuania	0	4	4
Slovakia	3	1	4
Others	32	5	37
Totals	356	75	431

Source: Based on figures supplied by the NSWQB and NISCC.

We now discuss the findings of this analysis in two sections: (1) NI and (2) ROI.

Northern Ireland

In recent years, both parts of Ireland have faced similar challenges arising from the global economic and financial recession. The decline in new registrations of social workers with international qualifications in NI, from 25 in 2008 to nine in 2013, coincides with the period of global economic recession. However, alongside economic drivers, it is possible that a range of other factors may have influenced social workers' motivation and their decision to seek employment in NI, including personal and family connections (Walsh et al, 2015). It is also likely that the rate of inward migration may have been influenced by other local contextual factors that have impacted on the availability of social work employment opportunities for non-UK nationals in NI during this period. During the 1990s, NI experienced recurring problems in retaining qualified social workers – particularly in the field of child and family care (Wilson and McCrystal, 2007). However, since the introduction in NI of a new degree in social work in 2004, with approximately 300 new social workers qualifying each year (2010 figure), there has been no need for recruitment drives outside the region (Walsh et al, 2010). Indeed, the indications are that social workers qualifying from education programmes in NI may now find it increasingly difficult to obtain qualified social work employment locally in the region. Clearly, the overall lack of qualified social work job opportunities will also have implications for migrant social workers seeking employment in NI in both community-based social work and residential social work/social care services.

At this point, it is too early to be definitive about whether the recent decline in registrations of social workers with international qualifications in NI is a temporary phenomenon or a long-term trend. However, since the referendum in June 2016, there have been growing concerns about the implications of Brexit for employment prospects and labour mobility more generally in NI. Although the UK as a whole voted narrowly to leave the EU, NI voted to remain by a margin of 56% to 44%. Since the vote, serious concerns have been expressed by both local politicians and policymakers about Brexit's possible detrimental impact, including anxieties about its implications for the status of NI's land border with the ROI, EU funding and the single market. Particular concerns have been expressed about how Brexit might jeopardise the free movement of labour given that both NI's private and public sectors depend on non-UK migrant workers, as well as cross-border workers from the ROI (Emerson, 2016). While it remains to be seen whether the fears and concerns expressed about Brexit become a reality in the future, it is likely that such uncertainties could inhibit future international job mobility, as well as unsettle migrant social workers already employed in NI. The legal decision in the UK High Court in November 2016 (now under appeal) that compels the government to bring any Brexit proposals to Parliament first creates more uncertainty and delays in the process.

Republic of Ireland

From the 1990s onwards, there has been evidence of immigration of social workers to Ireland beyond the traditional movements between ROI, NI and the UK. Rates of immigration have fluctuated with changing economic fortunes, both within the country and globally. This sits alongside rapid fluctuations in migration flows for Ireland more generally. Immigration rates exceeded emigration through the first half of the 2000s, spiking in 2007, with a sharp fall post-2008.

Figure 15.2: Immigration, emigration and net migration Ireland, 2000–16

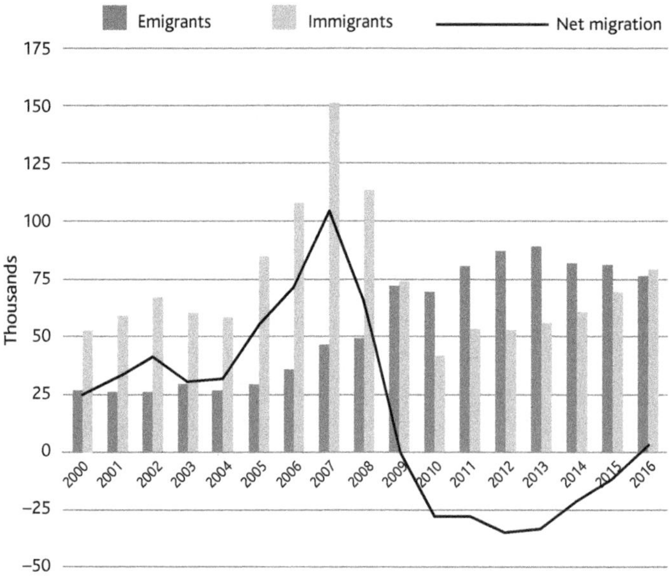

Source: EMN (2016).

From 2010 to 2015, figures show a net outward migration from Ireland. This trend has now reversed, with the number of immigrants to the ROI in the year to April 2016 estimated to have increased by almost 15%, from 69,300 in the year to April 2015 to 79,300, while the number of emigrants declined over the same period, from 80,900 to 76,200. These combined changes have resulted in a return to net inward migration for Ireland (+3,100) for the first time since 2009. Interestingly, Irish nationals continue to experience net outward migration, although at a much lower level than in the previous year, falling from 23,200 to 10,700.

Other indicators of economic recovery are also evident. The seasonally adjusted unemployment rate was 8.4% in April 2016, the lowest since November 2008 (CSO, 2016). If economic recovery is sustained, we are likely to see increased social work immigration to Ireland from within the EU and globally. However, the political realities of Brexit may have a detrimental impact on migration flows from NI and the UK.

Conclusions

On the basis of this analysis, we conclude that patterns of social work mobility reflect mobility patterns more generally in their sensitivity to economic and political change. In the Irish context, patterns of mobility changed rapidly in response to the economic expansion of the 'Celtic Tiger' era and later to the economic crisis of 2008. While this research focused on immigration, there is evidence of corresponding changes in the patterns of mobility of Irish social workers and those of other nationalities holding qualifications from Ireland. In addition, there is little known about onward mobility patterns of social workers who move to Ireland; therefore, patterns of emigration and onward migration warrant further research.

Political and social factors are also significant. Post-2004, figures for social workers from the EU accession states began to feature in the data on those applying for recognition of qualifications gained outside both jurisdictions, highlighting the benefits of free movement of labour within the EU. It is significant that Ireland, the UK and Sweden allowed free movement for the accession states from 2004 while the remaining 12 countries applied some restrictions in the transition period, typically of two years. Poland features as the most significant sending nation of the accession states. This may be due to the presence of an established Polish diaspora in both ROI and NI.

Pre-2008, we concluded that the European project can seemingly create differentiated migration regimes *within* and *outside* the EU, which could have the effect of creating a 'Fortress Europe' with significant barriers to mobility for those from outside the European zone (Walsh et al, 2010). The threat of 'Fortress Europe' has tragically come to pass, with the deaths of 3,771 migrants, the highest annual figure to date, attempting to cross the Mediterranean to Europe in 2015 (IOM, 2016). Mobility *within* Europe has also become more mired in complexity as the European project itself threatens to fracture due to conflict within and among member states on migration, the financing of indebted Eurozone countries and the implications of 'Brexit', as well as the uncertainty surrounding US economic and trade policy following the election of Donald Trump and the future dominance of the Republican Party in the US legislature from January 2017.

Withdrawal of the UK from the EU may increase transnational social worker mobility from anglophone countries such as Canada, Australia and New Zealand into the UK, including NI, but simultaneously restrict the mobility of social workers between the ROI and NI, from the rest of Europe to NI, and from ROI to England, Scotland and

Wales. While the situation for NI remains uncertain in the aftermath of Brexit, the economy of the ROI is showing signs of another upturn, which may give rise to a new phase of inward migration. In the most heavily pressurised service – that of child welfare – an announcement has been made that almost 200 new social work posts are to be created over the next three years (Oireachtas Report, 2016). Social workers, educators, employers, regulators and social work representative bodies in Ireland need to work together to avoid a second round of ad hoc assimilation efforts and instead contribute to a transnational professional space, as advocated by Bartley et al (2012).

References

Bartley, A., Beddoe, L., Fouché, C. and Harington, P. (2012) 'Transnational social workers: making the profession a transnational professional space', *International Journal of Population Research*, 1: 1–11.

Cairncross, F. (1988) 'Poorest of the rich (Ireland survey)', *The Economist* (US), 16 January.

CORU (Health and Social Care Professionals Council) (2016) *Annual report 2015*, Dublin: CORU. Available at: http://coru.ie/uploads/documents/AnnualReport2015.pdf

CSO (Central Statistics Office of Ireland) (2008) 'Ireland north and south: a statistical profile'. Available at: http://www.cso.ie/en/statistics/irelandnorthandsouth-astatisticalprofile/irelandnorthandsouth-astatisticalprofile-2008edition/

CSO (2016) 'Population and migration estimates, April 2016'. Available at: http://www.cso.ie/en/releasesandpublications/er/pme/populationandmigrationestimatesapril2016/

DHSS&PS (Department of Health, Social Services and Public Safety) (2007) 'Attitudes to migrant workers: results from the Northern Ireland Omnibus Survey'. Available at: www.delni.gov.uk/publicattitudestomigrantworkers

Emerson, N. (2016) 'Backing Brexit is a mistake Foster may never get to leave behind her', *Sunday Times*, 14 August, p 23.

EMN (European Migration Network) (2016) 'Population and migration estimates'. Available at: http://www.emn.ie/index.jsp?p=100&n=128&a=0

IOM (International Organization for Migration) (2016) *IOM Counts 3,771 Migrant Fatalities in Mediterranean in 2015*. Available at: http://www.iom.int/news/iom-counts-3771-migrant-fatalities-mediterranean-2015

Jacobs, D. and Maier, R. (1998) 'European identity: construct, fact and fiction', in M. Gastelaars and A. Ruijter (eds) *A united Europe: The quest for a multifaceted identity*, Maastrict: Shaker Publishing BV, pp 13–34.

Johnson, S. and Wolf, A. (2009) 'Qualifications and mobility in a globalising world: why equivalence matters', *Assessment in Education: Principles, Policy and Practice*, 16(1): 3–11.

Kearney, N. (2005) 'Social work education: its origins and growth', in N. Kearney and C. Skehill (eds) *Social work in Ireland: Historical perspectives*, Dublin: Institute of Public Administration, pp 13–32.

Labonte-Roset, C. (2007) 'EASSW and social work training in Europe', *European Journal of Social Work*, 10(1): 117–23.

Migration Observatory (2014) *Northern Ireland: Census profile*, Oxford: Oxford University Press.

Moran, J. (2004) *Induction study: A study of the induction needs of newly-qualified and non-nationally qualified social workers in the health boards*, Dublin: NSWQB.

Nicem (Northern Ireland Council for Ethnic Minorities) (2014) *Annual human rights and racial equality benchmarking report 2013/2014*, Belfast: Northern Ireland Council for Ethnic Minorities.

NSWQB (National Social Work Qualifications Board) (2008) *Annual report of 2007*, Dublin: NSWQB.

NSWQB and CCETSW (NI) (The Central Council for Education and Training in Social Work – Northern Ireland) (1998) *A cross-border analysis of social work qualifications in Northern Ireland and the Republic of Ireland*, Dublin and Belfast: NSWQB and CCETSW (NI).

Oireachtas Report (2016) 'Proceedings of the Irish Parliament and parliamentary questions', October. Available at: http://www.oireachtas.ie/parliament/oireachtasbusiness/parliamentaryquestions/

Pinkerton, J. and Campbell, J. (2002) 'Social work and social justice in Northern Ireland: towards a new occupational space', *British Journal of Social Work*, 32(6): 723–37.

Roche, S. (2015) 'An exploratory study of the experience of internationally qualified social workers practising in Ireland', unpublished master's dissertation in applied social research, Trinity College, Dublin.

Skuterud, E. (2016) 'An exploratory study of the experiences of internationally qualified social workers living in Ireland: sink or swim?', unpublished master's dissertation in applied social research, Trinity College, Dublin.

Traynor, C. (1998) 'Social work in a sectarian society', in CCETSW (NI) (ed) *Social work and social change in Northern Ireland: Issues for contemporary practice*, Belfast: CCETS.

Walsh, T., Wilson, G. and O'Connor, E. (2010) 'Local, European and global: an exploration of migration patterns of social workers into Ireland', *British Journal of Social Work*, 40(6): 1978–95.

Walsh, T., O'Connor, E. and Wilson, G. (2015) 'Local, European and global: mapping the changes in social work migration patterns into Ireland since the recession', unpublished conference paper, Joint Social Work Education and Research (JSWEC), Open University, Milton Keynes, UK.

Williams, C. and Graham, M. (2014) '"A world on the move": migration, mobilities and social work', *British Journal of Social Work*, 44(suppl 1): i1–17.

Wilson, G. and McCrystal, P. (2007) 'Motivations and career aspirations of MSW students in Northern Ireland', *Social Work Education*, 26(1): 35–52.

Wilson, G., O'Connor, E., Walsh, T. and Kirby, M. (2009) 'Reflections on practice learning in Northern Ireland and the Republic of Ireland: lessons from students' experiences', *Social Work Education*, 28(6): 631–45.

Wilson, G., Montgomery, L., Houston, S., Davidson, G., Harper, C. and Faulkner, L. (2015) *Regress? React? Resolve? An evaluation of mental health service provision in Northern Ireland*, Belfast: Action Mental Health/Queen's University, Belfast.

Yin, R. (1984) *Case study research design and methods*, Newbury Park, CA: Sage.

SIXTEEN

Conclusion

Liz Beddoe and Allen Bartley

Introduction

It has been our intention with this book to introduce readers to the phenomenon of transnationalism as it manifests within a single profession across a number of different national contexts. To conclude this introductory exploration of social work transnationalism, we draw together what we believe are the significant themes emerging from the contributions. The first theme concerns the impact on those social workers who cross borders of the nature of professionalisation and regulation in different jurisdictions. Second, we draw out the common difficulties faced by social workers and other stakeholders and the extent to which these challenge the ideals of social work as an international profession. Finally, we explore some potential solutions to these challenging circumstances.

Jurisdictional similarities and differences

It has been argued in a number of places in the book that social work is both global and local. As Karen Lyons points out in Chapter Two, social work is unified by a set of values and imperatives identified in the 'global definition' promoted by the International Federation of Social Workers (IFSW) as including social justice, human rights, collective responsibility and respect for diversities, as well as a commitment to promoting social change and development, social cohesion, and the empowerment and liberation of people. As the other chapters have made clear, the national, regional and local contexts in which social workers practise to uphold and promote those values and imperatives both have elements in common and differ widely. Clearly, each of the jurisdictions described in this volume has experienced social work as a transnational professional space. These countries' immigration policy settings and labour market regulations have not always perfectly aligned, but have generally encouraged those with professional qualifications and practice experience to cross international borders to fill (actual or perceived) skills shortages. The chapters in Part Two ('Practitioner perspectives') all recount the sorts of practice, cultural and linguistic differences encountered by transnational social workers (TSWs). Additionally, there are striking differences in the ways in which social work is structured and regulated in each jurisdiction.

Most apparent among those differences is the question of professional registration. Social workers across the countries of the UK and the provinces of Canada are all required to be registered. Registration has been voluntary in New Zealand, though legislation will have been introduced in August 2017 to provide protection of title for social work and require all social workers to be registered with the Social Workers Registration Board; professional registration of social workers does not exist in Australia, and is not likely to in the foreseeable future. Similar variance exists in the practice of protection of title: in the UK, for instance, roles entitled 'social worker' may only be filled by registered (and thus appropriately qualified) social workers. No such protection of title has been in place in New Zealand, though the Bill mentioned earlier will include this provision; in Australia, the professional body (the Australian Association of Social Workers [AASW]) has secured an informal agreement by major statutory employers to fill social work positions only with professionals eligible for AASW membership (see Chapter Fourteen). This makes it difficult to ascertain the number of social workers, including transnationals, in the workforce in some of the countries under discussion, and thus complicates the ability to compare the state of transnationalism across the profession.

The regulatory structures differ in terms of their centralisation or dispersion across the jurisdictions as well. Statutory child protection work and safeguarding social work with adults is centrally regulated in England, Scotland, Wales and Northern Ireland, and child protection and youth justice in Aotearoa New Zealand, though employment practices differ: there is a single, national statutory child protection and youth justice agency in Aotearoa New Zealand, whereas local authorities in England manage their own child protection and safeguarding regimes. Both regulation and labour market practices are dispersed across Canadian provinces and Australian states and territories. Similar divergence exists within the statutory health sector of all the jurisdictions. Again, this makes direct comparisons challenging; it also contributes to the initial disorientation of many TSWs.

On the other hand, social work in all the concerned jurisdictions has been subject to the entrenchment of neoliberal ideologies and the imposition of New Public Management (NPM), as well as the politics of austerity. This results in high caseloads, the use of output metrics to scrutinise social workers' labour and effectiveness, and increased levels of stress in the work (including the increasing strain on service users and their communities). In some jurisdictions, this has resulted in aspects of de-professionalisation as the intrusion by stakeholders outside the profession has limited the ability of social workers to determine the nature of their work. While the specific manifestations of these may vary across jurisdictions, TSWs may find themselves benefiting from neoliberal regimes (in the ways in which these promote globalised immigration and subject labour market policies to a 'market' logic). At the same time, they may struggle (along with their local colleagues) to find effective ways to action their social work values – particularly the commitment to social justice, empowerment and collective responsibility – within neoliberal regimes.

Challenges

With regard to TSWs, each of the chapters in the book canvasses a range of opportunities and challenges facing the social work profession and TSWs themselves, both within and across national borders. Some of these challenges are easily understood, such as language issues and the adjustment and accommodation required by all involved in the practice relationship, at least during periods of initial transition. Other challenges are more complex and entrenched, such as the politics and ethics of the regimes of certification and recognition in each receiving country to which TSWs are subject. Again, these vary widely across the jurisdictions studied in the preceding chapters – and even within several of them (as described in Chapter Four with regard to Canada). It is clear that despite the agreement on a single global definition, little progress has been made to develop consistent standards for assessing and comparing international social work qualifications – much less aligning such standards to immigration or labour-market policies. As highlighted by Marion Brown and her colleagues in Chapter Four and by Gai Harrison in Chapter Nine, the variance across the authorities responsible for these regimes reflects the diversity of the regulation arrangements. A number of authors describe the frustration experienced by many TSWs who, having been identified as 'desirable' migrants by immigration authorities on the basis of their professional qualifications and skills, find that they are scrutinised more critically by certification authorities, as well as subject to the biases and preferences of employers. This includes confronting what Brown and her colleagues eloquently refer to as the 'tautological relationship between getting a [local] job and needing [local] experience' (p 62, this volume). The resulting inconsistencies and contradictions between these various regimes reflect what Miller (1986) famously referred to as a 'policy ad-hocracy'.

There is consistent general agreement in all the chapters, and across all the jurisdictions under discussion, that the profession lacks a coherent or coordinated approach to offering programmes of transition for TSWs practising, or intending to practise, in a new local context. In the absence of a profession-wide initiative or expectation, the transition process becomes a proposition merely between TSWs and their employers; the experiences related in the pages of this volume suggest that most employers do not offer to TSWs a rigorous and comprehensive transition programme – if, indeed, they acknowledge that such a programme is even needed. The social work profession in the formerly colonised countries in the New World (Canada, Australia and Aotearoa New Zealand) has begun, albeit unevenly, to grapple with the need for ethical engagement and competent practice with their indigenous populations. In light of the global articulation of the profession's commitment to social justice, empowerment and liberation, it is reasonable to expect that TSWs would be assisted in those countries to engage meaningfully with indigenous populations and with post-colonising politics. Wheturangi Walsh-Tapiata and her colleagues (in Chapter Ten) compellingly describe how this might be done in one national context – though it is relevant to point out that while the profession in their country (Aotearoa New Zealand) requires all social workers to demonstrate competence to work with indigenous people, there is no systematic or coherent profession-wide programme to enable TSWs to gain the knowledge and skills to do so.

A final challenge that has not been articulated specifically in any chapter in this volume, but that might be implied by Angelika Papadopoulos in Chapter Fourteen, concerns the very existence of social work transnational professional spaces: in these 'austere' times (which we acknowledge are themselves products of a hegemonic neoliberal response to economic conditions), should increasingly scarce resources be invested to increase the number and capabilities of domestic social workers, rather than importing and retraining transnationals?

We suggest that the transnational exchange of social workers is positive – even necessary – for the profession. A number of the contributing authors articulate the benefits of this exchange, insisting that TSWs 'can bring fresh perspectives to the work of colleagues, teams and agencies' (Chapter Two, pp 27–28, this volume) and provide a productive cross-fertilisation of knowledge and skills from one professional field to another. With regard to cultural competency, TSWs may carry in their own cultural backgrounds the ability to engage with diverse migrant and refugee-background communities in their new countries (especially those from non-English-speaking backgrounds). The knowledge exchanges that can occur are able to give rise to a synthesis of ideas and novel responses to the increasingly complex problems with which social workers engage, in every jurisdiction.

Purposeful responses

A range of responses are suggested in this volume that have the potential to maximise the contribution that TSWs can make to the professional settings – and to the wider profession – in the new jurisdictions to which they travel. All such responses have as their foundation an acknowledgement or reaffirmation of core social work values as being fundamental to all social work practice – in the face of neoliberal imperatives to impose other imperatives, or to consider social work's core values to be external to the functions that social workers are asked to fulfil in many statutory organisations.

To address the complicated and often political issues related to recognition and certification, international social work organisations, such as the IFSW, could claim the task of developing protocols for social work education. These would not necessarily be for the development of a standardised global curriculum; rather, they could provide a single protocol for national authorities to use by which social work curricula could be assessed for commensurability. This could make more transparent and predictable the identification of knowledge gaps and skills mismatches from one jurisdiction to another, allowing prospective TSWs to reconsider or plan to upskill. In Chapter Fourteen, Angelika Papadopoulos highlights the four domains by which social work curricula are conceptualised in the IASSW (International Association of Schools of Social Work) global standards: the domain of the social work profession; the domain of the social work professional; methods of social work practice; and the paradigm of the social work profession. Papadopoulos argues that these could provide a universal framework for assessing social workers' capabilities and qualifications, and for making sense of national differences in social work education and professional practice.

We suggest that within each jurisdiction, whether at the national or state/provincial level, the profession itself should take a more active interest and role in the transition of TSWs to competent and effective practice in the local context. Leaving this transition to the vagaries of 'the market' results in inconsistent, ad hoc and too often unsatisfactory outcomes. This does a disservice both to the professionals involved and to the people and communities with whom they work. Resources should be developed under the 'ownership' of the profession (via professional associations) that enable TSWs (or prospective TSWs) to learn about the practice and policy context of a given jurisdiction even *before* migrating. In Chapter Twelve, writing from the Canadian context, Marion Brown and her colleagues highlight the two initiatives that have been developed in Canada as a result of their work that could be the prototypes for international efforts. These are the Immigrant Settlement Association of Nova Scotia (see: www.isans.ca) and the Social Work Migration Project (see: www.socialworkmigration.ca). Given the increasing diversity of all the societies under discussion in these chapters, we suggest that one of the essential components of transition initiatives could be the provision of the kinds of experiences described by Walsh-Tapiata and her colleagues in Chapter Ten, who advocate 'up close and personal' transformation through continuous 'cultural encounters' as being pivotal in the process of becoming culturally competent.

Absent in this volume are service users' accounts of engaging with TSWs. This reflects the gap in the international research. To date, no large or systematic studies have been found that explore this phenomenon from the perspective of the local populations with whom social workers work. We know from the studies that have been conducted with TSWs in Australia, Canada, the UK and Aotearoa New Zealand (cited in the pages of this volume) that TSWs themselves report not having been well prepared to practise effectively when they gained their first positions in the new jurisdiction. The field now requires research with service users to inform the development of effective induction programmes, and service users' voices should be prominent in future evaluations of those programmes.

While social work is a profession with global reach, it continues to be essentially a profession bound together by common aspirations to social justice and human rights. These rights extend to all stakeholders, including social workers themselves as they cross borders for myriad reasons, as well as for users of services in the host countries. In moving forward to better systems for the recognition of skills and experience and the integration of TSWs, we need to keep rights and justice in mind and examine our professional systems. This requires consideration of the social, cultural, economic and educational opportunities and mutual benefits in play in the transnational space.

Reference

Miller, M.J. (1986) 'Policy ad-hocracy: the paucity of coordinated perspectives and policies', *The Annals of the American Academy of Political and Social Science*, 485: 64–75.

Index

Note: page numbers in *italic* type refer to figures and tables, page numbers followed by n refer to notes.